A Social and Cultural History of Sport in Ireland

Sport has played a central role in modern Ireland's history. Perhaps nowhere else has sport so infused the political, social and cultural development and identity of a nation. During the so-called 'Decade of Centenaries' in Ireland (2014–2024), there has been an exponential growth in interest and academic research on Ireland's sporting heritage. This collection of chapters, contributed by some of Ireland's most preeminent sport and social historians, showcases the richness and complexity of Ireland's sporting legacy. Chapters on topics as diverse as the role of native Gaelic games in emphasising the emerging cultural nationalism of pre-Revolutionary Ireland, the contribution of Irish rugby to the broader British war effort in World War I, the emergence of Irish soccer on the international stage and the long-running battle to gain official recognition within international athletics for an independent Irish state are presented. The purpose of this work is to illustrate some of the latest and most vibrant research being conducted on Irish sports history. This book was published as a special issue of *Sport in Society*.

Richard McElligott lectures in modern Irish history at University College Dublin and is the author of *Forging a Kingdom: The GAA in Kerry, 1884–1934*. His research has been published in a range of journals including *Eire-Ireland* and *Irish Economic and Social History*. Since 2011, he has served as the Chairman of the Sports History Ireland Society.

David Hassan is the Head of the School of Sport at Ulster University. He is the author of 11 books and over 75 peer-reviewed articles and outputs dealing with sport and modern society. He holds a Distinguished Research Fellowship from Ulster in recognition of his outstanding contribution to research.

Sport in the Global Society – Contemporary Perspectives

Edited by
Boria Majumdar, *University of Central Lancashire, UK*

The social, cultural (including media) and political study of sport is an expanding area of scholarship and related research. While this area has been well served by the *Sport in the Global Society* series, the surge in quality scholarship over the last few years has necessitated the creation of *Sport in the Global Society: Contemporary Perspectives*. This series will publish the work of leading scholars in fields as diverse as sociology, cultural studies, media studies, gender studies, cultural geography and history, political science and political economy. If the social and cultural study of sport is to receive the scholarly attention and readership it warrants, a cross-disciplinary series dedicated to taking sport beyond the narrow confines of physical education and sport science academic domains is necessary. *Sport in the Global Society: Contemporary Perspectives* will answer this need.

Australian Sport
Antipodean Waves of Change
Edited by Kristine Toohey and Tracy Taylor

Australia's Asian Sporting Context
1920s and 1930s
Edited by Sean Brawley and Nick Guoth

Bearing Light: Flame Relays and the Struggle for the Olympic Movement
Edited by John J. MacAloon

Cricket, Migration and Diasporic Communities
Edited by Thomas Fletcher

'Critical Support' for Sport
Bruce Kidd

Disability in the Global Sport Arena
A Sporting Chance
Edited by Jill M. Clair

Diversity, Equity and Inclusion in Sport and Leisure
Edited by Katherine Dashper and Thomas Fletcher

Documenting the Beijing Olympics
Edited by D. P. Martinez and Kevin Latham

Ethnicity and Race in Association Football
Case Study Analyses in Europe, Africa and the USA
Edited by David Hassan

Exploring the Cultural, Ideological and Economic Legacies of Euro 2012
Edited by Peter Kennedy and Christos Kassimeris

Fan Culture in European Football and the Influence of Left Wing Ideology
Edited by Peter Kennedy and David Kennedy

Football, Community and Social Inclusion
Edited by Daniel Parnell and David Richardson

Football in Asia
History, Culture and Business
Edited by Younghan Cho

Football in Southeastern Europe
From Ethnic Homogenization to Reconciliation
Edited by John Hughson and Fiona Skillen

Football Supporters and the Commercialisation of Football
Comparative Responses across Europe
Edited by Peter Kennedy and David Kennedy

Forty Years of Sport and Social Change, 1968–2008
"To Remember is to Resist"
Edited by Russell Field and Bruce Kidd

Gender, Media, Sport
Edited by Susanna Hedenborg and Gertrud Pfister

Global Perspectives on Football in Africa
Visualising the Game
Edited by Susann Baller, Giorgio Miescher and Ciraj Rassool

Global Sport Business
Community Impacts of Commercial Sport
Edited by Hans Westerbeek

Governance, Citizenship and the New European Football Championships
The European Spectacle
Edited by Wolfram Manzenreiter and Georg Spitaler

Indigenous People, Race Relations and Australian Sport
Edited by Christopher J. Hallinan and Barry Judd

Legacies of Great Men in World Soccer
Heroes, Icons, Legends
Edited by Kausik Bandyopadhyay

Managing Expectations and Policy Responses to Racism in Sport
Codes Combined
Edited by Keir Reeves, Megan Ponsford and Sean Gorman

Mediated Football
Representations and Audience Receptions of Race/Ethnicity, Nation and Gender
Jacco van Sterkenburg and Ramón Spaaij

Modern Sports in Asia
Cultural Perspectives
Edited by Younghan Cho and Charles Leary

Moral Panic in Physical Education and Coaching
Edited by Heather Piper, Dean Garratt and Bill Taylor

Olympic Reform Ten Years Later
Edited by Heather Dichter and Bruce Kidd

Reflections on Process Sociology and Sport
'Walking the Line'
Joseph Maguire

Security and Sport Mega Events
A Complex Relation
Edited by Diamantis Mastrogiannakis

Soccer in Brazil
Edited by Martin Curi

Soccer in the Middle East
Edited by Alon Raab and Issam Khalidi

South Africa and the Global Game
Football, Apartheid and Beyond
Edited by Peter Alegi and Chris Bolsmann

Sport – Race, Ethnicity and Identity
Building Global Understanding
Edited by Daryl Adair

Sport and Citizenship
Edited by Matthew Guschwan

Sport and Communities
Edited by David Hassan and Sean Brown

Sport, Culture and Identity in the State of Israel
Edited by Yair Galily and Amir Ben-Porat

Sport in Australian National Identity
Kicking Goals
Tony Ward

Sport in the City
Cultural Connections
Edited by Michael Sam and John E. Hughson

Sport, Memory and Nationhood in Japan
Remembering the Glory Days
Edited by Andreas Niehaus and Christian Tagsold

Sport, Music, Identities
Edited by Anthony Bateman

Sport, Race and Ethnicity
The Scope of Belonging?
Edited by Katie Liston and Paddy Dolan

The British World and the Five Rings
Essays in British Imperialism and the Modern Olympic Movement
Edited by Erik Nielsen and Matthew Llewellyn

The Changing Face of Cricket
From Imperial to Global Game
Edited by Dominic Malcolm, Jon Gemmell and Nalin Mehta

The Consumption and Representation of Lifestyle Sports
Edited by Belinda Wheaton

The Containment of Soccer in Australia
Fencing Off the World Game
Edited by Christopher J. Hallinan and John E. Hughson

The History of Motor Sport
A Case Study Analysis
Edited by David Hassan

The Making of Sporting Cultures
John E. Hughson

The Olympic Movement and the Sport of Peacemaking
Edited by Ramón Spaaij and Cindy Burleson

The Olympic Games: Meeting New Challenges
Edited by David Hassan and Shakya Mitra

The Other Sport Mega-Event: Rugby World Cup 2011
Edited by Steven J. Jackson

The Politics of Sport
Community, Mobility, Identity
Edited by Paul Gilchrist and Russell Holden

The Politics of Sport in South Asia
Edited by Subhas Ranjan Chakraborty, Shantanu Chakrabarti and Kingshuk Chatterjee

The Social Impact of Sport
Edited by Ramón Spaaij

The Social Science of Sport
A Critical Analysis
Edited by Bo Carlsson and Susanna Hedenborg

Towards a Social Science of Drugs in Sport
Edited by Jason Mazanov

Twenty20 and the Future of Cricket
Edited by Chris Rumford

Who Owns Football?
The Governance and Management of the Club Game Worldwide
Edited by David Hassan and Sean Hamil

Why Minorities Play or Don't Play Soccer
A Global Exploration
Edited by Kausik Bandyopadhyay

Women's Football in the UK
Continuing with Gender Analyses
Edited by Jayne Caudwell

Women's Sport in Africa
Edited by Michelle Sikes and John Bale

A Social and Cultural History of Sport in Ireland
Edited by David Hassan and Richard McElligott

A Social and Cultural History of Sport in Ireland

Edited by
Richard McElligott and David Hassan

LONDON AND NEW YORK

First published 2016 by Routledge

2 Park Square, Milton Park, Abingdon, Oxfordshire OX14 4RN
711 Third Avenue, New York, NY 10017

Routledge is an imprint of the Taylor & Francis Group, an informa business

First issued in paperback 2018

Copyright © 2016 Taylor & Francis

All rights reserved. No part of this book may be reprinted or reproduced or utilised in any form or by any electronic, mechanical, or other means, now known or hereafter invented, including photocopying and recording, or in any information storage or retrieval system, without permission in writing from the publishers.

Notice:
Product or corporate names may be trademarks or
registered trademarks, and are used only for identification and explanation without intent to infringe.

British Library Cataloguing in Publication Data
A catalogue record for this book is available from the British Library

ISBN 13: 978-1-138-10129-6 (hbk)
ISBN 13: 978-0-367-00205-3 (pbk)

Typeset in Times
by diacriTech, Chennai

Publisher's Note
The publisher accepts responsibility for any inconsistencies that may have arisen during the conversion of this book from journal articles to book chapters, namely the possible inclusion of journal terminology.

Disclaimer
Every effort has been made to contact copyright holders for their permission to reprint material in this book. The publishers would be grateful to hear from any copyright holder who is not here acknowledged and will undertake to rectify any errors or omissions in future editions of this book.

Contents

	Citation Information	xi
	Notes on Contributors	xiii
1.	Introduction: Irish sports history Richard McElligott and David Hassan	1
2.	Contesting the fields of play: the Gaelic Athletic Association and the battle for popular sport in Ireland, 1890–1906 Richard McElligott	3
3.	The *Cork Sportsman*: a provincial sporting newspaper, 1908–1911 David Toms	24
4.	Ireland – soccer champions of the world Cormac Moore	38
5.	The GAA and revolutionary Irish politics in late nineteenth- and early twentieth-century Ireland David Hassan and Andrew McGuire	51
6.	The emergence of hurling in Australia 1877–1917 Patrick Bracken	62
7.	Irish-born players in England's Football Leagues, 1945–2010: an historical and geographical assessment Conor Curran	74
8.	Irish rugby and the First World War Liam O'Callaghan	95
9.	Hardy Fingallians, Kildare trippers and *'The Divil Ye'll Rise'* scufflers: wrestling in modern Ireland Paul Ignatius Gunning	110

CONTENTS

10. The National Athletic Association of Ireland and Irish Athletics, 1922–1937: steps on the road to athletic isolation 130
    Tom Hunt

    Index 147

Citation Information

The chapters in this book were originally published in *Sport in Society*, volume 19, issue 1 (January 2016). When citing this material, please use the original page numbering for each article, as follows:

Chapter 1
Introduction: Irish sports history
Richard McElligott and David Hassan
Sport in Society, volume 19, issue 1 (January 2016) pp. 1–2

Chapter 2
Contesting the fields of play: the Gaelic Athletic Association and the battle for popular sport in Ireland, 1890–1906
Richard McElligott
Sport in Society, volume 19, issue 1 (January 2016) pp. 3–23

Chapter 3
The Cork Sportsman: a provincial sporting newspaper, 1908–1911
David Toms
Sport in Society, volume 19, issue 1 (January 2016) pp. 24–37

Chapter 4
Ireland – soccer champions of the world
Cormac Moore
Sport in Society, volume 19, issue 1 (January 2016) pp. 38–50

Chapter 5
The GAA and revolutionary Irish politics in late nineteenth- and early twentieth-century Ireland
David Hassan and Andrew McGuire
Sport in Society, volume 19, issue 1 (January 2016) pp. 51–61

Chapter 6
The emergence of hurling in Australia 1877–1917
Patrick Bracken
Sport in Society, volume 19, issue 1 (January 2016) pp. 62–73

CITATION INFORMATION

Chapter 7
Irish-born players in England's Football Leagues, 1945–2010: an historical and geographical assessment
Conor Curran
Sport in Society, volume 19, issue 1 (January 2016) pp. 74–94

Chapter 8
Irish rugby and the First World War
Liam O'Callaghan
Sport in Society, volume 19, issue 1 (January 2016) pp. 95–109

Chapter 9
Hardy Fingallians, Kildare trippers and 'The Divil Ye'll Rise' scufflers: wrestling in modern Ireland
Paul Ignatius Gunning
Sport in Society, volume 19, issue 1 (January 2016) pp. 110–129

Chapter 10
The National Athletic Association of Ireland and Irish Athletics, 1922–1937: steps on the road to athletic isolation
Tom Hunt
Sport in Society, volume 19, issue 1 (January 2016) pp. 130–146

For any permission-related enquiries please visit:
http://www.tandfonline.com/page/help/permissions

Notes on Contributors

Patrick Bracken is a researcher in sports history at De Montfort University, UK. His PhD thesis explored the development of a range of sports in Co. Tipperary, Ireland, during the second half of the nineteenth century.

Conor Curran is a researcher in sports history at De Montfort University, UK, and tutor at St. Patrick's College, Ireland. His current project focuses on the migration of Irish footballers to Britain from 1945 to 2010. He is author of the book *Sport in Donegal: A History* (2010).

Paul Ignatius Gunning is an independent scholar who researches the history of sport in Ireland. His recent publications can be found in *Sport in Society: Cultures, Commerce, Media, Politics*.

David Hassan is the Head of the School of Sport at Ulster University, Northern Ireland. He is the author of 11 books and over 75 peer-reviewed articles and outputs dealing with sport and modern society. He holds a Distinguished Research Fellowship from Ulster in recognition of his outstanding contribution to research.

Tom Hunt is an independent researcher in Waterford, Ireland. His work focuses on the history of sport. He is author of *Sport and Society in Victorian Ireland: The Case of Westmeath* (2007).

Richard McElligott lectures in modern Irish history at University College Dublin, Ireland, and is the author of *Forging a Kingdom: The GAA in Kerry, 1884–1934* (2013). His research has been published in a range of journals including *Eire-Ireland* and *Irish Economic and Social History*. Since 2011, he has served as the Chairman of the Sports History Ireland Society.

Andrew McGuire is a PhD candidate in History and Politics at Ulster University, Northern Ireland. His research focuses on the Irish in Britain and Irish nationalism in the late nineteenth and early twentieth centuries.

Cormac Moore is a PhD candidate in sports history at De Montfort University, UK. His most recent book, *The Irish Soccer Spilt*, was published in 2015.

NOTES ON CONTRIBUTORS

Liam O'Callaghan is a Senior Lecturer at Liverpool Hope University, UK. His research examines the social history of modern Ireland, with a particular focus on comparative histories of sport and leisure.

David Toms is a Lecturer in the School of History at University College Cork, Ireland. His research has focused on the history of sport in Ireland, and his first monograph, *Soccer in Munster: A Social History, 1877–1937*, was published in 2015.

Introduction: Irish sports history

Richard McElligott[a] and David Hassan[b]

[a]School of History and Archives, University College Dublin, Republic of Ireland
[b]School of Sport, University of Ulster, Northern Ireland

Sports history as a discipline in Irish academia has had a long gestation. Perhaps this was inevitable, considering that a substantial move away from the study of traditional political history and towards social history only really began in Ireland in the early 1980s. For much of the twentieth century, the historiography of Irish sport, such as it was, was monopolized by studies of the Gaelic Athletic Association (GAA): the largest sports organization on the island. The GAA's importance as a pillar of the Irish cultural revival movement of the 1890s and its connection with radical Irish nationalism at the turn of the twentieth century meant that histories of the Association were invariably dominated by the perceived role of the organization and its members during the Irish revolutionary period.

While there was no denying the nationalist credentials of the GAA, and therefore no impediment to writing its story in the decades after the formation of the new Irish state, the situation was far more complicated for advocates of soccer, rugby and other imported sports. The perceived link between 'British' sports and unionist sentiment in Ireland, along with the political partition of the island, made it difficult for those wishing to investigate soccer, rugby or cricket's development there. For much of the past 100 years, a lack of success in such sports, at least at the international level, further stifled interest in documenting their impact on Irish life.

The 1990s finally saw the emergence of a generation of cultural and sports historians in Ireland who, influenced by what had been developing in British and American academia, sought to place the history of Irish sport in the wider international context of the Victorian Sports Revolution. Works by Mike Cronin, Paul Rouse and others further sought to move the historiography of Irish sport away from politics and place it within the broader context of Irish social, economic and cultural history (Rouse 1990; Cronin 1999). Their pioneering research laid the groundwork for an explosion of interest in Irish sports history since the turn of the current century. Crucial studies produced in the past decade, such as those by Neal Garnham, Tom Hunt, Rouse, Cronin and Mark Duncan, Liam O'Callaghan and James Kelly, give categorical proof to the strength and virility of the discipline in modern Irish academia (Garnham 2004; Hunt 2007; Cronin, Duncan, and Rouse 2009; O'Callaghan 2011; Kelly 2014). There are now more students than ever before researching the history of Irish sport and its role in Irish society at undergraduate, post-graduate and post-doctoral level. Moreover, 2015 will see the publication of several more important works on Irish sport including four books by contributors to this collection; Conor Curran's study of the development of sport in Donegal, Tom Hunt's official history of the Irish Olympic Council, Cormac Moore's investigation of the administrative split in Irish soccer in 1921 and David Toms' social history of soccer in Munster.

Much of the credit for the increasing visibility of sport in Irish historiography must go to the foresight of Dr Paul Rouse and Dr William Murphy for organizing the inaugural Sports History Ireland Conference at University College Dublin on 18–19 February 2005. Shortly afterwards, the Sports History Ireland society was officially formed and it has since grown and thrived. The society's annual conference continues to attract large numbers of high quality papers and has become the main platform for Irish sports historians to present their research to an enthusiastic national and international audience. On 20 September 2014, Sports History Ireland hosted its 10th anniversary conference in Dublin: its largest and most successful event to date. The impetus for this special collection was both to recognize the work the society has done in promoting the discipline in Ireland over the past 10 years and a desire to present to an international audience a sample of the latest research being conducted within Irish sports history. The contributors to this volume are all veterans of past Sports History Ireland conferences and all the papers included were presented at either the 2013 or 2014 events.

In conclusion, we wish to thank all those who have attended and contributed to the Sport History Ireland conferences over the past 10 years. We also extend our deep thanks to the contributors of this volume for all their hard work. Finally, we thank Routledge for their generous support of the Sport History Ireland conference in the past and for the publication of this assembly of papers. It is hoped that this collection will offer an important and stimulating addition to the ever-growing volume of work on Irish sport history as well as a fitting testimony to the continuing role of the Sport History Ireland society in promoting such research.

References

Cronin, Mike. 1999. *Sport and Nationalism in Ireland, Gaelic Games, Soccer and Irish Identity Since 1884*. Dublin: Four Courts Press.

Cronin, Mike, Mark Duncan, and Paul Rouse, eds. 2009. *The GAA: A People's History*. Cork: Collins Press.

Garnham, Neal. 2004. *Association Football and Society in Pre-Partition Ireland*. Belfast: Ulster Historical Foundation.

Hunt, Tom. 2007. *Sport and Society in Victorian Ireland, The Case Study of Westmeath*. Cork: Cork University Press.

Kelly, James. 2014. *Sport in Ireland 1600–1840*. Dublin: Four Courts Press.

O'Callaghan, Liam. 2011. *Rugby in Munster a Social and Cultural History*. Cork: Cork University Press.

Rouse, Paul. 1990. "The Politics of Culture and Sport in Ireland: A History of the GAA Ban on Foreign Games 1884–1971. Part 1: 1884–1921." *International Journal of the History of Sport* 10 (3): 330–360.

Contesting the fields of play: the Gaelic Athletic Association and the battle for popular sport in Ireland, 1890–1906

Richard McElligott

School of History and Archives, University College Dublin, Dublin, Republic of Ireland

> The Gaelic Athletic Association's (GAA) meteoric rise to dominance in the 1880s reflected its success in tapping into an Irish sporting constituency left largely untouched by the games of the British Empire. However by the early 1890s, the GAA verged on extinction as the broader economic, social and political climate conspired against it. In its wake, sports as diverse as rugby union, cricket and soccer sought to capitalize and gain increasing popularity among Irish sportsmen. This article sets out to explore sporting developments in provincial Ireland during the 1890s to illustrate how the Association's demise was a major factor in the consolidation and spread of rival sports at that time. With the rejuvenation of the GAA in the years after 1900, it will explore the campaign conducted by the Association and its membership against those games that now gravely endangered its once powerful local and national monopoly.

Introduction

The establishment of the Gaelic Athletic Association (GAA) in November 1884 ushered in a sporting revolution in Ireland. Its inaugural meeting was the harbinger for the democratization of modern, codified and competitive sport on the island. Previously the sporting creations of the British Empire, introduced to Ireland in the second half of the nineteenth century, had struggled to make an impact outside of the country's larger urban centres (Bracken 2004; O'Dwyer 2006; Hunt 2007).[1] Sports such as cricket, rugby and soccer remained predominantly the plaything of either a largely Protestant, educated, upper class or the garrisoned police and military forces in the country (see Cronin 1999, 104). As Mike Cronin (2011, 2758) has recently argued, before the coming of the GAA, organized sport in Ireland was mostly controlled by, and in the interests of, a social and sectarian elite. The Association's advent dramatically altered this situation. For the first time, the majority of Irish sportsmen had access to competitive games that were overseen by a national organization. In addition, many enthusiasts were given their first opportunity to administer clubs and local governing boards affiliated to the new sports body.[2] The GAA's arrival thus signified a fundamental shift in organized sports participation in Ireland (Cronin, Duncan, and Rouse 2009, 19).[3] The GAA's success in tapping into a sporting constituency, left largely untouched by the sports of the British Empire, explains its stellar rise to prominence. Within five years, the Association numbered 777 affiliated clubs with over 41,000 members across the island of Ireland (NAI, CBS Index, 4467/S; 2792/S).[4] Such statistics are all the more impressive when compared to its biggest sporting rivals.[5]

While few scholars dispute the Association's achievement in introducing organized sport *en masse*, much ink has been spilled on postulating the reasons why.[6] Traditional histories have sought to explain the Association's success in terms of its kinship with Irish political nationalism (see O'Sullivan 1916; Devlin 1935). More recently, Irish sport historians have sought to place the GAA's development in the wider international context of the Victorian Sports Revolution and have highlighted the GAA's achievement in terms of its ability to ape contemporary developments in British sport while also appealing to native social, economic and cultural idiosyncrasies (see Rouse 1993; Mullan 1996; Cronin 1999; Garnham 2004a; Hunt 2007; Cronin, Duncan, and Rouse 2009).[7]

Nevertheless, few studies have been devoted to the GAA's ruinous collapse in 1890s Ireland.[8] Within 10 years of its formation, the GAA neared extinction, the victim of a ceaseless tide of broader economic, social and administrative problems. With some notable exceptions, little has been done to explore the interplay between Gaelic games and its sporting rivals at this time (see Hunt 2007; O'Callaghan 2011; Curran 2012b). Ireland was a rare example internationally of how the global sports of the Victorian Sporting Revolution were confronted by codified and nationally administered native games. This article will assess sporting developments in provincial Ireland during the 1890s to firstly illustrate how the Association's demise was a major factor in the consolidation and spread of rival sports. Concentrating on the rejuvenation of the GAA in the years after 1900 spurred on by the emergence of a strong Irish cultural nationalist movement, it will analyse the fight-back conducted by the Association and its membership on ideological and practical grounds against those sports that now gravely endangered its once powerful local and national monopoly.

National decline of the GAA in 1890s Ireland

From a seemingly unassailable position of dominance over Irish popular sport in 1889, it is extraordinary that within a further five years the GAA neared ruin. This remarkable implosion was directly related to the broader economic situation. It is important to remember that agriculture represented the dominant employment industry in Ireland at that time.[9] By 1890, an economic depression had descended on Ireland, which resulted in weak aggregate demand for Irish agricultural produce in its principal market of mainland Britain (Donnelly 1975, 151/313).[10] Since its foundation, the GAA had evolved as a predominantly rural organization in terms of its membership profile and club structure and nearly 62% of its players were directly employed in agriculture (McDevitt 1997, 269).[11]

The economic situation led to the reappearance of mass emigration, which accounted for an almost 15% (716,000) decrease in the Irish population between 1881 and 1900 (Vaughan and Fitzpatrick 1978, 3).[12] In 1896, 39,226 people alone left Ireland, 83.7% of who were aged between 15 and 35. This was precisely the age group of young rural men upon which GAA membership largely depended.[13] Emigration had a devastating impact on the Association resulting in the lifeblood of many clubs being swept away. The popular newspaper, *Sport* bemoaned that emigration was now the 'deadliest enemy of all' for the GAA (*Sport*, January 2, 1892).

Already labouring to stem the haemorrhaging of its membership, the Association's ability to combat the devastating effects of mass emigration and widespread economic decline was severely compromised by the great schism in Irish nationalist politics caused by the downfall of Charles Stewart Parnell as leader of the Irish Home Rule movement in December 1890.[14] Parnell was one of the three original patrons of the GAA and like other sections of Irish society the Association became bitterly divided over the issue. The revolutionary Irish Republican Brotherhood (IRB) decided to use the influence it had gained among the upper echelons of the GAA to throw the official support of the Association behind Parnell and his political supporters (NAI, CBS, DICS Reports Box Two, 521/S/2493).[15] However, such actions resulted in the alienation of those in the organization opposed to Parnell politically.[16] *Sport* lamented that the rupture in Irish politics was having a profound effect on the GAA across rural Ireland where it had caused 'our people to devote all their attention ... to politics and to fighting one another' (*Sport*, January 2, 1892). By January 1894, the combination of all of these factors had reduced the Association to a spectre of its past glories. Club numbers had collapsed from a height of 777 to 118 and its national membership now numbered as little as 5183.[17]

The GAA's organizational structure made it particularly susceptible to the impact of emigration and economic volatility. A principal cause for the GAA's vulnerability was the ad hoc nature of the vast majority of its clubs. Reflecting the structure of rural Irish society, many GAA teams formed around a nucleus of local town land farming communities and as a result most were little more than 'ephemeral combinations', rather than permanent organized sports clubs (McAnallen 2009, 160).[18] In addition, GAA clubs were often at a severe financial disadvantage compared to their sporting rivals. Unlike rugby or cricket, Gaelic games, due to their implied nationalist outlook, did not attract the patronage of local landlords and gentry.[19]

Another major problem for the GAA was that compared to rugby and soccer, Gaelic games lacked clearly defined and universally understood playing rules. Richard Blake, one of the GAA's most prominent referees, argued that the principal reason for declining popularity was the vagueness surrounding its rules, which, he wrote, continually caused uncertainty and forced referees to interpret the laws for themselves (*Sport*, January 28, 1893).[20] As a consequence of its ill-defined rulebook, early Gaelic matches were plagued by contests being abruptly ended as disputes with referees over a scoring decision or the sending off of a player erupted and objections were sought.[21]

The broader economic and social situation would have tried the strength of any mass sporting organization, especially one whose membership relied mostly on the rural, lower-middle and working classes. Yet, the incompetence and bungling of the Association's administrative structure was also pinpointed as the major cause of teams and players withdrawing in droves. Objections and counter-objections to the awarding of matches would be a persistent feature of local and national contests throughout the 1890s. Often this led to bitter recriminations between local clubs and their county boards and between those boards themselves and the Central Executive.[22] The *Kerry Sentinel* argued that what lay behind the decimation of the Association was:

> [T]he bad management of the County Committee. County Boards are largely responsible for the disappearance of many clubs, which, smarting under the bungling and unjust treatment of the governing body became disorganised, and eventually disbanded. (*Kerry Sentinel*, January 2, 1892)

The *Anglo-Celt* echoed these sentiments arguing that the collapse of the GAA was caused by a combination of emigration and those left at home showing 'a coldness to' Gaelic games:

> One way or another people commenced to tire of the Association and the manner in which it was conducted ... Incompetent referees, small unsuitable playing bounds, and bad management of committees conducting local tournaments, were greatly to blame. (*Anglo-Celt*, October 14, 1893)

The threat of rival sports to the Association's dominance had precipitated the introduction of a rule in September 1886, which banned members from playing non-Gaelic games (O'Sullivan 1916, 35).[23] A year later, the GAA, under heavy IRB influence, introduced a prohibition on members of the police and British military joining the organization (*Sport*, February 26, 1887). While this action had a much more implicit ideological imperative, it was rescinded in April 1893 as the GAA desperately sought to bolster its dwindling membership following the catastrophic consequences of the Parnell split (O'Sullivan 1916, 103). Its leadership was forced to revoke the ban on members playing rival sports in 1896 in another attempt to augment its national membership (Rouse 1993, 345–346). While the removal of both the police and non-Gaelic games bans was intended to augment the GAA, instead it often had the opposite effect. As a consequence of the bans' initial introduction, police and British army personnel serving in Ireland had tended to concentrate their sporting activities on rugby, cricket and Association football. They continued to provide a powerful local impetus for those sports during the GAA's decline in the 1890s.[24]

With the effective collapse of the GAA in many areas, thousands of would-be athletes found themselves without a sporting outlet. Doubtlessly due to the economic situation, many had more pressing matters than simple sporting considerations. However, there remained a sizeable proportion of former GAA members who were able to retain their sporting interests. Across Ireland those who could afford to, turned to other sports. Economic downturn and mass rural emigration impacted less significantly on cricket, rugby and soccer. The national collapse of the Association would thus prove to be a significant stimulus to the consolidation and spread of such games across provincial Ireland. This helps to explain the marked growth in popularity of rugby in southwest Munster, soccer in the northeast and cricket across much of the Irish midlands.

Rugby Union's expansion in Southwest Ireland

O'Callaghan (2011, 146–147) has highlighted the remarkable fluidity between popular footballing codes in Ireland at this time and how, particularly in Munster, sports clubs often switched affiliation between rival sports bodies. For example in Kerry, the Killorglin Laune Rangers club had initially played rugby before transferring to the GAA in 1887 and becoming one of the most renowned early Gaelic football teams (Foley 1945, 172). In Munster, the collapse of the local GAA allowed rugby union to make significant inroads into the sporting constituency of urban and rural workers who had been predominant within the GAA there. In the aftermath of the Parnell split, the Limerick County Board disbanded for most of the 1890s due to a bitter internal power struggle (Ó Ceallaig 1937, 82). In Kerry, the County Board became defunct in the mid-1890s due to continued dissention within the local GAA's leadership (*Kerry Sentinel*, March 31, 1897). As a result, rugby began to expand and thrive in the larger urban centres of the southwest. For instance before 1914, the Tralee RFC was the most successful team based outside the cities of Cork and Limerick to compete in the Munster Senior Cup, the premier rugby competition in the region (O'Callaghan 2011, 36). In the absence of organized Gaelic games activity in Kerry, those young men who were socially and economically in a position to, switched to rugby.[25] The significant uptake in rugby, despite the harsh economic conditions, can be explained by examining the social profile of a sample of rugby players in Kerry.[26] This sample used the same class categories employed by the census. Therefore, we find that Class I, or professionals, amounted to 17.5% of rugby players examined. Class II, which were defined as those engaged in various commercial activities such as merchants and clerks, totalled 42.5%. Class III, those employed in agriculture, made up 2.5%. Class IV was defined as those in industrial labour, of which 2.5% were unskilled and 30% skilled. Corroborating these findings with a survey of 308 Kerry GAA players from 183 clubs (61.2% of which were urban based) active between 1896 and 1905, we find an enormous disparity between the 40.7% of GAA members engaged in agriculture as opposed to 2.5% in rugby (see McElligott 2013, 140–141).

Likewise, those in commercial activity are more than double their equivalents in the GAA: 19.2%. More than three times as many professionals were involved in rugby as opposed to GAA: 4.7%. Finally, both skilled and unskilled industrial labourers amounted to 32.5%, strikingly similar to the 32.1% for GAA members. The evidence suggests that in contrast to their GAA counterparts, most rugby players in Kerry were engaged in occupations that were less directly affected by the harsh agricultural situation. Many were also higher up the social echelon and had a more stable income than GAA members. Thus, they could afford to play sport even in economically bleak times. The almost equal participation of industrial labourers in both sports in largely urban teams indicates that there were few socio-economic barriers to GAA players from such background's crossing over to the rival code. It is likely that many of the 19.2% of white collar workers (often young clerks and shop assistants) previously involved in the GAA would also have found little difficulty in switching codes. With no organized Gaelic activity, men in the larger Kerry towns who may otherwise have played GAA turned to rugby.

From the mid-1890s, public meetings were held in larger Kerry towns such as Castleisland and Dingle to form rugby clubs. The attendances were comprised primarily of members of former Gaelic football teams (*Kerry Sentinel*, November 26/December 31, 1893). In 1898, a large gathering of Killarney GAA supporters established a rugby club there under the guidance of Dr William O'Sullivan.[27] Significantly it was expressly stated that the club was being formed in response to the local collapse of Gaelic games and potential members were assured that involvement would not hinder them participating in Gaelic games if they were reorganized in the town.[28] The status rugby was attaining in the county was apparent when Tralee was chosen as the venue for the high-profile inter-provincial test match between Munster and Leinster in January 1900. Media reports highlighted the large crowd that attended and how gate receipts were 'beyond all expectation'. The town was selected by the Irish Rugby Football Union's (IRFU) Munster branch 'which urged that such a match would tend to stimulate Rugby in County Kerry' (*Kerry Sentinel*, January 17, 1900).[29] That April, Tralee caused the shock of the Munster Senior Cup by beating Cork Constitution in the semi-final. They therefore qualified for their first final appearance (*Kerry Sentinel*, April 7, 1900). The local press commented that: 'Up to the present Rugby football [in Kerry] had a chequered existence ... Now things have begun to look up ... and the interest taken in the sport is keen' (*Kerry Sentinel*, March 17, 1900).

As O'Callaghan (2011, 76) has shown, the introduction of junior competitions and Sunday play in both Limerick and Cork by local rugby authorities also led to a significant increase in the number of clubs and the expansion of the geographical and social appeal of the game across the province. The facilitation of Sunday play also allowed rugby advocates in Limerick to encroach significantly on the social and cultural territory of the GAA (32/81). Larger rugby clubs in Limerick City took a prominent role in helping to spread the code in the towns of west Limerick and north Kerry, which, up until then, had been strongholds of Gaelic football.[30] Indeed in west Cork, where competition for players between rugby and GAA clubs was intense, the resurgence of rugby clubs in local towns was seen as a grave threat to the GAA's survival in the area (*Southern Star*, December 24, 1892). By 1900, rugby was revelling in a new found popularity across much of south and west Munster.

A cricket revival

Undeniably, the unprecedented boom in cricket in several counties during the 1890s illustrates that the game was able to take advantage of the decline in the local GAA to boost participation in such areas (Bracken 2004, 108; O'Dwyer 2006, 55–62). In counties like Tipperary, Kilkenny and Westmeath, the sport reached its peak of popularity between the years 1894 and 1900. During those years, the number of active cricket clubs in Tipperary and Westmeath remained in the high 20s, while in Kilkenny numbers peaked at 50 in 1896 (Bracken 2004, 109; O'Dwyer 2006, 157; Hunt 2007, 119). Several factors explain why cricket was in a position to benefit from the turmoil within the local GAA there. The early nature of GAA competitions often meant that there were few competitive hurling or football matches for rural GAA teams in a typical playing season. Once a team was defeated in the knock out county championship structure, they were frequently denied another competitive match until the following year.[31] However, Tom Hunt (2007, 156) has argued that cricket offered players a competitive structure, which ran the length of a summer and guaranteed a comprehensive series of matches. Furthermore, while Sunday play was a major stimulus to the popularity of the GAA among the Irish working class, in Westmeath, Sundays had already been well established as the principal playing day for cricket since the 1880s (2007, 157). It is therefore not surprising that many former GAA members turned to cricket to maintain their interest in organized sport following the GAA's decline. This is further supported by the fact that in counties such as Westmeath, the economic background of the majority of cricket players at this time corresponded broadly to the same economic classes previously involved in the GAA. For example, a study of 312 Westmeath cricket players conducted by Hunt illustrates that 53.5% were classified as farmers, farmers' sons or farm labourers (2007, 136).

Evidence for sportsmen turning to cricket in the GAA's absence is widespread. In Westmeath, the Mullingar GAA club, after winning the 1892 county championship, retired from football activities for the summer and established the Mullingar Cricket Club, which was comprised of players from the two Gaelic football teams in the town.[32] In Kilkenny, the popularity of cricket was such that the *Kilkenny Journal* argued its clubs should be utilized as a base to reform the local GAA. The paper believed that it was up to the local cricket captains and club secretaries to spearhead a revival in the county's native games (*Kilkenny Journal*, September 21, 1895).[33]

Soccer's growth in Northwest Ireland

The final major sport to show significant growth in parts of provincial Ireland following the GAA's collapse was soccer. Particularly in Ulster, soccer began to gain popularity among the working class of the region, principally due to the relative proximity of Belfast, which became the main stronghold of the sport on the island (Garnham 2004b, 5). There the GAA had been much slower to organize than elsewhere in Ireland.[34] Also the GAA's reliance on Sunday play had initially deterred participation by Sabbatarian and evangelical Protestants who formed a significant majority of the population in much of the region (Garnham 2004a, 40). In contrast to the GAA's misfortunes, the Irish Football Association's (IFA) decision in May 1894 to legalize professionalism indicated the growing strength and vitality of the Association's main sporting competitor in major urban centres like Belfast and the numbers of clubs affiliating to the IFA showed a steady progression throughout the 1890s (43/72). Again, the economic situation and effects of mass emigration seemed to have been far less damaging to soccer's popularity.[35]

In the northwest of Ulster, especially in counties Donegal and Derry, the decline of the local GAA secured the dominance of soccer in the region (Curran 2012b, 135). In Derry, a Football Association was established in 1886 and its influence allowed soccer to spread through neighbouring northeast Donegal in the early 1890s. Meanwhile in 1888, a GAA county board was organized in Derry (*Derry Journal*, October 29, 1888). As with soccer, Derry's influence also had a telling effect on the spread of the GAA in those areas of Donegal close to the city (Curran 2010, 36–38). Such was the popularity of soccer, however, that a number of Derry GAA clubs were actively fielding soccer players and incidents of players transferring between the rival codes was said to be a major problem (*Derry Journal*, August 18/27, 1890).[36] Moreover, in the wake of the Parnell split, the Catholic clergy in Derry City began to strongly support and actively promote the game of soccer among the city's catholic working class, not least as a way of countering what they saw as the subversive political influence of the GAA (Murphy 1981, 171).[37] The intense clerical opposition had a profound effect on the Derry GAA with prominent clubs such as the Young Emeralds, the McCarthy's and the Young Irelands electing to reorganize themselves as soccer clubs (Curran 2012b, 127). By 1892, the GAA had effectively collapsed in the city and within three years soccer had completely monopolized the sporting interests of the Catholic working class there (Murphy 1981, 172). The downfall of the Derry GAA heavily contributed to the Association's collapse in Donegal. In its absence, sportsmen looked to soccer to fill the void. As Conor Curran (2012b, 111) has shown, the number of soccer teams in Donegal began to increase significantly in the early 1890s. In 1891, there were at least 17 and this figure more than doubled in the following year. This illustrates a significant growth from the handful of teams in the county in the mid-1880s. The dominance of soccer in Derry meant the city's teams played an increasing role in spreading the code into Donegal. Seven northeast Donegal clubs were already affiliated with the Derry FA when an independent Donegal FA was formed in March 1894 (*Derry Journal*, March 9/30, 1894). While soccer went from strength to strength, only two Gaelic football matches were recorded in Donegal between the years 1891 and 1892 (Curran 2012b, 119).[38]

The revival and reorganization of the GAA, 1898–1905

By the mid-1890s, the GAA had effectively collapsed across most of rural Ireland. Thousands of its members had been forced to break their ties with the Association due to economic necessity, emigration or because of the effects of bitter political in-fighting. With the disbandment of the local GAA, many other would-be athletes had turned instead to cricket, soccer and rugby to satisfy their sporting passions. The year 1894 represented the GAA's nadir and in reaction to its national impotence those in charge now looked to recast the Association along more inclusive and less confrontational lines. In 1895, Richard Blake was elected as the GAA's National Secretary (*Sport*, April 13, 1895). Observing its poor health and regarding the influence radical nationalists exercised on its ruling body as the primary cause for this, Blake was determined not to let another political upheaval wreak havoc within the GAA. A month after his appointment, the GAA declared their organization to be non-political and non-sectarian.[39] Blake realized that the Association's survival was dependent on it distancing itself from nationalist politics and instead reorganizing as a governing body of sports that would attract 'mass spectator support' (Mandle 1987, 95). He immediately set about restructuring the playing rules for both hurling and football in order to eliminate their glaring defects. This, he hoped, would increase interest and popularity in the games at the expense of their growing rivals: soccer and rugby.[40] The changes pioneered by Blake would lead to a faster, more open, scientific and higher scoring game, which could now compete with more illustrious, international rival sporting codes for public interest. Blake represented the first of a new breed of GAA administrators: those drawn increasingly from the growing Irish professional Catholic middle classes who wished to restructure the Association on a more proficient model and govern it according to the best practice of contemporary sporting bodies. His administrative competence and energy salvaged the GAA at a time when it faced extinction and laid the foundations for the GAA's remarkable renaissance at the turn of the twentieth century.[41]

Ironically despite Blake's efforts to keep the GAA apolitical, the Association's national revival was greatly stimulated by the organization fully integrating itself into the emerging Irish cultural nationalist movement that was already becoming the dominant ideological force in Irish politics and society.[42] The development of popular cultural organizations, such as the Gaelic League, helped to stimulate the widespread reorganization of the GAA across much of provincial Ireland in the years surrounding 1900.[43] Police reports noted the symbiotic relationship between the Gaelic League and the GAA as the former spread rapidly with one 'educating the mind' while the other trained 'the body' (NAI, CBS, IG & CI Box 2, 24242/S).[44] In Longford, Westmeath, Dublin, Derry and Donegal, Gaelic League clubs played an instrumental role in forming hurling clubs and promoting the popularity of the game among its membership and the general public (Hassan 2009, 81; Hunt 2009, 200–201). Likewise, the Ancient Order of Hibernians (AOH) also played a key role in the reorganization of the GAA, especially in Ulster.[45] At its 1905 National Convention, a unanimous motion was passed asking its branches across Ireland to help foster Gaelic games in their localities (*Derry Journal*, September 6, 1905). In Tyrone, the AOH voted to fine or expel members taking part in sports other than Gaelic games and the organization was praised for being 'the backbone' of the GAA in the county (*Fermanagh Herald*, October 6, 1906).[46]

The emergence of cultural nationalism as a force within Irish society fostered an atmosphere among the country's youth that was conducive to the GAA's message. But even more significantly, it would feed into the Association a new generation of educated, professional officials who would become prominent at both a local and national administrative level. In place of the farmers, labourers and tradesmen, who had hitherto composed the bulk of its national membership, a new class of members emerged drawn increasingly from teachers, office clerks and civil servants, or in effect those within Irish society for whom the emerging ideology of cultural nationalism exerted its most powerful psychological appeal (Hutchinson 1987, 152; De Búrca 1999, 66; Nolan 2005, 69). For example, in Kerry, participation in the Association by members drawn from the professional classes increased by 67.5% between 1888 and 1916, while the numbers classified as shop assistants and clerks quadrupled (McElligott 2013, 140–141). This new class of enthusiastic and well-educated young men rejuvenated the Association in the years after 1900. Their professional and administrative talents helped to turn the Association into a profitable, ordered and efficient organization at all levels. In 1900, the Association approved what would prove to be one of its most important pieces of administrative legislation: the formation of provincial councils to deal with the running of the GAA in the country's four provinces.[47]

With its resurrection, the Association was now in a position to again contest the control of popular sport in Ireland. This fight would take place on both an ideological and practical level. The new breed of cultural nationalists who now infused the leadership of the GAA was determined to place it at the heart of Ireland's nationalist revival. These individuals fervently believed that the Association should be engaged primarily in a project of national and cultural liberation (Rouse 2010, 289–290). By 1901, much of the GAA's leadership found themselves caught up in the all-encompassing cultural nationalism of the era. Little wonder that at its Annual National Convention, delegates approved a motion proposed by Thomas F. O'Sullivan of the Kerry GAA that members would:

pledge ourselves to resist by every means in our power the extension of English pastimes to this country as a means of preventing the Anglicisation of our people. That County Committees be empowered to disqualify or suspend members of the Association who countenance sports which are calculated to interfere with the preservation and cultivation of our distinctive National pastimes. (Croke Park Archive (CPA), GAA/CC/01/01, 15 December 1901)[48]

With this motion, the GAA reintroduced its ban on foreign games, specifically the British sports of rugby, soccer, cricket and hockey. If the administrative evolution of the GAA by1901 gave the Association its platform, the ideology of cultural nationalism and the existence of the 'Ban' now gave it a weapon to wrestle back control of popular sport in Ireland. For many, presenting the Ban as a crusade against the Anglicization of Ireland's culture could also ensure the survival and triumph of native games in areas where its popularity was being undermined. In the following years, a bitter struggle, cloaked in the ideology of the cultural revival movement, would take place across the media and sports fields of provincial Ireland; a struggle to destroy the threat of rival codes to the previous dominance of Gaelic games.

Campaigns against rugby and cricket

Eoghan Corry (2009, 100) has contended that the Irish press was arguably the most important catalyst in sustaining the GAA through its early crisis-ridden years. Many within the Association were deeply aware of the immense potential of the print media to reach and influence a far wider audience than at any other time in Irish history. Profoundly affected by the cultural nationalism of the time, a new class of GAA journalists emerged who utilized the press as a stage to attack what they saw as the corrupting influences of Anglicized sports. This propaganda campaign, conducted throughout provincial Ireland, played its role in helping to divert large numbers of athletic young men back into the GAA's ranks. Sports perceived as British were now challenged and their supporters stigmatized (Hunt 2007, 194–195).[49]

Thomas F. O'Sullivan was typical of this new breed of journalists. After being appointed secretary of the Kerry GAA following its re-establishment in May 1900, O'Sullivan became the *Kerry Sentinel*'s official GAA correspondent.[50] From its pages, O'Sullivan launched a crusade to secure the county as a Gaelic games stronghold. Given the real danger that rugby was posing to the pre-eminence of Gaelic games there, it was no surprise that the sport's advocates bore the brunt of O'Sullivan's wrath. In a heated debate with one correspondent on the necessity of a foreign games ban, O'Sullivan declared 'I am not in favour of crushing all imported sports ... merely ... athletic exercises like rugby ... which are calculated to injuriously affect National pastimes' (*Kerry Sentinel*, February 22, 1902). In December 1901, O'Sullivan lamented that the game had a foothold in most Kerry towns and it was necessary that decisive action should now be taken before it spread into rural districts 'bringing with it the pestilential spirit of Anglicisation' (*Kerry Sentinel*, December 18, 1901). O'Sullivan was instrumental in the Ban being reactivated within the GAA's constitution. By presenting it as a crusade against the Anglicization of Ireland's culture, he also wished to ensure the survival and dominance of Gaelic games in Kerry through undermining the threat posed by rugby's popularity there. He argued that:

> the persons who are promoting the extension of Rugby, Association, and the other anglicising agencies ... are doing more to blot out our Nationality than the British Government. If our people were self-respecting, ... if instead of hob-nobbing with the avowed enemies of their country, and aping foreign manners and customs, and as a result, degenerating from sterling Irishmen into contemptible West Britons ... they endeavoured to realise the passionate

aspiration of nationhood, there would be no fear of the ultimate triumph of our National cause, the success of which is imperilled not by British treachery or brute force, but by the recreantcy of un-Irish and anti-Irishmen ... [We have] every desire to prevent our young men from becoming anglicised cads ... Irish games which are superior from an athletic standpoint should be good enough for self-respecting Irishmen who have no ambition to renounce their nationality. (*Kerry Sentinel*, January 11, 1902)

Following Tralee's RFC's defeat in the 1902 Munster Cup, O'Sullivan, with unmistakeable glee, inserted a mock obituary into his column proclaiming that the team had succumbed and 'died ... after an hour's painful illness. Regretted by a large circle of shoneens – R.I.P' (*Kerry Sentinel*, March 22, 1902).[51] In the aftermath of this defeat, O'Sullivan reported satisfactorily that many of Tralee's players 'have given up the ghost as far as rugby is concerned' (*Kerry Sentinel*, March 29, 1902). He also mocked the attempts by the Listowel Rugby club president Jack Macaulay to keep the sport alive by applying for a £50 grant from the IRFU to try and promote the sport in the district, claiming that he could 'not even get his own employees to play the game' (Kerry Sentinel, 29 March 1902). The patrons of rugby in Kerry, lacking the countywide organization of the revitalized local GAA and without a voice in the increasingly nationalist popular media, could not hope to fight off such a determined attack on its status.[52] Kerry was distant from the heartland of Munster rugby, and the province's branch of the IRFU, based in Cork city, was dominated by officials from there and Limerick city. Weak local administration of the game was compounded by O'Sullivan's persuasive tirades. In Kerry, O'Sullivan helped to change the popular perception of rugby by arguing that it represented simply another extension of the 'British garrison' in Ireland. Among the local nationalist press, the reporting of the game virtually ceased after late 1902. Once the county captured its maiden All Ireland football title in 1905, rugby effectively slipped into the background of Kerry's sporting history.

In the southwest, it was the organizational strength of the revitalized GAA at a local level that allowed the Association to benefit in membership terms from the propaganda campaign conducted by the likes of O'Sullivan. Outside the cities of Cork and Limerick, rugby was in want of a strong administrative structure. In rural areas, the combination of the GAA's ban, along with accompanying press campaigns that vilified British sports, decidedly stymied rugby's potential development and those clubs that survived struggled for any level of permanence (O'Callaghan 2011, 52). In west Limerick, many GAA clubs were reformed, including the Newcastle West Boer GAA club that declared their intention 'to do away with English pastimes that had lately been making serious encroachments to the determinant of national pastimes in the area' (*Limerick Leader*, May 13, 1901). However in Limerick City, where rugby had its strongest foothold in the region, many Gaels looked with envy at the success of the re-established Kerry GAA in combating its popularity. The *Limerick Leader* found it:

> depressing to contemplate that the fire of athleticism which kindled such a brilliant blaze wherever a branch of the GAA sprang into life in Limerick some two years back, and which has been instrumental in touching those sterling Kerry Gaels into their former life and strength, should now have burned so low, that the void from which the present splendid board of the Kingdom sprang, is now threatened to become the destiny of that of Garryowen' rugby. (*Limerick Leader*, October 30, 1901)

In November 1902, O'Sullivan was instrumental in a more stringent resolution on foreign games being adopted by the national GAA. This rendered it compulsory for county boards to expel Gaelic players 'participating in, or encouraging in any way West-British pastimes' like rugby, cricket, and Association football (CPA, GAA/CC/01/01, 30 November 1902). Yet conscious of the popularity of rugby among the city's working class, the Limerick County Board feared the effect that the rule would have on its membership who played both Gaelic and rugby (*Limerick Leader*, December 1, 1902). Similarly in Cork, the popularity of rugby among GAA members in the city meant that resistance to the Ban by those who controlled the Cork GAA was marked. The *Cork Weekly Reporter* argued that 'enforcement as far as Cork city and a large part of the county is [*sic*] concerned, will result in the disorganization of many prominent clubs'.[53] The County Board's tolerance of foreign games received censure from many rural Cork clubs. A meeting of representatives from those in east and south Cork in April 1901 rued that at a time 'when anti-Irish sports such as hockey, soccer and rugby were everyday increasing and gaining ground in county, the good old native games were becoming unknown and fast dying out', a situation 'chiefly due to the unsportsmanlike and unpatriotic actions of the so-called Cork County Board' (*Cork Weekly Examiner*, April 13, 1901). O'Sullivan enjoyed remarkable success in destroying the appeal of rugby among the GAA's sporting constituency in Kerry. However, similar campaigns in Cork and Limerick cities proved less successful, as a consequence of rugby's stronger organizational structure there. Nevertheless, the combination of the ban and media campaigns against rugby played a key role in halting the spread and appeal of rugby in rural districts of the southwest.

Areas of provincial Ireland where cricket had overtaken the GAA in popularity were similarly targeted by those who wished to reassert the dominance of Gaelic games. Individuals, especially those from Catholic and therefore ostensibly nationalist backgrounds who continued to play and promote the game, were especially pilloried.[54] In Kilkenny, the local GAA sought to wrestle back control over popular sport in the wake of the reintroduction of the Ban. Dan O'Connell, the Kilkenny GAA Secretary, denounced the widespread practice of illegal tournaments and games being held by GAA clubs that had not affiliated with the county board because cricket players on their teams would then be liable for automatic expulsion. He called for this practice to be eradicated and for the Ban to be 'utilised for the purpose of organizing means in different districts against the furtherance of games of Saxon invention' (*Kilkenny People*, June 24, 1905). The number of active cricket clubs there did decline significantly from 30 to 21 between 1905 and 1906. Despite this, cricket, though weakened by the resurgence of the GAA in Kilkenny, was still played relatively widely in the county for several years after (O'Dwyer 2006, 66–67). However in Tipperary, where cricket enjoyed similar popularity, Bracken (2004, 120) has concluded that the introduction of the foreign games ban and the ideological fervour that accompanied it represented 'the death knell' for the previous success of cricket in rural areas.

Westmeath offers one of the best examples of how the combination of local GAA reorganization and intense media campaigns eliminated the threat posed by cricket to Gaelic games. On the back of the reestablishment of the Westmeath County Board in 1904, local nationalist newspapers like *The Midland Reporter* began a determined assault on cricket's credibility (Hunt 2007, 194). The newspaper declared that it 'constantly advocated the upholding of Gaelic pastimes and preached a crusade against the games of the foreigner'(*Midlands Reporter*, September 29, 1904).[55] Commenting on a cricket match near the village of Stoneyford, the paper announced:

> English and imported games … in the larger centres … have been slowly but surely eradicated by the voice of popular opinion; and even as a beaten enemy will retire to their mountain fastness in the hour of defeat, so the thrust-out-of-place game of cricket in Westmeath betakes itself to obscure villages like Stoneyford and others of that ilk to sulk in their obscurity. (*Midlands Reporter*, June 30, 1904)

Such places were condemned as 'simply useless so far as Ireland is concerned' (*Midlands Reporter*, July 28, 1904).[56] So effective was the paper's campaign against cricket that at a meeting of the Westmeath GAA in March 1905, delegates declared the no one had done more than the editor of the *Midland Reporter* 'to place the GAA in its present sound state, it has practically annihilated West British games in our county' (*Midland Reporter*, March 25, 1905). As Hunt has shown, once the GAA revived in Westmeath, cricket clubs proved an important source for players of the game.[57] By 1905, cricket's dominant position in rural Westmeath was eclipsed by Gaelic games (Hunt 2007, 215). As in Kerry, much of this was due to the administrative weakness of the game once the county's GAA had been reorganized.

The GAA versus Association football

What is significant about the campaigns against cricket and rugby is that invariably the game subjected to harshest denouncement in a given area was the one that had the most success in penetrating the former sporting consistency of the GAA. Where soccer's popularity had usurped the local GAA, advocates of the game were similarly targeted and like other parts of provincial Ireland, it was in the pages of the local press that the propaganda campaign between both was most keenly contested. In April 1906, the nationalist *Donegal News* argued that soccer's 'evil effects on the moral of the people would of themselves call loudly for their suppression'. Gaelic sports imbued players:

> with a good national and healthy moral spirit ... [and] not only do they develop the muscular parts of the body in proper proportion and thereby lend grace and easy dignity to their movement, but also ... strengthen the voice and lend a greater facility for its development, [yet] the foreign game ... has done for the Irish physique what the foreign language has done for the Irish mind. (*Donegal News*, April 21, 1906)

As exemplified in the above passage, the dominant image constantly being reinforced was Gaelic players who were morally and physically superior athletes and whose skill and bravery contrasted sharply with practitioners of Anglicized sports, tainted as they were by their associations with professionalism, modernity and social degeneration. This imagery fitted into the developing national consensus of the superiority of traditional Irish life over modern and increasingly Anglicized society.[58]

However, soccer would prove an entrenched opponent and tackling its popularity proved a much sterner challenge. A principle reason was that more so than rugby and cricket, the social base that comprised the GAA and IFA and from which they sought to enhance their membership, was, generally, the same socio-economic group. This ensured that by the 1900s, the IFA was seen as the main challenge to the GAA in terms of club strength, while soccer was clearly the most popular sport in many regions, particularly Ulster (Connolly and Dolan 2013, 856). There, the battle between both codes for the affections of young Irishmen was often most intense. Soccer's popularity in Ulster had much to do with the continued organizational weakness of the GAA there. It was only in 1903 that an Ulster GAA Council was finally formed and it took until 1906 before all nine counties had a functioning County Board (Curran 2012a, 139). Writing in 1905, R.A. Whyte, a member of the GAA's Central Executive, acknowledged that the province had been 'thoroughly and effectively saturated with the glamour of foreign games' (*Anglo-Celt*, August 12, 1905). Calls by Monaghan delegates to exempt the province from the Ban at that year's Ulster GAA Convention is evidence of how much its membership in such areas still relied heavily on teams backboned by soccer players.[59]

In Fermanagh, the reorganization of the local GAA in 1904 resulted in soccer promoters there petitioning the IFA for a £50 grant to reassert the game in the region. In turn, the Fermanagh Division of the AOH called a meeting 'to tackle the Belfast Mongrels who would dare to bribe with £50 the boys of the county to forsake the game of their forefathers'. With the help of the Fermanagh County Board, they resolved to organize a GAA club in every single parish (*Fermanagh Herald*, October 6, 1906). Despite this, the Fermanagh GAA struggled and by April 1905, only 10 clubs had affiliated to the body (*Derry Journal*, April 19, 1905).[60] For much of the next decade, soccer's growth in the county curtailed the development of the GAA (Brock 1984, 22/32). This was largely due to the relatively strong local organization of the game there. The donation of £50 from the IFA allowed a new Fermanagh and Western League to be created in 1907, giving soccer players access to a competitive football programme.[61] Yet as Curran has observed, such financial assistance on the part of IFA was exceptional (Curran 2014, 80).[62]

Donegal serves as perhaps the most interesting example of a region where the attempted resurgence of the GAA failed to impact on soccer's popularity. The battle against soccer there was taken up by Seamus MacManus, a prominent local IRB member and leading local organizer of the Gaelic League (Curran 2010, 80). As with O'Sullivan's campaign in Kerry, MacManus used the local nationalist press to publicly attack the popularity of soccer in the region. In March 1905, he declared it:

> a great pity that while the other counties of Ireland have awakened to the fact they are Irish, and have adopted again their own Irish games in preference to games introduced by the foreigner, Donegal alone, one of the most Gaelic counties in Ireland, should not realise its duty. There are many great football clubs in Donegal, almost all of them playing football under foreign rules ... the time has come, however, when they must fall into line with the rest of Ireland, or else seem to take sides against their country. (*Derry Journal*, March 1, 1905)

MacManus utilized his position within the local Gaelic League to continue his appeal and in April 1905, he put forward a resolution for its members to discard the playing of Association football in the region (*Derry Journal*, April 14, 1905). He also demanded that representatives of soccer clubs in Donegal should hold a meeting and resolve to introduce Gaelic games throughout the county. This, he felt, would see 'the conclusion of the Association regime' (*Derry Journal*, March 1, 1905). An added spur to MacManus' efforts was news that a County Board had been re-established in neighbouring Derry (*Derry Journal*, May 26, 1905). Following this, a meeting of members of the Donegal United Football Club decided to abandon soccer and revive a GAA club in the town. The *Derry Journal* also reported that in Mountcharles, Dunkineely and St John's point, GAA clubs were being formed (*Derry Journal*, April 19, 1905). Nevertheless the problems MacManus would face in Donegal were foreshadowed at a meeting of the revived Derry GAA that September. Its secretary complained that popularizing Gaelic games in the county was very difficult as 'the roots of the foreign games have struck very deep' and the work of undoing its success will 'undoubtedly be long and arduous' (*Derry Journal*, September 11, 1905). As the summer progressed further reports of soccer teams willing to change allegiance were not forthcoming and Curran has speculated that MacManus' failure to immediately offer any competitive alternative to local soccer tournaments was a factor (Curran 2012b, 245). Only in late October did MacManus succeed in establishing a working County Board in Donegal (*Derry Journal*, February 12, 1906). Despite its formation, Gaelic games there, similar to the experience in Derry and Fermanagh, struggled against soccer's popularity among the local population.[63] At the end of 1905, 32 soccer clubs were recorded in Donegal, while the County Board had affiliated just three teams (Curran 2012a, 431). Local Unionist papers, such as the *Derry Sentinel*, also began to attack the reformed Derry GAA, stating that its members were nothing but 'parochial humbugs and tin-pot warriors' and that 'sensible Irishmen' would not support it (*Derry Journal*, February 12, 1905).[64]

Notwithstanding the best efforts of men like MacManus neither the Donegal nor Derry GAA succeeded in establishing itself as a serious threat to the popularity of soccer in the region at this time.[65] By October 1908, the *Donegal Independent* reported that GAA matches there were 'a thing of the past' (Curran 2010, 114).[66] Donegal thus represents a prime example of how the entrenched popularity of foreign games and the lack of strong local GAA administration limited the influence of cultural nationalists to spread Gaelic games at the expense of British sports and reassert control over popular sport in the region.

Conclusion

In the 15 years under consideration, an earnest, often bitter, battle for supremacy between native and imported sports was played out across much of provincial Ireland. Ireland was a unique case where the global sports of the Victorian sporting revolution came up against popular native games that had successfully aped the codification and administrative templates of their rivals. This was the GAA's great strength. It offered its members the chance to run and administer clubs affiliated to a national sports body and the chance to participate in local and national competitions according to standardized rules while simultaneously catering for the idiosyncrasies of Irish life and culture (see Garnham 2004b). Yet, perversely, this was also the Association's weakness. When the GAA collapsed, there were few impediments for many of its former sportsmen to become actively engaged in rugby, soccer or cricket. The club and competitive structures of those sports were easily recognisable to Gaelic athletes. In the absence of Gaelic games activity, former players became increasingly involved in rugby in the rural southwest, cricket across the Irish midlands and soccer in many parts of the northwest. It is evident that the surge in interest and participation in these sports in the three regions considered bears a direct correlation with the local collapse of their main sporting rival, the GAA.

Once the Association began to restructure itself and, crucially, reaped the benefits of the emerging cultural nationalist movement, it was again able to contest control of popular sport in Ireland. The pervasive ideology of the Gaelic Revival and determination to eradicate the vestiges of Anglicization within Irish life gave advocates of Gaelic games a powerful weapon to brandish at supporters of 'British' sports. Yet it is surely significant that while all 'British' games were denounced, only specific sports were actively targeted in each of the regions studied here. These were the sports that had most successfully appealed to would-be GAA members and that threatened most seriously the Association's sporting monopoly on a local level. Media campaigns and patriotic considerations took their toll, but it is noteworthy that the counties in which such appeals had the most success, (Kerry/Westmeath) were areas where the GAA's rival (rugby/cricket) was weakly organized. For the likes of Donegal or Limerick city, the strong organizational structure of soccer and rugby respectively and the continuing feebleness of local County Boards ensured that despite the cultural atmosphere of the day, the games of the 'Saxon' remained dominant.

Disclosure statement

No potential conflict of interest was reported by the author.

Notes

1. Although in the case of cricket, by the 1870s the game had reached a level of popularity in many rural parts of counties such as Westmeath, Tipperary and Kilkenny.
2. The GAA's administrative structure consists of a Central Executive (later renamed the Central Council), which administers the games nationally under which are individual county boards, which administer and run competitions within their own county bounds.

3. For a discussion on motivations behind the GAA's formation and Michael Cusack's determination to open up Irish sport to the ordinary working Irish men, see Rouse (2009).
4. Membership numbers are estimated from police statistics on the GAA's strength, which indicated that there was an average membership of 53 men per affiliated club (NAI, CBS Index, 2792/S).
5. By 1889, the Irish Football Association (IFA) numbered only 65 clubs eventually rising to 199 by 1902. The Irish Rugby Football Union meanwhile had a mere 47 registered clubs by the time the GAA was formed (Garnham 2004b, 43; O'Callaghan 2011, 40).
6. A recent exception is Gerry Finn (2010, 2255–2287) who has argued that elite public schools in Ireland and Trinity College actually played a key role in disseminating sports of British origin among the Irish population.
7. Yet as more regional studies of the Association emerge the likes of Dónal McAnallen have begun to further critique this view, arguing that the peculiarities of the GAA's development and expansion across Ireland show it 'was, in fact, more counter-Victorian than Victorian'(McAnallen 2014, 63).
8. A notable exception is Mandle (1994).
9. More than 56% of the total economically active male population of the country was directly employed in farming in 1891, while in more rural counties that figure was as high as 72.5% (*Census of Ireland, 1891. Part II. General Report, with Illustrative Maps and Diagrams, Tables, and Appendix*, [C. 6780], H.C. 1892, XCI.1, p. 356).
10. The inevitable result was a sustained slide in prices for Irish farmers. Over the next decade, rural Ireland would witness a prolonged depression, interspersed with frequent potato crop failures.
11. A total of 61.8% of GAA members depended on agriculture for employment, a figure that does not include the thousands of GAA players whose employment was geared towards a supporting role for the agricultural economy. For example, occupations such as shop assistants and office clerks were a popular career choice for younger farmer's sons and these groups formed the majority of the 16.2% of the GAA's membership identified in Hunt (2009, 184–186) national survey as belonging to the commercial class.
12. Better economic opportunities in Britain and North America for those families decimated by the agricultural situation in Ireland, accounted for this steep rise (Fitzpatrick 1980, 129).
13. During the period 1886–1905, 96.7% of GAA members were aged between 15 and 35 (Hunt 2009, 192).
14. In November 1890, Parnell's political power was at its zenith but it quickly unravelled once his affair with his married mistress Kitty O'Shea made headline news across Britain and Ireland. The scandal caused outrage among political and church leaders. Parnell's allies in Parliament disowned him while on the 6 December 43 members of his own party voted to remove him as leader (Mandle 1994, 103–105).
15. For example, a national conference of the Association's affiliated club representatives in July 1891 pledged its memberships support 'to the leadership and ideals of Charles Stewart Parnell'. *Sport*, July 25, 1891.
16. Before long police reports were observing that the GAA was being torn asunder due to this internal dissension and if this breach was not soon repaired it would become inseparable (NAI, CBS, DICS Reports Box Two, 521/S/2817).
17. Only three County Boards held annual meetings during the 1893 and apart from the counties of Kerry, Cork, Dublin, Waterford, Kildare and Roscommon, which contested that year's All Ireland football championship, the Association remained defunct elsewhere. By January 1894, only 38 clubs survived in the midlands, 33 clubs in the southwest, 17 in the southeast, only 1 in Ulster and a further 29 in the west of the country (NAI, CBS Index, 4467/S/ 7828/S; *Sport*, March 24, 1894).
18. To take the example of Kerry, there were no less than 539 separate GAA teams recorded as being active between 1890 and 1905 (see McElligott 2013, 467–468).
19. This was in stark contrast to areas like central Scotland where 89% of sports club patrons and presidents were either members of the nobility or large landowners. Patronage of GAA clubs by such groups was almost non-existent (Tranter 1989, 232).
20. Blake stressed that the varied interpretation of the GAA's limited rules by individual referees negated a common understanding, 'resulting in players losing all confidence in these officials while spectators were left bewildered by their decisions' (*Sport*, January 28, 1893).

21. One famous example was the 1893 All Ireland Football Final between Cork and Wexford when, following an altercation with an opponent, the referee sent off the Cork player responsible. However, his team-mates refused to play on and left the field, an action which resulted in Wexford being awarded the game and title (*Sport* June 30, 1894).
22. For example, the Kerry County Board refused to affiliate with the Central Executive and take part in the All Ireland in 1896 owing to a dispute with officials in Dublin over the match venue for that year's Munster final (*Kerry Sentinel*, February 15, 1896).
23. As Rouse (1993, 341) argues, there was no political or ideological motivation to the ruling, rather it was simply a measure designed to force GAA clubs to affiliate to the ruling body so as to gain as much revenue as possible from their affiliation fees.
24. In Kerry, the local RIC played a key role in the resurgence in popularity of cricket in the county in the mid-1890s. Meanwhile, association football was first introduced to the county at this time by military regiments, such as the Durham Light Infantry being stationed in the military barracks in the county's capital Tralee (*Kerry Sentinel*, February 10, 1894/June 19, 1895/April 8, 1896).
25. Indeed, before its collapse many within the Kerry GAA were already concerned at the growth of the rival sport. When one attendee asked at a meeting of the County Board in 1894 if the organization was being too 'conservative' in not allowing its members to play rugby, the members response was that the class of men who run that game 'would poison and hang everything Gaelic' given the chance'(*Kerry Sentinel*, April 17, 1894).
26. The sample consisted of selecting a pool of 32 players from various rugby combinations from 1897 to 1900 and matching them to census material from 1901. Players names taken from following teams: Tralee RFC 1897/1899/1900, Tralee Wreckers 1900, Tralee Pioneers RFC 1900, Killarney RFC 1898/1899, St Brendan's Seminary Killarney team 1899.
27. O'Sullivan was a Killarney native who had gained fame in 1895 by captaining Queen's College Cork to victory in the Munster Senior Cup. He also became the first Kerry man to be capped internationally by Ireland (Larner 2005, 259).
28. Indeed the meeting chairman argued 'that the rugby game improved the condition of players who had afterwards looked to play in Gaelic matches' (*Kerry Sentinel*, November 26, 1898).
29. Such was the growing local enthusiasm for the sport that for the first time, the rail network arranged special match day services travelling from Kerry to Dublin for the upcoming Irish rugby internationals (*Kerry Sentinel*, February 10, 1900).
30. For example, the inaugural meeting of the Listowel rugby club in October 1899 was presided over by John Macaulay, one of the founding members of the Garryowen RFC (Dillon 2010, 13).
31. This lack of competitive matches became all the more common as local county boards became inactive and championships were abandoned or left to drag on for years at a time. The Kilkenny County Board collapsed in 1891, while the Westmeath county board suffered a similar fate in 1893 (O'Dwyer 2006, 54; Hunt 2007, 150).
32. That May, the local Independent Wanders GAA club also decided to change their allegiance to cricket (Hunt 2007, 156–157).
33. Meanwhile in Galway, the collapse of the local GAA helped to inject new life into cricket's appeal in the county. The Tuam Stars club had been favourites to win the 1891 Galway football championship but were defeated in its early rounds. Following their bitter defeat, the club quickly disbanded due to inactivity and the growing acrimony within the county's GAA leadership over the Parnell split. In the club's absence, the Tuam Cricket Club prospered, being augmented by players from Stars. The influx of these trained and competitive players emboldened the club to affiliate to the Connacht Cricket Union and subsequently win the inaugural Connacht Senior Cricket Cup that same year (O'Donoghue 1987, 132).
34. For example, by January 1894, only one affiliated GAA club, located in Belfast, was recorded as still being active (CBS Index, 7828/S, 31 January 1894).
35. Garnham (2004b, 95–96) study has shown that 63.6% of contemporary professional soccer players in Ireland were registered as either skilled labourers, artisans or white collar workers, occupations that in large urban centres like Belfast or Dublin would be little impacted by decline in wider agricultural economy.
36. This is further evidenced by the Derry Board's decision to ban the handling of the ball in Gaelic football matches, contrary to the GAA's own rules. The intention was to help facilitate soccer players (*Derry Journal*, March 12/26, 1890).

37. In November 1891, the Bishop of Derry publicly denounced the playing of Gaelic games on Sundays (Corry 1993, 55).
38. The decline of GAA clubs at the expense of soccer in the region can be traced using the example of Buncrana club, Cahir O's from the Inishowen peninsula. They were the most active GAA club in the area, playing 13 matches in 1889. Yet in 1890, the Cahir O's participated in only eight matches and in August were said to have become inactive. In April 1893, a Derry soccer team played a match against Buncrana and this indicates that the GAA club had since switched to soccer (Curran 2012b, 126–127).
39. Likewise, a rule was passed stating that 'no political questions of any kind shall be raised at any of its meetings and no GAA club shall take part as a club in any political movement' (*Sport*, May 4, 1895).
40. For example, he clearly defined the previously continuous rules surrounding the catching of and running with the ball in Gaelic football, stating that once caught, the ball must now be kicked immediately and cannot be hopped, thrown or carried. Carrying was defined as moving more than four steps with the ball in hand. He also introduced comprehensive rules empowering referees to terminate matches due to interference of players and spectators. Clubs were also now expected to take precautions to prevent spectators from threatening or assaulting referees, officials or players during or after matches (*Sport*, May 4, 1895; Lennon 2010, 42–52).
41. During his tenure, the number of clubs affiliated to the Association grew from 114 to 357, while income mushroomed from £284 to £1176 (See Blake 1900). However, Blake's tenure was not to endure. In 1898, he was dismissed from office over claims of his mismanagement of the GAA's finances (4–6). Yet both RIC reports and Blake's own account claim this was only a pretext and in fact, IRB elements within the GAA, led by its president, Frank Dineen, wanted him deposed because of his hostility to their own influence (NAI, CBS, Precis Box 2, 11 February 1898, 15506/S).
42. This 'Gaelic Revival', as it was termed, would ultimately transform the entire cultural, political, economic and social fabric of Ireland. This reawakening of cultural nationalism within Irish society had already been given an impetus by the Home Rule campaign itself which had encouraged many Irish intellectuals to give serious thought as to what shape the society and culture of a politically independent Ireland would be (Hutchinson 1987, 155/168).
43. Douglas Hyde had established the Gaelic League in 1893 to preserve and revive the Irish language. Hyde also wished the organization would stand as a bulwark against the increasing Anglicization of Irish society before the country and its people lost forever a sense of their separate nationality (Comerford 2003, 141). The energetic idealism generated by the League was seen as having the potential to revive the ailing fortunes of the Association (Nolan 2005, 69).
44. This close relationship is not surprising, considering the Association's stated mission to preserve and promote native games against the encroaching Anglicization of Irish sport was for many cultural nationalists a natural extension of their promotion of an independent Gaelic culture and identity personified in the growth of organizations such as the Gaelic League.
45. The Ancient Order of Hibernians was an Irish Catholic and nationalist society that emerged in Ulster in the late nineteenth century and was closely associated with membership of the Irish Parliamentary Party (Garvin 2005, 107–110).
46. At the 1906 Tyrone Annual GAA Convention, up to 65 members representing almost every local AOH branch were recorded as attending the meeting.
47. Their formation resulted in a much greater degree of organization and control at provincial level than the GAA's Central Executive alone could provide. It was a key factor in the revival of the GAA nationally from 1900 onwards. CPA, GAA/CC/01/01, 9 September 1900. By 1907, the number of affiliated GAA clubs stood at 784, with 101 in Ulster, 124 in Connaught, 222 in Munster and 337 in Leinster (De Búrca 1999, 73).
48. As De Búrca (1999, 71) argued, this re-imposition of the ban on GAA members playing foreign games 'was a practical application in the realm of sport of the policy of de-Anglicization, which had been advocated by cultural nationalists like Hyde as far back as 1892'.
49. Any connection with the British establishment could now leave GAA members open to media condemnation. In Kilkenny, a prominent GAA referee and Gaelic Leaguer, Jack McCarthy, drew the scorn of the *Kilkenny People* because he attended a ball being held to celebrate the return from the Boer War of a local British Army Colonel. 'Union-Jack', as he was labelled,

50. The *Kerry Sentinel* was at that point the most popular paper in Kerry and its editor, Edward Harrington, was a staunch support of Irish Parliamentary Party.
51. *Shoneens* and *West Britons* were pejorative terms for Irishmen who imitated English ways. Moreover, they were men 'who never shied away from toasting the health of the English King' (see for example *Kerry Sentinel*, January 11/March 22, 1902).
52. Under O'Sullivan's shrewd administration, the Kerry GAA blossomed and as secretary he laid the foundation for the county's dominance of Gaelic football in the years after 1905 (McElligott 2013, 124–127).
53. Indeed, while O'Sullivan argued that the time had come 'when a line should be drawn between the friends and the enemies of the GAA, and the more coercion that was applied, the better', Mat O'Riordan, representing the Cork Board, said every club in Cork would suffer if rugby men were excluded from GAA's ranks (*Cork Weekly Examiner*, December 6, 1902).
54. In his autobiography Patrick Heffernan, a Catholic middle-class doctor from rural Tipperary, bitterly recalled how he was decried as an 'imperialist' and 'shoneen' for his continuing involvement with the game (Heffernan 1958, 1/9). Prominent local advocates of the Irish revival who engaged in such exports of British cultural colonialism were subjected to particular social ostracization. In Claremorris, a prominent member of the local Gaelic League who joined the town's cricket team was heckled by the *Connaught Telegraph* as 'the latest addition to the ranks of West Briton shoneens' who had betrayed his conviction by 'joining the nation killers'. The paper threatened that he had 'one week to withdraw from the cricket club' or else they would expose him to the whole community (*Connaught Telegraph*, June 2/16, 1906). Evidently he heeded this warning and within a few weeks the paper was reporting that the individual was no longer involved with the club (*Connaught Telegraph*, July 14, 1906).
55. The paper began to carry a weekly satirical column entitled 'In Lighter Vein' written by the anonymous 'The Man in the Street', which specialised in taunting Westmeath cricketers.
56. Moreover such people were accused of looking

> to the Saxon with admiration, and they imitate him in every respect … They are incapable of thinking for themselves, and like a moth around a candle, they hanker after English ideals, although their limited intelligence does not allow them to successfully imitate. (*Midland Reporter*, September 7, 1905)

57. To take one example, the Ringtown hurling club was founded in February 1904 and shared direct lineage with the area's cricket team (Hunt 2007, 199–201).
58. McDevitt (1997, 263) argues that such constant reinforcement of the supremacy of Gaelic games allowed them to become a 'hallmark of the Gaelic Renaissance', with hurling and football producing examples of Irish masculinity which gave contemporary Irish society an image to be proud of. Such romantic views, especially of hurling, remained common with historians of the GAA well into the 1940s. Carbery (1946, 57–59), for example, credited the establishment of the GAA and the ensuing popularization of hurling, as bringing about the regeneration of Irish culture and the 'spiritual emancipation' of the Irish people.
59. The Monaghan delegates argued that the GAA was still only finding its feet in a district that was 'run all over' by soccer and such draconian measures would set back the GAA's progress terminally. In the end, the Ulster convention decided to recommend to the Central Executive that the foreign games ban should not apply in Ulster (*Anglo-Celt*, December 30, 1905). Despite this when the motion came before the GAA's annual convention on 27 January, it was defeated by an overwhelming majority (*Anglo-Celt*, February 3, 1906).
60. Indeed the body blamed much of this on the local press for not giving enough prominence to GAA matches, while instead devoting most of its sports pages to soccer (*Derry Journal*, January 29, 1906).
61. I am indebted to Dr Conor Curran for allowing me to use some of his most recent research.
62. During this period, the IFA failed to take the lead in establishing county football associations to effectively administer soccer in individual counties. As a result, only five local football associations were registered with the IFA by 1900.

63. In mid-November, a meeting of the Donegal GAA stated that the Killybegs and Barnesmore football clubs had voted to remain playing soccer as their players considered it to be a superior game to Gaelic football (*Derry Journal*, November 17, 1905). The rules of soccer certainly seem to be far more commonly understood in the region. A report of a Gaelic football county championship match held in Derry City in December 1906 complained that not only were both clubs unable to gather together a full side, but both goalkeepers persisted in picking the ball off the ground and throwing it to their players, soccer style, which is illegal under Gaelic rules (*Derry Journal*, January 1, 1906).
64. There was obviously a degree of sectarian tensions between both codes, with the *Derry Journal* remarking that opposition to the GAA 'by the Unionist people ... simply arises out of religious and political prejudice towards everything Irish and Catholic ... Are the Derry Catholics going to allow this Irish movement to be killed by Protestant objectors?' (*Derry Journal*, April 16, 1906).
65. In May 1906, the Donegal Board was reported to have 20 clubs affiliated but by 1907, this number had fallen to seven with Donegal and Derry sharing the lowest number of affiliated clubs to Ulster Council (Curran 2012b, 140–141).
66. Significantly MacManus' decision to emigrate to the USA precipitated the collapse of the County Board less than two years later.

References

Blake, Richard. 1900. *How the G.A.A. Was Grabbed*. Dublin: Richard T. Blake.
Bracken, Patrick. 2004. *Foreign and Fantastic Field Sports Cricket in County Tipperary*. Thurles: Liskeveen Books.
Brock, Gabriel. 1984. *The Gaelic Athletic Association in County Fermanagh*. Enniskillen: Fermanagh GAA.
Carbery, Mehigan, P. D. 1946. *Hurling, Ireland's National Game*. Dublin: Gaelic Publicity Services.
Comerford, R. V. 2003. *Ireland: Inventing the Nation*. London: Arnold.
Connolly, John, and Paddy Dolan. 2013. "The Amplification and De-Amplification of Amateurism and Professionalism in the Gaelic Athletic Association." *The International Journal of the History of Sport* 30 (8): 853–870. doi:10.1080/09523367.2012.763031.
Corry, Eoghan. 1993. *Oakboys: Derry's Football Dream Comes Through*. Dublin: Poolbeg Press.
Corry, Eoghan. 2009. "The Mass Media and the Popularisation of Gaelic Games, 1884–1934." In *The Evolution of the GAA, Ulaidh, Eire agus Eile*, edited by McAnallen, David Hassan and Roddy Hegarty, 100–112. Armagh: Stair Uladh.
Croke Park Archive (CPA). 1911. *GAA/CC/01/01 Central Council Minute Books: 1899–1911*.
Cronin, Mike. 1999. *Sport and Nationalism in Ireland, Gaelic Games, Soccer and Irish Identity since 1884*. Dublin: Four Courts Press.
Cronin, Mike. 2011. "Trinity Mysteries: Responding to a Chaotic Reading of Irish History." *The International Journal of the History of Sport* 28 (18): 2753–2760. doi:10.1080/09523367.2011.626223.
Cronin, Mike, Mark Duncan, and Paul Rouse, eds. 2009. *The GAA: A People's History*. Cork: Collins Press.
Curran, Conor. 2010. *Sport in Donegal: A History*. Dublin: History Press Ireland.
Curran, Conor. 2012. "The Development of Gaelic Football and Soccer Zones in County Donegal, 1884–1934." *Sport in History* 32 (3): 426–452. doi:10.1080/17460263.2012.724699.
Curran, Conor. 2012b. "Why Donegal Slept: The Development of Gaelic Games in Donegal, 1884–1934." PhD diss., De Montfort University.
Curran, Conor. 2014. "Networking Structures and Competitive Association Football in Ulster, 1880–1914." *Irish Economic and Social History* 41 (1): 74–92. doi:10.7227/IESH.41.1.5.
De Búrca, Marcus. 1999. *The GAA: A History*. 2nd ed. Dublin: Gill & Macmillan.
Devlin, P. J. 1935. *Our Native Games*. Dublin: Gill & Son.
Dillon, Thomas. 2010. *Listowel Rugby Club Celebrating 110 Years, 1900–2010*. Listowel: Listowel Rugby Club.
Donnelly, James. 1975. *The Land and the People of Nineteenth-Century Cork: The Rural Economy and the Land*. London: Routledge and Kegan.

Finn, Gerry. 2010. "Trinity Mysteries: University, Elite Schooling and Sport in Ireland." *The International Journal of the History of Sport* 27 (13): 2255–2287. doi:10.1080/09523367.2010.508874.

Fitzpatrick, David. 1980. "Irish Emigration in the Later Nineteenth Century." *Irish Historical Studies* 22 (86): 126–143.

Foley, Foley. 1945. *Kerry's Football Story*. Tralee: The Kerryman.

Garnham, Neal. 2004a. "Accounting for the Early Success of the Gaelic Athletic Association." *Irish Historical Studies* 34 (133): 65–78.

Garnham, Neal. 2004b. *Association Football and Society in Pre-Partition Ireland*. Belfast: Ulster Historical Foundation.

Garvin, Tom. 2005. *The Evolution of Irish Nationalist Politics*. Dublin: Gill & Macmillian.

Hassan, David. 2009. "The GAA in Ulster." In *The Gaelic Athletic Association 1884–2009*, edited by M. Cronin, W. Murphy, and P. Rouse, 77–92. Dublin: Irish Academic Press.

Heffernan, Patrick. 1958. *An Irish Doctor's Memories*. Dublin: Clonmore & Reynolds.

Hunt, Tom. 2007. *Sport and Society in Victorian Ireland: The Case Study of Westmeath*. Cork: Cork University Press.

Hunt, Tom. 2009. "The GAA: Social Structure and Associated Clubs." In *The Gaelic Athletic Association 1884–2009*, edited by M. Cronin, W. Murphy, and P. Rouse, 183–202. Dublin: Irish Academic Press.

Hutchinson, John. 1987. *The Dynamics of Cultural Nationalism: The Gaelic Revival and the Creation of the Irish Nation State*. London: Allen & Unwin.

Larner, Jim, ed. 2005. *Killarney, History and Heritage*. Cork: Collins Press.

Lennon, Joe. 2010. *The Playing Rules of Football and Hurling 1602–2010*. Gormanstown: Northern Recreation Consultants.

Mandle, W. F. 1987. *The Gaelic Athletic Association and Irish Nationalist Politics 1884–1924*. Dublin: Gill & Macmillan.

Mandle, W. F. 1994. "Parnell and Sport." *Studia Hibernica* 28: 103–116.

McAnallen, Dónal. 2009. "The Greatest Amateur Association in the World? The GAA and Amateurism." In *The Gaelic Athletic Association 1884–2009*, edited by M. Cronin, W. Murphy, and P. Rouse, 157–181. Dublin: Irish Academic Press.

McAnallen, Dónal. 2014. "Review of Forging a Kingdom: The GAA in Kerry, 1884–1934." *History Ireland* 22 (1): 63.

McDevitt, Patrick. 1997. "Muscular Catholicism: Nationalism, Masculinity and Gaelic Team Sports, 1884–1916." *Gender and History* 9 (2): 262–284. doi:10.1111/1468-0424.00058.

McElligott, Richard. 2013. *Forging a Kingdom: The GAA in Kerry, 1884–1934*. Cork: Collins Press.

Mullan, Michael. 1996. "The Devolution of the Irish Economy in the Nineteenth Century and the Bifurcation of Irish Sport." *The International Journal of the History of Sport* 13 (2): 42–60. doi:10.1080/09523369608713935.

Murphy, Desmond. 1981. *Derry, Donegal and Modern Ulster 1790–1921*. Londonderry: Aileach Press.

National Archives of Ireland (NAI). 1895. *Crime Branch Special (CBS), District Inspectors' Crime Special (DICS) Reports*.

National Archives of Ireland (NAI). 1892. *Crime Branch Special (CBS) Index*.

National Archives of Ireland (NAI). 1902. *Crime Branch Special (CBS), Inspector General and County Inspector (IG & CI) Reports*.

Nolan, William, ed. 2005. *The Gaelic Athletic Association in Dublin 1884–2000, Vol. 1 1884–1959*. Dublin: Geography Publication.

O'Callaghan, Liam. 2011. *Rugby in Munster A Social and Cultural History*. Cork: Cork University Press.

O'Donoghue, Noel. 1987. *Proud and Upright Men*. Tuam: Clódóirí Lurgan Teo.

O'Dwyer, Michael. 2006. *The History of Cricket in County Kilkenny: The Forgotten Game*. Kilkenny: O'Dwyer Books.

O'Sullivan, T. F. 1916. *Story of the GAA*. Dublin: Abbey Street.

Ó Ceallaig, Séamus P. 1937. *History of Limerick G.A.A. from Earliest Times to the Present Day Part 1, 1888–1908*. Tralee: Anvil Press.

Rouse, Paul. 1993. "The Politics of Culture and Sport in Ireland: A History of the GAA Ban on Foreign Games 1884–1971." *The International Journal of the History of Sport* 10 (3): 333–360. doi:10.1080/09523369308713835.

Rouse, Paul. 2009. "Michael Cusack, Sportsman and Journalist." In *The Gaelic Athletic Association 1884–2009*, edited by M Cronin, W Murphy, and P. Rouse, 47–61. Dublin: Irish Academic Press.

Rouse, Paul. 2010. "Empires of Sport: Enniscorthy, 1880–1920." In *Enniscorthy: A History*, edited by Colm Toibín, 275–296. Wexford: Wexford County Council Public Library Service.

Tranter, Neil. 1989. "The Patronage of Organised Sport in Central Scotland, 1820–1900." *Journal of Sport History* 16 (3): 227–247.

Vaughan, W. E., and A. J. Fitzpatrick, eds. 1978. *Irish Historical Statistics, Population, 1821–1971*. Dublin: Royal Irish Academy.

The *Cork Sportsman*: a provincial sporting newspaper, 1908–1911

David Toms

Department of History, University College Cork, Cork, Republic of Ireland

> This article examines the regional, Cork-based sporting newspaper, the Cork Sportsman, for its lifespan of 3 years, when it was published weekly from 1908 to 1911. The article seeks to place this sporting newspaper in the context of the development of a specialist sporting press in Ireland from the late nineteenth century as well as in the context of the development of sporting coverage in the traditional newspaper trade developing simultaneously both nationally and regionally. Moreover, this article seeks to address why the newspaper had such a short lifespan at a time when coverage of sport in newspapers was growing and expanding in scope in the region. In so doing, this article argues that close examination of sporting newspapers is an important element of understanding the way in which sports history is written, given the significance of newspapers as a source in the methodology of many historians of sport.

Introduction

The relationship between sport and the popular press is a symbiotic one, as examples around the world show. One of the most famous is from Italy, where the winner of the Giro d'Italia wears a pink jersey, symbolising that race's origins and relationship to *La Gazzetta dello Sport*, whose news was printed on pink paper (Foot 2011, *passim.*; Martin 2011, *passim.*) In America, Oriard (1998) argued on American football that without the popular press it would not have been the spectacle of the popular imagination it became. The development of a specialist sporting press followed soon after the emergence of a popular press from the late eighteenth century onwards (Brailsford 1997, 131). Even those early newspapers carried sporting notices. That early impetus of the press to include sporting notifications has been characterised by Tony Collins as part of sports development in line with the emergence of modern capitalist society. Recent scholarly work on sport in late-early modern Ireland gives further credence to Collins' assertion (Kelly 2014, 21 and 22). The emergence of codified sporting practice throughout the nineteenth century saw a further expansion of the specialist sporting press, and the practice was not restricted to Britain, with the sporting press in Italy, France, USA and Japan all vitally important not just in reporting sporting activity, but in many cases assisting in the creation of new competitions (Collins 2013, 57–59). The late nineteenth century in Ireland was marked like England, the USA and several European countries by the emergence of a specialist sporting press with newspapers like *Irish Field and Gentleman's Gazette* (1870), *Sport* (1880), *Ireland's Saturday Night* (1894) and the *Irish Wheelman* (1894), all delivering weekly sporting news to the people of Ireland. As Eoghan Corry Corry (2009, 100) has remarked 'rapid progress in technology, literacy and the self-confidence of newspaper contributors all converged to produce a body of writing that serves as a window into the social mores, concerns and debates of the time'. This was as true for the sporting press as it was for daily newspapers. Equally, the role of the localised press at this time in Ireland is also worth bearing in mind. As Marie-Louise Legg has argued 'the Irish provincial press should not ... be considered as subsidiary or inferior to the national press. It performed an essential role in the development of the idea of the nation and in understanding its parts and varieties' (1998, 174 and 175). Since sporting newspapers emerged with national or single-sport focuses, it is unsurprising that a regionally based sporting newspaper emerged in Ireland as well. Most sporting newspapers published in Ireland from the end of the nineteenth century onwards were usually national in scope or sport-specific, but the *Cork Sportsman* was unique for having a regional focus as its editorial basis in an Irish context.

The relationship between sports history and the newspaper might be seen as equally intertwined. In many respects, the newspaper is a vital part of the methodology of a good deal of sports history. In the Irish context, it is especially valuable. The scholarly work which has emerged in Ireland since the early 2000s on the history of sport has been built in some respects on the back of newspapers – national, local and sporting. Liam O'Callaghan has written that in his work on the social and cultural history of rugby in Munster, the local provincial newspapers 'were particularly valuable', sentiments echoed by Tom Hunt in his work on Westmeath's Victorian sporting culture (O'Callaghan 2011, 243; Hunt 2007, xiii). Given the significant part played by newspapers in underpinning the methodology of much Irish sports history, it is surprising perhaps then that with a number of notable exceptions – chiefly the work of Paul Rouse – the historiography of Irish sport has not seen more in-depth analysis of particular periodicals (2004, 7–22; 2011a, 49–60; 2011b, 117–132).

Rather than focus solely on the coverage of one sport, this article, taking its cue from Conor McCabe's work on the *Football Sports Weekly* (2011), seeks to explore in some detail the *Cork Sportsman*'s short 3-year run considering the paper's development and eventual decline in light of the emerging market for sports coverage in nonspecialist newspapers. What follows will argue that this paper's decline was driven by the three main factors: first, the paper's reliance on voluntary contributions for content. Second, the limited market in which it was operating and finally an inability to keep pace with the technological innovation and economies of scale available to the other non-sporting press in the city that also increasingly reported sporting news.

This will be argued while at the same time illustrating the newspapers ability, thanks to its close connections to local sporting bodies, in particular the local Gaelic Athletic Association (GAA), for outstanding and rich journalism. This will be done by analysing the newspaper's coverage of a 1910 exhibition tour undertaken by two hurling teams to Belgium. This tour has received scant attention in the historiography of Irish sport thus far though it was significant as the first such tour to Europe (King 1998, 11 and 12). Yet, this tour received in-depth coverage from the *Cork Sportsman* and forms the paper's greatest achievement. The *Cork Sportsman* offers us a unique glimpse into Ireland's sporting world in the early twentieth century: it tells us much about the relationship between sport and the printed media; the beginnings of a specialist sporting press and the pioneers of sports journalism in Ireland. It helps us get to the heart of sport in early twentieth century Ireland: sport was a part of popular culture, and the *Cork Sportsman* was a place where this popularity was given expression. Thus, despite being relatively unknown, and underutilised, it proves itself another vital source in the emerging field of Irish sports history.

Sporting Cork: the *Cork Sportsman* and its context

What it was about Cork in this period that saw it become the cradle of just such a regional sporting newspaper? A wide range of sporting activity was engaged by the inhabitants of the city and surrounding countryside by 1908, when the *Cork Sportsman* first appeared. The GAA, founded in November 1884, held its second ever meeting in the city in 1885, and the Association grew rapidly from there. In 1901, the Munster Football Association, a body for the organising of association football in the region had been founded in Cork. Rugby football had emerged in the city in the early 1870s with the local university, University College Cork, founding a rugby football club in 1874. Aside from these field sports, other sports also flourished in the city, with the Sunday's Well Boating and Tennis Club founded in 1899, Dolphin Swimming Club formed in 1901, while rowing went back as far as 1850 when the Lee Rowing Club was founded. Given such a vibrant sporting culture it is unsurprising a sporting newspaper emerged there. Of course, Cork was not unique in the province of Munster for sporting activity, so this in itself is not a sufficient explanation for the emergence of the *Cork Sportsman*. More crucially, Cork was in this period the most significant city in Munster, with a developed commercial base, a sizeable professional middle class, a university, and strong British military presence in the form of both the navy and the army. In the year that the *Cork Sportsman* ceased trading, the population of Cork city and county in that year's census was 392, 104 (Census 1911). Compared with the populations of the two other counties in the province with large cities, Waterford (83, 966) and Limerick (143, 069), Cork was by some way the most populous. One outcome of this greater population was that Cork developed a more varied newspaper culture with a number of daily and weekly newspapers circulating in the city including the *Cork Examiner* (1841), *Evening Echo* (1892), *Cork Constitution* (1873) and *Cork Weekly News* (1883). Other newspapers also emerged, including newspapers that served as organs for particular political parties, such as the O'Brienite *Cork Free Press* (1910).[1] In a city with such a well-developed sporting and newspaper culture the emergence of a specialist sporting newspaper seems less surprising.

General newspaper reporting of sport in Ireland in the 1870s was quite sporadic, with an increase in the 1880s and 1890s until it became a firm fixture in many newspapers at the start of the twentieth century, aided particularly by the increased ability to provide photographic plates in the relaying of a news story. As Tranter notes of the British example 'many ... specialist newspapers and periodicals launched to cash in on the demand for sporting news ...' which were often 'also short-lived' (Tranter 1998, 76). The pattern was somewhat similar in an Irish context. The majority of papers were not hugely successful, but some were. As Rouse (2004, 9) argued, the Irish sporting context called for a compromise 'weekly special'. This compromise was a Dublin-based newspaper simply entitled *Sport*. *Sport* was the first major weekly sporting newspaper in Ireland and was to remain the most successful such paper in early twentieth century Ireland thanks in no small part to its parent paper the *Freeman's Journal*. By having a larger parent company in which it operated, *Sport* was less vulnerable to the difficulties of economy of scale and competition that would ultimately see the *Cork Sportsman* cease printing. Work by Rouse (2004, 9 and 10) situates *Sport* firmly into the story of the Victorian popular press, while noting that it was the quality of the journalism, and not its price or any other factor which ensured its success. As Eoghan Corry has noted of the example of another national daily in Ireland, the *Irish Independent*, it was sport's popular appeal that saw its circulation more than quadruple in a 5-year period (2009, 100–112). As well as boosting the sales of local and national dailies, the corollary of this was to take readers away from the specialist sporting press in time. In England, Richard Holt noted that from the 1920s 'sports reporting and photography was accepted as a crucial and specialized component of popular journalism' (1989, 309). He writes that the cause of sport was taken up by the national dailies 'with a vengeance', not unlike what happened in an Irish context with the emergence in the 1930s of the *Irish Press* (Cronin, Duncan, and Rouse 2009, 192).

As well as the weekly specials that emerged like *Sport*, other sport-specific titles emerged in Ireland: for instance, the *Irish Field and Gentleman's Gazette* provided not just a dedicated sporting weekly, but did so almost primarily for horseracing, hunting, coursing and other sports of the turf. *Gaelic Athlete* (1912) was an exclusively GAA-based newspaper. There are other examples of an Irish paper that catered almost solely for a single sport such as the *Football Sports Weekly* (1925). This paper, produced, circulated and concerned in the main with soccer (though not exclusively) ran for 3 years between 1925 and 1928. This paper has received little enough scholarly attention thus far, though Conor McCabe has written of it that it 'was not part of the establishment: it was much more important – it was part of the everyday' (2011, 158). Similarly, the *Gaelic Athlete* was an organ of the GAA, and it too had a sporadic shelf life, appearing both before and after Ireland's war of independence. *Football Sports Weekly* was something of a mouthpiece for the soccer establishment in Dublin but was highly encouraging of the game elsewhere, particularly in Munster. A similar venture was the *Irish Coursing Calendar*, a newspaper set up by the Irish Coursing Club in 1924. Although a largely coursing and greyhound racing centred newspaper, it also reported on other sports (*Report of the Advisory Committee on the Greyhound Industry 1952*, 44). The proliferation of these titles shows, despite their sometimes uncertain existence, a real appetite for sporting news amongst the Irish public. So it was that in Munster one such paper developed to satisfy the needs of a province where sport was flourishing. That newspaper, the *Cork Sportsman*, was another paper which saw the opportunity to expand the market as *Sport* had done in the 1880s. By the time it began publishing, *Sport* had been the market leader for 28 years. No wonder then that the *Cork Sportsman* also took the weekly special as its publishing model. The *Cork Sportsman* came out on a Saturday, with a roundup of a huge range of sports, which varied depending on the time of the year.

The *Cork Sportsman* was published for just 3 years between 1908 and 1911. In that short time span however it managed to make itself central to the culture of sport in Cork particularly, but to the Munster region of Ireland more generally. By its final year of publication, the newspaper was widely distributed with copies available in some 48 different locations in Cork city alone. Along with 23 locations in the county, the paper was available in Kerry in Tralee and Killarney, Dublin, Waterford and Limerick city and county. It could be purchased on the Cork, Blackrock and Passage Railway, the Cork and Bandon Railway, Cork and Macroom Railway, the Great Southern and Western Railway and the Cork and Muskerry Railway stations (*Cork Sportman*, May 20, 1911).

High distribution levels in the Cork region suggest that the paper was in high demand. The availability of the paper in all the major railway points in the region is important too. Much is often made of the link between the growth of railways and the ability for localised regional sports to become nationally organised (Cronin and Higgins 2011, 43–49) but the newsagents in places like railway termini was surely also crucial to the spread of newspapers as the *Cork Sportsman*'s case indicates. In the second issue of the *Cork Sportsman*, the editor notes that 'one thing has pleased us immensely in connection with our critics – they are united in saying that our paper is "too small", and ... are "asking for more"' (*Cork Sportsman*, May 30, 1908). The early signs were good, with an editorial shortly after noting 'the enthusiastic support we have received from all classes of sportsmen couple [sic] with the fact that advertisers have taken to us' (*Cork Sportsman*, June 6, 1908). Nonetheless the advertising revenue was not sufficient to offset the need for a price-rise. The *Cork Sportsman* was for part of its life sold for a halfpenny, the price later rising to a penny, like its other sporting and general newspaper counterparts. The price rise may be explained by the need to cover the costs of printing, especially since the paper began as four page paper, expanding to eight pages due to demand. Yet, the end of its life had reduced it to just four pages once more (*Cork Sportsman*, May 14, 1909). The anniversary issue was jubilant in its assertion that the paper had achieved its aim of providing more fulsome coverage than the more traditional press with the editor recalling the first editorial and feeling they have matched their ambitions set out there, stating that 'our confident expectation of the co-operation of all classes of sportsmen has been more than realised' (*Cork Sportsman*, May 22, 1909). The paper carried a huge range of notes with everything from association football, rugby, Gaelic games, to water polo and cricket, much of it contributed by passionate followers of these sports who were involved. Much of the material in the paper thus gives us not a dispassionate view from a professional journalist, but most often a view of the sports from practitioners themselves. This was both a great strength and a great weakness in the newspaper. It provides us with a unique insight into the emergence of dedicated sports journalism.

When association football began to develop in Cork at the end of the first decade of the twentieth century, the *Cork Sportsman* closely followed it. As the game spread out from Cork city to Limerick, Tipperary and Waterford, the paper followed these developments closely, writing of the games emergence in Waterford that 'gates of nearly 1,000 have been taken in Waterford City, and if the rate of progress is kept up, Cork will soon be outdistanced' (*Cork Sportsman*, May 22, 1909). The Cork newspaper perhaps ran away with itself when they said there were hopes of a league emerging at that time. Likewise, it was through the pages of the *Cork Sportsman* that we learn that when Manchester City visited the city to play in 1909, that the players as part of their trip kissed the Blarney Stone! (*Cork Sporstman*, April 24, 1909; May 8, 1909). It was invaluable to many of these sports as a place to publish fixture lists and club notices as well as letters exchanges – more than simply reporting matches, it was a crucial element in the sporting culture of Cork and Munster for its short life. More than just a source of news, it was a public forum for discussion about sporting matters. The paper was alive with letter exchanges being conducted between people over the paper's lifespan. This particular function that the newspaper served highlights the important role a periodical like the *Cork Sportsman* had in fostering a sporting community in Ireland. As the season's changed so too did coverage, in winter association football took up the front page while in summer, it was cricket that was often given front billing, while the GAA notes were usually the most detailed. The GAA notes covered the huge range of emerging Gaelic sport in Cork city and county. There was great colour to be found in the journalism in the pages of the *Cork Sportsman* such as when in 1908, the Bohemian Cricket Club in Cork celebrated their championship victory at their end of season dinner. In the report of the dinner, we are let in on the fun of the party:

> The following contributed to an excellent musical programme: – Messrs. A Young, CA Boyle, JM Cullinane, P Riordan, P O'Flynn, V O'Connell, F Leech, F Cussen etc. Mr P Belas acted in his usual capable manner as accompanist. 'The Song of the Beaux' – otherwise the topical duet – was one of the features of the evening, and was sung with much sprightliness by Messrs. Welsby and Carleton, who were also the authors of the amusing verses. When the last encore – and there were many – had been responded to, the duettists were presented with a floral tribute (uncooked) in reward for their efforts. (*Cork Sportsman*, October 24, 1908)

With such lively copy peppered throughout its pages, the editors perhaps had a right to be confident about their publication. Like much of sporting culture in Ireland then, this particular snippet indicates something of the decidedly male contributors and readership of the paper. The advertisements indicate this too: along with the obvious sporting requisites stores and fishing tackle shops that advertised in the pages of the paper, the chief advertisers tended to be drinks companies, bars, suit shops, dry cleaners and similar businesses. Women are noticeable by their absence from the pages of the paper, either as players or as targets of the paper's advertisers. Such confidence in the newspaper's development reached its climax in 1910, when the organ covered in detail the tour of Cork and Tipperary hurlers to Belgium as part of that year's Pan-Celtic Congress. The Pan-Celtic Congress was an initiative to bring together people with an interest in the histories, cultures and languages of the 'Celtic' nations including Ireland, Scotland, Wales and Brittany. The addition of a hurling exhibition to the 1910 Congress held in Namur, Belgium was the brainchild of J. J. Walsh, a stalwart of Cork GAA administration.

The GAA's Belgian tour 1910 and the *Cork Sportsman*

In Ireland, the GAA had by 1910 cemented itself as the foremost sporting organisation on the island. It had recovered from the bleakest days of the 1890s and the Parnell split to re-emerge in the twentieth century as a body with significant popular support and participation.[2] The introduction of a rule that banned the GAA's membership from either attending or playing what it considered 'foreign' games in 1905, described by Richard Holt as '... the most audacious and successful challenge to British sports mounted anywhere in the world' (1989, 240) helped cement the GAA's place as the dominant sporting force in the country. Such was the success of the GAA that J. J. Walsh, then chairman of the Cork County Board, was quoted as saying:

> For centuries past that little Green Isle of theirs had been entirely excluded from the Councils of the Nations of the earth ... for some years the GAA had attained to such a state of development as to need little further advancement at home – and as a consequence it was thought advisable to look further afield. (*Cork Sporsman*, September 3, 1910)

Tours had been a part of the GAA's history from the very foundation of the organisation with the American 'Invasion' of 1888 being perhaps the most famous example. The venture was an attempt by the early GAA to promote the sport by undertaking an exhibition tour while also trying to raise £5,000 to stage the Aonach Tailteann. The tour was a failure financially as American sporting bodies were then quarrelling with each other, depriving the tourists of suitable opposition (Cronin, Duncan, and Rouse 2009, 345 and 346). The failure of the 1888 tour to America is important in understanding the 1910 tour to Belgium. Equally important to understanding the 1910 tour is its presentation as a travel narrative through the pages of the *Cork Sportsman*. This narrative was provided from September to November 1910 by a journalist going under the moniker "Kinalea". Mike Cronin has argued that the journalist who followed the GAA's tour to America in 1888 did more than just report on matches, he observed America 'and the ways in which his comments illuminate the Irish understanding of its western neighbour' mattered (Cronin 2007, 191). Thus was it the case for the 1910 tourists and their accompanying journalist's writings in the *Cork Sportsman*. Kinalea's role as conveyor of the events, and giving a sense of the tour shape still how we as historians understand the Belgian tour. That he did so in the pages of a regional sporting newspaper says something about that paper's significance at that time (Cronin 2007, 190–216).

If Kinalea had an important part to play as the journalist who conveyed the tour to readers back home in Ireland, then an equally important role was played by J. J. Walsh, who as Cork county board chairman, was central to the development of this tour to Belgium. Walsh was Postmaster General in Cork, a member of the Irish Republican Brotherhood, and under his command the Cork GAA was re-organised and vastly improved in its structure.[3] He was a vociferous chairman to have at Central Council meetings in Dublin for the Cork GAA. Walsh's politics were no secret – his reforms of the Cork GAA came largely from a desire to use the GAA as a training ground for men linked to physical force nationalism. As Walsh put it: 'In 1909 we decided to take over the whole responsibility of the GAA in the County. Up to then our efforts were subject to ultimate control by the County Board' (1948, 17 and 18). As a businessman, Walsh was highly dismissive of how the GAA was being run in the county up to that point. He felt that a lack of turnstiles, no proper accounting, and the poor conduct of the Annual Congress was highly damaging to the image, effectiveness and economy of the organisation. Walsh stated that 'the cold truth is that the GAA was, if anything, on the down grade [at the time he took over as chairman in Cork], while all the educated and influential classes were switching over to alien games' (1948, 18). Clearly Walsh felt that the GAA needed to appeal to the greatest number of people possible. Walsh's abilities at organisation excelled themselves in his business dealings:

> A feature of this advance unknown to GAA bodies elsewhere was the fact that we were able to buy shares in the Great Southern Railway, a circumstance that gave us the necessary pull where travel facilities counted for a great deal indeed. (*The Irish Nation*, June 19, 1909)

The Great Southern Railway was to prove a sound investment for Walsh and the Cork GAA. Walsh's forceful nature and his determined mind is perhaps best summed up from this glowing tribute offered to him in the *Irish Independent* on the opening of Aonach Tailteann in 1924:[4]

> We heard his voice declaring the great festival open – the 'JJ' voice that had roared his club to victory on the playing fields of Cork, that had dominated Gaelic Athletic Councils, that had wooed a Railway Co. Directorate to more Sunday passenger traffic and bigger receipts, that had defied British Courts martial to do their darndest, and that later urged on his fellow-prisoners in the sensational breakout of Mountjoy. (*Sunday Independent*, August 3, 1924)

Walsh went on from his job as Postmaster general of Cork, and Cork county board chairman in the GAA to be a Sinn Féin TD for Cork in the 1918 General Election, and was later Minister for Posts and Telegraphs in the Free State Government. Without such a man at the helm, it seems unlikely that Cork, Tipperary or indeed the Munster Council could have got this tour underway. Walsh's determination to improve the lot of the Cork GAA was manifested in his organisation of the 1910 tour, and his access to the *Cork Sportsman* ensured his organisational success would have a public outlet.

The idea of the tour was a simple one: both the Cork and Tipperary senior hurling teams would go to the continent to play exhibition games to showcase the sporting aspects of Gaelic culture as part of the 1910 Pan-Celtic Congress. Cultural nationalism was an important element in broader nationalism not alone in Ireland but across Europe since the middle of the nineteenth century. Sport, especially indigenous sport, was an important signifier of cultural difference. As Derek Sayer has noted of the Sokol movement in the Czech lands 'the organization sought to embody the national ideal in a very literal sense, as photographs of its muscular male gymnasts show' (1998, 106). In the same way, those involved in Ireland's own cultural revival saw Gaelic games as a means of distinction from those in Britain. On this very subject, Douglas Hyde, founder of the Gaelic League, argued as early as 1892 that:

> The work of the [Gaelic athletic] association in reviving our ancient national game of *caman*, or hurling, and Gaelic football, has done more for Ireland than all the speeches of politicians for the last five years ... the physique of our youth has been improved in many of our counties; they have been taught self-restraint, and how to obey their captains; they have been, in many places, weaned from standing idle in their own roads or street corners. (1973, 156 and 157)

In 1910 Belgium, a fellow Catholic and Celtic nation hosted the Pan-Celtic Congress. As part of the event's programme, an exhibition of hurling was arranged. The Pan-Celtic Congress was an international expression of the Gaelic revival then underway in Ireland. It placed the attempts by the Gaelic League to foster and encourage Irish people to speak their own language into a broader transnational attempt to revive minority languages that were understood as belonging to the Celtic race. This was thus called Pan-Celticism (O'Leary 1986, 106). Pan-Celticism and Ireland had a late blooming relationship, due to some opposition to Pan-Celticism in the Gaelic revival movement. Nevertheless Dublin hosted the first congress in 1901. One manifestation of Pan-Celticism (which included the Breton, Manx and Gaelic languages) in Ireland was the monthly journal, *Celtia*. In the journal was to be found grammars, vocabulary and verb tables for various Celtic languages as well as songs and ballads, and editorials and opinion pieces about the part the language revival had to play in the gaining of nationhood. In the very first issue, this was the leading article:

> The opening of the twentieth century finds the Celtic race in the beginning of a new phase of existence. From John O'Groats to the banks of the Loine, and from Galway Bay to the Welsh Marches, the racial instinct is asserting itself in manifold forms, all tending in one direction – the preservation of those characteristics which distinguish the Celtic nationalities from their more powerful neighbours. (*Celtia*, vol. 1, issue 1)

Another form of the 'racial instinct' to which the above extract appealed was the playing of Gaelic games. For an ambitious organiser such as J. J. Walsh, the opportunity to provide a sporting display of Irish national games at a major cultural event like the Pan-Celtic Congress undoubtedly appealed. The tour proved to be one of mixed results. Financially, it was quite disastrous. In terms of attendance and gaining notoriety it was somewhat successful, in Munster at least (De Búrca 1980, 83). There was some preparation in the lead up to the tour to ensure its success, although a variety of factors mitigated the tours success – the rushed organisation of the tour, poor advertising in Belgium itself along with factors like poor weather all ensured that the tour, though it came off, was costly. With little time between the gestation of the idea and its execution, mobilising of volunteers to help drum up support for the tour happened rapidly. In early August, shortly before the teams left, there was a great deal being done to raise funds for the venture. A meeting of the Munster council of the GAA reported on by the *Cork Free Press* on 8 August 1910 saw the following transpire:

> The Council had under consideration the granting of a subscription to the two hurling teams who were to travel from Cork and Tipperary to give an exhibition at the Pan-Celtic Congress. It, however, transpired that the application had not been received in time to admit of its being put on the agenda .... (*Cork Free Press*, August 8, 1910)

There was yet another meeting reported on the 10 August in which an application was made for a loan of £40 for the tour, the issue not being resolved for at least another four days, when a report in the *Cork Free Press* stated that a proposed a loan of some £100 for the tour was passed unanimously (*Cork Frees Press*, August 14, 1910).

In the meantime, there were a number of fundraising matches to be played, with the gate receipts from the games to go to the tour. The first of these was a Dungourney versus Thurles match, since both of these teams made up the bulk of the Cork and Tipperary sides respectively. A game had been organised to be played in Thurles on the 14 August, however, after some complaints, the game was moved to the Athletic Grounds in Cork. The purpose of this game was twofold. As well as being for fundraising purposes, it was also to be used to decide who would play in Belgium. In the event, the game provided neither. Due to a horrendous thunderstorm, the match was abandoned. This meant the tour started out underfunded, hence the £100 loan, and without a team selected on current form.

The Belgian tour received extensive coverage in the *Cork Sportsman* coming in the form of a weekly serialisation. These instalments covered every aspect of the tour, from the journey back and forth, to the matches played and the various receptions the players received along the way from the Belgian people and from the great and good of Belgian life, including Archbishops and Cardinals. Indeed, the tour was seen to be in direct opposition to the spread of British sports on the continent, and an attempt to challenge this emerging hegemony. We are told that 'They decided to give a display of hurling in Belgium, and let the people of Continental Europe decide whether the programme offered by the Kelts or the Saxons was the better one' (*Cork Sportsman*, September 3, 1910). The narrative Kinalea spun turned the tour from a simple exhibition as part of a larger cultural event into where Irish manhood was on display for Europe to see. He wrote of the game played at Fontenoy as part of the tour:

> At times they regarded us with awe as the match got fast and exciting, and like many other foreigners they realised what Irish soldiers in wrath must be like when the Irish even in play can be so fierce. How men could wield such formidable weapons so wildly and still so skilfully they could not imagine. (*Cork Sportsman*, October 8, 1910)

Kinalea finished by noting the Belgians had their stick and ball game reminiscent of hurling, 'but of course not at all so manly or fast' (*Cork Sportsman*, October 8, 1910). There is an attempt to both 'other' the Irishmen for their athletic prowess, while also recognising the common cause of those involved in Pan-Celticism.

Kinalea's travel narrative also had something of the secular pilgrimage about it. This was especially evident in the recounting of the trip to Fontenoy – quoted from above – the centre-piece of the tour. Fontenoy was the site of a battle in May 1745 during the Wars of Austrian Succession, in which the Irish Brigade in the French army particularly distinguished itself (Murphy 2007). As such it was seen to be hallowed turf for Irish nationalists, the symbolism of playing Ireland's national game on a European field where Irish blood was spilled, appealed to Kinalea. In all of this, Kinalea was playing up to the symbolic nature of what such Pan-Celtic congresses were meant to be about: they were transnational expressions of cultural nationalism that was so prevalent in Europe since the nineteenth century. The religiosity, the masculinity, the fearsomeness of the 'Gael' was key to the narrative spun by the lengthy instalments Kinalea provided.

The journey undertaken to Belgium was an intense one. The first leg to England saw a train ride from Cork to Waterford to Dublin to ferry across to England and then a drive to London to travel to the Continent by train. Their journey was relayed with much detail, and one gets a sense of intense fun from the proceedings and the men certainly did not shy away from enjoying their time:

> Dr. Edwin related experiences of the Belgians and their manners, while from the far end of the carriage a crowd seemed to gather in conspiracy, the purpose of which was soon located as the "Cork Accent" of Steven, announced that "he'd go four!" .... On the Continental Express were all sorts of Nationalities and they soon woke to the significance of the fact of the existence of Ireland. (*Cork Sportsman*, September 10, 1910)

Certainly it is likely that this was the first time outside of Ireland for a good many of these men, and no doubt they were taking full advantage of the trip. Each player was expected to carry £3 of their money for the duration of the tour; a considerable sum of money for these men. As research by both Hunt and McElligott has shown, those who played Gaelic games in the early twentieth century tended to come from rural backgrounds, or else were members of the working and lower middle class in Ireland's towns and cities (McElligott 2013, 135–146; Hunt 2009, 183–203). Many of these men would have formed a similar socio-economic demographic, and £3 would have been hard to come by for most.

The two teams were undoubtedly the strongest hurling teams in the country at the time, and contained some of the most well-known hurlers in the country. One of the key figures in the Tipperary side, was Tom Semple; a man described '... of the tall sinewy type, more of a thoroughbred than a hunter.' He was further described as 'a tall athletic man with a great stride and sweep of arm ... he was a smooth stylish hitter with great ball control' (Kilfeather 1984, 25). Semple is one of the most famed hurlers in the history of Tipperary, with the hurling grounds in Thurles now bearing his name. The Tipperary side was made up of those who had won both the 1908 All-Ireland and the 1909 Munster Championship.

The Cork captain was Jim 'Jamesy' Kelleher, a Dungourney man: 'With a wonderful variety of strokes, it is a pleasure to any ardent student of the game to watch him ...' he also called him 'a broad-shouldered wedge of a man ... but powerfully built, active and tireless'(Kilfeather 1984, 25). It is hardly surprising then, when you consider this pedigree, that the games themselves were so well attended when they did come off in Belgium. Certainly as far as exhibitions of the finer points of hurling, you could not find a better display of hurling and all its attendant skills.

However, the level of sporting success of the tour can only have been minor in reality. Like many of the exhibitions of the period, the performance of a hurling match would have been seen as little more than a curio, for all their brilliance, by a good deal of the spectators, this was an afternoon's entertainment rather than a serious exhibition of a sport for the people of Belgium. Indeed as Kinalea noted of the very final game they played, which was at the exhibition grounds of the Pan-Celtic Congress, though in front of a poor crowd 'due to a want of advertising':

> The Belgian ladies were much interested in our game, but some of our non-players were too interested in them to let them appreciate it properly. We heard afterwards that a few who had learned the wiles of the world down Castlemartyr way, played a nice game on the side line. But, perhaps, it is not fair to tell tales out of school. (*Cork Sportsman*, October 29, 1910)

More prosaically, Kinalea's extensive narrative of the trip was serialised over a long period. The first instalment appeared in the September 10 issue and the final instalment appeared in the November 12 issue of the paper. That means there were some 10 instalments in the serialisation of this narrative, a remarkable feat of writing especially since Kinalea claims in that final instalment that:

> Originally it was never intended that the account of the Brussels tour should extend beyond one week's issue, but they unconsciously drew their weary length across several editions. They got out of control of the writer altogether. Some were written between the mouthfuls of tasty of a tasty meal in a London hotel, some were scribbled on the back of a suitcase in a railway carriage, some were rushed off at odd intervals from the overloaded hours of business. (*Cork Sportsman*, November 12, 1910)

This was done in order to encourage people to continue buying and reading the paper. The style employed by Kinalea was often florid, utilising French to often comic effect. Kinalea carries on in that final instalment to demure that these thousands of words:

> ... have no virtues of style or coherence. They are written with one object only – to afford a fairly true account of a pleasant time, which, in the writer's memory at least, will always be hallowed by the pleasantest recollection. (*Cork Sportsman*, November 12, 1910)

Despite this false modesty, Kinalea's narrative stands as the most sustained piece of journalistic writing to appear in the newspaper over its lifespan. It was a significant undertaking of logistics to provide all of the copy under the circumstances. It does say something about those logistics that the narrative was not published until after the tour had ended. It can be seen as a crowning achievement for the paper: the *Cork Sportsman* through their correspondent Kinalea provides us with a picture of a little known tour that otherwise would be largely lost to posterity. The tour and how we understand what happened on it is mediated almost entirely through Kinalea's narrative.

The most successful evening of the entire tour was the homecoming of the Cork players to the city. There was a huge crowd to greet them at the Galnmire terminus and a procession from there was led by several marching bands that 'evoked much well deserved admiration for their superb and inspiring playing all the way through the City' (*Cork Sportsman*, September 3, 1910). At the reception, J. J. Walsh gave the following rousing speech, some of which has been quoted above:

> ... the members of the Association laboured under no misapprehension as to the feelings of which the citizens of Cork and indeed the people of the whole country entertained regarding the work of which the Gaelic Athletic Association was doing for Ireland, and their sympathies for the movement .... (*Cork Sportsman*, September 3, 1910)

Walsh went on to say:

> they also saw the golden opportunity of showing the world and telling those people of Europe in particular who regarded Irishmen as mere nonentities from the standpoint of being a potent unit in the universe – they saw the opportunity of proving to those peoples that though centuries of persecution had followed on the trail of the history of the country, the Irish race was still there, not only a potent factor, but a proud and independent factor in the constitution of the human race. (*Cork Sportsman*, September 3, 1910)

While the tour had started out underfunded and requiring a £100 loan as we saw above, when the tourists returned, the Cork versus Tipperary game was rescheduled, doubtless to recoup some of the costs of the tour. However, the organisers of the match yet again were forced to cancel:

> The Cork County Board are to be sincerely sympathised with. They are evidently not in good graces with the Clerk of the Weather. All arrangements were complete for the long looked-forward-to contest between Cork and Tipperary – between the teams that made History on Belgian soil recently. (*Cork Free Press*, October 3, 1910)

In Tipperary, a public lecture was organised to bring one of the organisers of the Pan-Celtic Congress over to help recoup the costs also, but this too proved to be an unsuccessful measure. A combination of bad luck with the weather was compounded by the hasty organisation of the tour, something to which Kinalea's narrative attested; combined, it all meant that the tour was financially unsuccessful.

Conclusion

While J. J. Walsh's career would continue in the ascendant for many years to come following the Belgian tour of 1910, it was to mark a highpoint of the ability of a small newspaper like the *Cork Sportsman* to deliver high-quality journalism into the homes of Irish readers. Within a year of Kinalea's last instalment of his day-by-day account of the trip, the *Cork Sportsman* had ceased appearing of a Saturday morning throughout the newsagents of Munster. Similar self-congratulation to that which marked the newspaper's first anniversary was not to be found the paper's subsequent anniversaries. Indeed what was the third anniversary issue carried instead a rather bristling notice to contributors that

> the Editor wishes that he could invent some form of language which would really convince Contributors that unless "Copy" reaches the office by a certain date each week, there is no likelihood of it being included in the issue for which it was intended ... we must impress upon our Correspondents that we have no option in the matter. (*Cork Sportsman*, May 20, 1911)

This reliance on irregular contributions was not viable in the long run and stands in stark contrast to the editorial of the second issue where it was felt that with the help of their correspondents, described as 'some of the ablest', the paper would be a success (*Cork Sportsman*, May 30, 1908). As well as relying on largely voluntary contributions of material, providing just one form of news for the same price as newspapers providing everything from local, provincial, national and international news, not to mention sporting news, always meant that servicing only a small provincial area in a specialist interest was unlikely to remain profitable in the long-term. In many respects, the paper was a casualty of the very forces that allowed it to exist in the first place: a greater demand for sporting news, and greater communications networks among them. These developments were to be harnessed by much larger competitors, with whose scale the *Cork Sportsman* and its printers, the Landon brothers, could not compete. That the organ was in decline becomes apparent from early September of 1911 until its final issue on Thursday 19 October 1911. Up until this point the paper was coming out weekly on a Saturday morning. But from September of 1911, the day and the intervals between the papers changed. An edition of the paper came out on 2 September 1911, a Saturday, followed quickly by an issue on the Wednesday, 6 September 1911. It then came out the following Wednesday, 13 September 1911, followed then by an issue on the 20 September and another does not appear until Thursday, 28 September (*Cork Sportsman*, September 2, 1911; September 6, 1911; September 13, 1911; September 20, 1911; September 28, 1911). While this would appear to be a switch simply to publication on a Wednesday rather than a Saturday, the dates again become erratic. With issues coming out on Friday, 6 October 1911, followed by a Wednesday edition on 11 October 1911 and then the final issue on the following Thursday 19 October 1911, it appears that the paper was simply struggling to meet its own deadlines (*Cork Sportsman*, October 6, 1911; October 11, 1911; October 19, 1911).

Another indicator of the paper's decline was its increasing reliance English news to fill out the pages, with reportage of the Football League and English horse-racing occupying a more prominent place among local reporting. There were also increasingly large ads for the papers printers Landons, indicating that the *Sportsman* is not just printed by the company, but is intimately tied up with the paper. Landon Brothers printed the *Cork Sportsman* at their stationery and chandlery business at 16 Bridge Street in Cork. This premise was also listed as the office of the paper. This would suggest that the brothers owned as well as printed the paper. It is little wonder then that their going out of business would coincide with the decline of the paper. The premises at 16 Bridge Street were in the hands of another proprietor by the following year (*Guy's Cork Directory* 1912).

Local competition from the *Cork Examiner*, *Cork Constitution* and even the *Cork Free Press*, all of which carried considerable sporting coverage. The *Cork Examiner* was able to print photographs from matches, making it especially popular and difficult for the much smaller operation of the *Sportsman* to match. As Legg (1998, 175) pointed out 'new nationalist newspapers founded ... were short-lived, finding themselves unable to compete against the well-established press in the area, which itself was changing over to nationalist politics'. In the same vein, the specialist sporting press in Ireland, although many would have a brief flowering, in the end could not compete against the more established press. This is interesting in light of how J. J. Walsh, more or less the architect of the Cork GAA at the beginning of the twentieth century, saw the paper: 'In addition to the powerful assistance accorded by the *Cork Examiner* and the *Cork Free Press* in those days, we also had our own weekly, the *Cork Sportsman*. There was, therefore, no lack of propaganda' (1948, 17). Under Walsh's direction, the Cork GAA fully understood the importance of a weekly sporting organ such as the *Cork Sportsman* in terms of being able to use it to promote Gaelic games, attested to by the amount of space the GAA takes up in the pages of the paper especially for a major event like the 1910 Tour of Belgium. Nevertheless the paper did not exist solely to cater for the needs and interests of one sporting body was equally important for those who played cricket, association football, rugby, hockey, water polo and a whole range of other sports. In any case, its short life as an organ for sport in Cork and the rest of Munster indicates that even in Ireland, the demand for a localised dedicated sporting press could be fulfilled, even if only briefly. The fact was though larger provincial and national newspapers increased their sporting coverage as time went on and were better able to absorb the costs of such expansion. The growth of the specialist newspapers alerted the bigger newspaper concerns to the value and necessity of dedicated sports coverage, which in some cases they promptly excelled at, surpassing their specialist counterparts at providing. This milieu created a first celebrity sports journalist in PD Mehigan, best known to readers of the *Cork Examiner* as 'Carbery' and readers of the *Irish Times* as 'Pato', in an era just before the emergence of radio commentators like Micheál Ó'hÉithir. Of all the specialist papers to emerge, *Sport* was best placed to thrive since it was run as part of a larger parent company, the *Freeman's Journal*, rather as a self-sustaining business like the *Cork Sportsman*, which proved to be an unsustainable business model. The larger dailies benefited from economies of scale, with which specialist enterprises like the *Cork Sportsman* could not compete, thus the paper became one more sporting newspaper title whose editions are littered across Irish newspaper history and acts now as a rich source to the sports historian as the examination of the 1910 Belgium Tour indicates.

Disclosure statement
No potential conflict of interest was reported by the author.

Notes
1. William O'Brien (1852–1928) was an Irish journalist and politician of the late nineteenth and early twentieth century. He was the leader of both the United Irish League and later the All-For-Ireland League, and presented serious opposition at one point, especially in Cork, to John Redmond's Irish Party. Both were grassroots political organisations that attempted to challenge the hegemony of the Redmond-led Irish Party.
2. For an in-depth analysis of the impact of the various schisms within the GAA during this period see McElligott, *Forging a Kingdom: The GAA in Kerry, 1884–1934*, 65–107; The Parnell split was a schism in Irish popular politics when it was revealed that the leader of the Irish parliamentary party in Westminster, Charles Stuart Parnell, was romantically involved with a divorcée, Kitty O'Shea. Causing a scandal among the majority Catholic population of Ireland, it saw those who wished to continue supporting Parnell splitting away from those who did not.
3. The Irish Republican Brotherhood was a secret, oath-bound society that sought to achieve Irish freedom from the UK by violent means. The structure of the GAA in Cork in the early twentieth century was as follows: a number of subcommittees comprised of those elected to the Cork county board looked after the various leagues in both hurling and football in the city and county. Members of the county board were in turn elected to represent Corks interests both at provincial level at the Munster Council and nationally the GAA's Central Council.
4. The Aonach Tailteann was an event held three times from 1924 to 1932, a kind of 'Irish' Olympics which saw Irish athletes and those from the Irish diaspora competing in a variety of events over the course of a fortnight in Ireland's capital city in Dublin. J. J. Walsh was a key figure in seeing these events come to fruition.

References
Brailsford, Dennis. 1997. *British Sport: A Social History*. Cambridge: Lutterworth Press.
Collins, Tony. 2013. *Sport in Capitalist Society: A Short History*. London and New York: Routledge.
Corry, Eoghan. 2009. "The Mass Media and the Popularisation of Gaelic Games, 1884–1934." In *The Evolution of the GAA: Ulaidh, Éire agus Eile*, edited by Donal McAnallen, David Hassan, and Roddy Hegarty, 100–112. Belfast: Ulster Historical Foundation.

Cronin, Mike. 2007. "The Gaelic Athletic Association's Invasion of America, 1888: Travel Narratives, Microhistory, and the Irish American 'Other'." *Sport in History* 27 (2): 190–216.
Cronin, Mike, Mark Duncan, and Paul Rouse. 2009. *The GAA: A People's History*. Cork: The Collins Press.
Cronin, Mike, and Roisín Higgins. 2011. *Places We Play: Ireland's Sporting Heritage*. Cork: The Collins Press.
De Búrca, Marcus. 1980. *The GAA: A History*. Dublin: Gill & MacMillan.
Foot, John. 2011. *Pedalare! Pedalare! A History of Italian Cycling*. London: Bloomsbury.
Hunt, Tom. 2007. *Sport and Society in Victorian Ireland: The Case of Westmeath*. Cork: Cork University Press.
Hunt, Tom. 2009. "The GAA: Social Structure and Associated Clubs." In *The Gaelic Athletic Association, 1884–2009*, edited by Mike Cronin, Will Murphy, and Paul Rouse, 183–203. Dublin: Irish Academic Press.
Kelly, James. 2014. *Sport in Ireland, 1600–1840*. Dublin: Four Courts Press.
Kilfeather, Seán, ed. 1984. *Vintage Carbery by PD Mehigan*. Dublin: Beaver Row Press.
King, Seamus J. 1998. *The Clash of the Ash in Foreign Fields: Hurling Abroad*. Cashel: King.
Legg, Marie-Louise. 1998. *Newspapers and Nationalism: The Irish Provincial Press, 1850–1892*. Dublin: Four Courts Press.
Martin, Simon. 2011. *Sport Italia: The Italian Love Affair with Sport*. London: IB Tauris.
McCabe, Conor. 2011. "Football Sports Weekly and Irish Soccer 1925–28." *Media History* 17 (2): 147–158.
McElligott, Richard. 2013. *Forging a Kingdom: The GAA in Kerry, 1884–1934*. Cork: The Collins Press.
Murphy, David. 2007. *The Irish Brigades, 1685–2006: A Gazetteer of Irish Military Service, Past and Present*. Dublin: Four Courts Press.
O'Callaghan, Liam. 2011. *Rugby in Munster: A Social and Cultural History*. Cork: Cork University Press.
O'Leary, Philip. 1986. "Children of the Same Mother: Gaelic Relations with Other Celtic Revival Movements 1882–1916." *Proceedings of the Harvard Celtic Colloquium* 6: 103–130.
Oriard, Michael. 1998. *Reading Football: How the Popular Press Created an American Spectacle*. Chapel Hill: University of North Carolina Press.
Rouse, Paul. 2004. "*Sport* and the Irish in 1881." In *Sport and the Irish: Histories, Identities, Issues*, edited by Alan Bairner, 7–22. Dublin: UCD Press.
Rouse, Paul. 2011a. "Newspapers, Journalists and the Early Years of the Gaelic Athletic Association." In *Irish Journalism Before Independence: More a Disease than a Profession*, edited by Kevin Rafter, 49–60. Manchester: Manchester University Press.
Rouse, Paul. 2011b. "Journalists and the Making of the Gaelic Athletic Association, 1884–1887." *Media History* 17 (2): 117–132.
Sayer, Derek. 1998. *Coasts of Bohemia: A Czech History*. Princeton, NJ: Princeton University Press.
Tranter, Neil. 1998. *Sport, Economy and Society, 1750–1914*. Cambridge: Cambridge University Press.
Walsh, J. J. 1948. *Recollections of a Rebel*. Tralee: The Kerryman.

Ireland – soccer champions of the world

Cormac Moore

Department of History, De Montfort University, Leicester, UK

> This paper examines Ireland's first outright victory of the British Home Championship in 1914, the annual soccer competition between the countries of England, Scotland, Wales and Ireland inaugurated in 1883, first played in 1884. This paper will look at the primary reasons why the Irish international team struggled against the other British teams, particularly England and Scotland, in the early years of the competition. It will demonstrate that the increased popularity of the game across Ireland allowed it to compete more competitively against its rivals in Britain from the turn of the twentieth century, culminating in the success of 1914.

Introduction

Sports history in Ireland has grown as an area of academic interest over recent years. Much of the interest has focused on the Gaelic Athletic Association, with little emphasis placed on other sports. Soccer, despite being one of the most popular sports in Ireland, has been the subject of very little academic attention. The one notable exception is Neal Garnham's *Association Football and Society in Pre-Partition Ireland* which provides the most comprehensive study of the beginnings of soccer in Ireland to date up until the split in Irish soccer of 1921. Ireland's British Home Championship win of 1914 was the subject of a paper by Colm Kerrigan published in *History Ireland* in 2005. This paper draws on the earlier research of Garnham and Kerrigan and focuses on the primary reasons why the Irish international team became competitive in competition with the other home countries leading to success in 1914. This, Ireland's first outright victory of the British Home Championship, came about over 30 years after the competition had begun. The annual international tournament was the first ever international soccer competition, established in 1883 and first played in 1884. Ireland's record up until 1914 was abysmal, only once previously sharing the title with England and Scotland in 1903. Most years consisted of heavy defeats to England and Scotland, punctuated with the odd moral victory and a yearly scrap with Wales for the wooden spoon that Ireland invariably lost.

This paper will look at Ireland's record in the tournament pre-1914 up until it reached its peak in 1914, assessing the progress soccer made in Ireland during that period, enabling the international team to reach a level of parity with the other home nations. During that period the game had grown from being localized to Belfast and its surrounding environs to a sport enjoyed by the masses spread across different geographical regions. The campaign of 1914 will be looked at in depth as well as the profile of the players, players from many different parts of the country, who contributed to Ireland's success.

It was believed by many that the victory of 1914 was the beginning of a bright future for the Irish team. However, months later the world was plunged into war. As a consequence of the First World War, Home Rule was shelved and the Easter Rising of

1916 saw the country move in a different direction towards independence. Irish soccer also veered on a path towards division through localized leagues during the war and a split between North and South in 1921 which still survives today, dashing all hopes of ever repeating the success of 1914.

International beginnings

Organized soccer came later to Ireland than anywhere else in the UK. The Football Association (FA) in England was founded in 1863, Scotland's first club, Queen's Park was formed in 1867 with the Scottish Football Association following in 1873 and the Football Association of Wales was up and running with a domestic trophy by 1877 (Garnham 2004, 4).

The man most responsible for the introduction of codified soccer into Ireland was County Down man, John McCredy McAlery, manager of the Irish Tweed House gentleman's outfitters in Belfast (Garnham 2004, 4). It is believed, whilst on honeymoon in Scotland, McAlery witnessed a game of soccer. So enthralled was he with the sport that he invited the captain of the Caledonians football club, J.A. Allen, to bring a match to Belfast (Garnham 2004, 4). Allen brought Caledonians to Belfast where they played an exhibition match against Queen's Park of Glasgow on 24 October 1878 at the Ulster Cricket Ground. This is considered to be the first game of football played in Ireland under association rules. Queen's Park was believed by many to be the great innovating club of the game at the time, pioneering the passing or combination game which soon overtook the dribbling game favoured by teams in England (Robinson 1920, 27). McAlery, who was Treasurer of the Cliftonville Cricket Club, established a soccer team within Cliftonville in 1879, based on the rules of the Scottish Football Association, it not being uncommon for soccer clubs to gestate from cricket clubs at the time (Mason 1980, 31). The club was soon playing practice matches against other clubs. Cliftonville played Quidnuncs, a team of rugby players on 29 September 1879, the first time two Irish teams played a soccer match. By 1880 four clubs were regularly playing against each other: Cliftonville and Knock in Belfast, Moyola Park in Castledawson, Derry and Banbridge Academy from County Down. In its first season, Cliftonville played 14 matches, winning 8, drawing 2 and losing 4 (Garnham 1999, 163).

The Irish Football Association (IFA) was established in 1880 to organize, govern and promote the game of soccer in Ireland. Cliftonville sent an invitation to other clubs in the Belfast and District area to organize a soccer governing body for Ireland with the first meeting taking place on 18 November 1880, at the Queen's Hotel in Belfast (IFA 1880). In attendance were representatives from Cliftonville FC, Avoniel FC, Distillery FC, Knock FC, Oldpark FC (all Belfast), Moyola Park FC (Castledawson) and Alexander FC (Limavady). At that meeting a sub-committee was formed to agree on rules for the IFA as well as the introduction of a cup competition, the Irish Cup which would become the blue-riband competition of Irish soccer. The IFA realized from the beginning, it needed a vibrant competition to allow soccer to grow, with a cup worth fighting for needed to be awarded to the winner (Mason 1980, 16). The IFA commissioned William Gibson & Co. in Belfast who designed a trophy which according to the *Belfast Newsletter* in an article from 19 February 1881 was:

> of solid silver, vase shape, of most artistic design, and high-class workmanship, being richly chased with Irish shield, surrounded with shamrocks, and its beauty is much enhanced by being surmounted with a finely modelled athlete holding an association ball, the whole resting on a handsome ebony plinth, ornamented with silver.

The IFA could look back with satisfaction on its first year in operation. It had successfully organized a cup competition and it made a profit of 13 pounds, 1 shilling and 5 pence in its first year (IFA 1881). At that meeting, another was mentioned, a gathering involving the 'kindred Associations throughout the United Kingdom to be held in Manchester on 25 April' (IFA 1881). It was a Conference of the Football Secretaries of the British associations, chaired by C.W. Alcock of the English FA. At that meeting, it was agreed to arrange for internationals between Ireland against England and Wales the following year (*Leeds Mercury*, April 26, 1881).

Ireland's first foray into international soccer took place on 18 February 1882. Ireland played England at Bloomfield, the ground of Knock football club, in Belfast. In a preview of the match on 16 February, the *Freemans Journal* described it as a meeting of Ulster versus England, a 'semi-international match in Belfast between an association eleven picked from the various local clubs and the English international team'. The paper concluded by saying, 'the affair is likely to prove a financial success, but a football failure'. On the same day, the *Belfast Newsletter* also expressed doubts that the match would go well for the Irish team considering most players representing Ireland had about two years practice pitted against the experienced FA team from England. The fears were to prove well founded as Ireland slumped to a 13 to nil loss. Dressed in royal blue jerseys and hoses, with white knickers and wearing a badge consisting of an Irish cross, with a harp in the centre and surrounded with a wreath of shamrocks, the Irish were no match for the all-white Saxons (*Belfast Newsletter*, February 18, 1882, 3). To make the score line even more humiliating, it came immediately after England's largest ever home defeat, also to this date, a 6–1 rout by Scotland (*Belfast Newsletter*, February 20, 1882). It has been commented that McAlery, who was captain that day, wept at the result (Brodie 1980, 3). The Irish team consisted of players from just four clubs, all recently founded, Cliftonville, Knock, Distillery and Avoniel. All were based in the vicinity of Belfast. England fielded a team made up of players from seven clubs, Cambridge University, Oxford University, Blackburn Rovers, Nottingham, Aston Villa, Swifts and Royal Engineers from London (*Belfast Newsletter*, February 20, 1882). Ireland played Wales in Wrexham a week later and lost by seven goals to one. There would be no international victory for five years, the first coming against Wales in 1887 (Garnham 2004, 35)

Preceding the match against England came a request from McAlery 'asking if the English team would agree to play their International match with them under the Scotch' rules. Two of the main differences between the Scottish and English rules centred on the offside and throw-in rules (Robinson 1920, 55). It was met with the haughty rebuke of the English FA 'that the Association recognizes no other rule than their own and as they have always strictly adhered to them they cannot deviate from their principle for the match in question' (FA 1882). This request from the IFA may have prompted the English FA to seek uniformity on one code being played throughout the UK. It called for a conference with the Scottish FA a few months later in Sheffield to come to such an agreement, a conference the Scottish FA declined to attend (FA 1882). This rejection stung the English FA deeply who responded with the following reproach:

> That the answer of the Scottish Association to the letter of this Association respecting the announcement of withdrawing from the Conference is not at all satisfactory and as it is the almost unanimous desire of the Football Association to have one uniform code of rules throughout the United Kingdom and the present diversity of the rules is not conducive to the interests of the game; the Committee of this Association cannot take any further steps towards arranging the International match until the Scottish Association appoints representatives to meet representatives of the Football Association, the Irish and the Welsh Associations. (FA 1882)

Fearing the loss of international fixtures, the Scottish FA soon agreed to change their minds and a conference of the four home nations was held in December 1882 in Manchester where new uniform codes were agreed upon (*Glasgow Herald*, December 7, 1882). Despite misgivings from some English FA council members on the wisdom of the potential of 'Associations having no authority as compared with this one (the parent Association, the English FA)' (FA 1883) to dictate the rules of the game, most council members welcomed the move and soccer journeyed on the path towards uniformity.

This led to the formation of the International Football Association Board (IFAB) to approve changes to rules on football, a body which met for the first time in 1886 (IFAB 1886). It was also decided that an annual championship should be played between the four home countries which became the British Home Championship. Ireland played Scotland in the first ever match of the tournament, held in Ormeau Road, Belfast on 26 January 1884. In the build-up to the match, *The Belfast Newsletter* in an article from 14 January 1884 was optimistic that Ireland would give a good account of themselves 'on account of the great popularity of the dribbling code' with 'new clubs ... springing up in all parts of Ireland, several clubs playing in and around Dublin, the head centre of Rugby football'. By 1884 there were two clubs in Dublin, the Dublin Association Football Club and one based in Trinity College Dublin. The paper went further by predicting that Ireland would soon 'be "second to none" in the exposition of association football, and those "knowing ones" who prophesised its downfall and utter annihilation must feel small as they see its bright prospects and increasing popularity'.

Despite this optimism, Ireland lost to Scotland by five goals to nil. This was followed up with a 6–0 defeat to Wales and an 8–1 loss to England. Ireland's first win in the competition was in 1887 against Wales, their second win was another four years later in 1891, also against Wales. The 1890s and the early 1900s followed a similar pattern with Ireland regularly losing with the exception of some wins and draws against Wales. The first Irish victory over Scotland occurred in 1903, the first year Ireland shared the title. Ireland also defeated Wales that year resulting in Ireland finishing on a total of four points, the same as England and Scotland. Ireland's first victory over England did not come until 1913, the two team's 30th meeting in the Home Championship. Of the previous 29 meetings in the tournament against England, Ireland had lost on 26 occasions, drawing just 3 times.

Ireland's overall record in the British Home Championship up until 1914 highlighted how far behind the country was to the other home nations. Out of a total of 90 matches played over 30 years, Ireland lost 67, drew 9 and won just 14, scoring 99 goals and conceding 331, a goal difference of minus 232 (see Table 1).

A contributing factor to these poor results was the late development of the game in Ireland compared to the other home associations. The progress of soccer in Ireland was initially slow and geographically confined to Belfast and its adjoining areas. By 1886, there was still less than 40 clubs affiliated to the IFA (Garnham 2004, 5). The first soccer club was not established in Dublin until 1883 (*Freemans Journal*, October 15, 1883, 1). One Dublin paper described the players as 'butting at the ball like a pack of young goats'

Table 1. Ireland's British Home Championship record: 1884–1913.

Played	Won	Drew	Lost	For	Against	±
90	14	9	67	99	331	−232

Source: Richard Samuel, The British Home Football Championships 1884–1984 (South Humberside: Soccer Books Ltd 2003).

and stating it being unlikely that 'the natives will take kindly to the innovation' (Garnham 2004, 4). Despite this, the game did catch on in Dublin and in some surrounding counties in Leinster, leading to the establishment of the Leinster Football Association in 1892 (Briggs and Dodd 1993, 26). The Munster Football Association was not formed until 1901 and there was no regional soccer body in Connacht before the Irish Free State was founded in 1921. By contrast, the English FA by the mid-1880s was an association with a membership of over 1000 clubs (Mason 1980, 16). In central Scotland alone, club membership increased from 66 in 1880 to over 500 by 1890 (Taylor 2008, 40).

Ireland also lagged far behind England and Scotland in introducing professionalism, another key factor in producing the poor results up until 1914. England accepted professionalism in the mid-1880s (Mason 1980, 74), Ireland not until 1894 (Garnham 2004, 69). Professionalism officially came into Irish soccer at the IFA Annual Meeting of 1894 by a vote of 64 to 30. Ironically, it was the votes of the staunchly amateur club, Cliftonville and the Leinster delegates who would not introduce professionalism for another decade themselves, that saw the motion pass. Professionalism would be slow to develop in Ireland. By 1903 there were just 104 professionals in Ireland, all confined to Ulster, many of them part-time, and most of them professional for just one season (Garnham 2004, 86). It did lead to larger crowds at matches and improved standards, most aptly demonstrated by Ireland's sharing of the British Home Championship with England and Scotland in 1903, it is best season in that competition to date by a considerable distance. The IFA granted each regional division a lot of autonomy on introducing professionalism, the North West division introducing it in 1902 followed three years later by the Leinster Football Association (Byrne 2012, 21).

Many also felt that the IFA was biased in its selection policy for the international team, leaning heavily towards selecting players from Belfast and its surrounding environs. After a heavy international defeat in 1892, Thomas Kirkwood Hackett, one of the Leinster Football Association's founding members, stated, 'All this has come upon us because of the prejudice of five men [IFA International Selection Committee members] who select the teams preventing anyone outside the Belfast area being chosen to represent their country' (Briggs and Dodd 1993, 22). The national side was often just referred to as 'Belfast' in the media. The Dublin-based newspaper, *Sport* on 3 March 1894 blamed the IFA of 'behaving most unfairly' in 'overlooking the Dubliners'. Of the 605 internationals caps awarded between 1882 and 1900, just 23 were awarded to players playing for Leinster clubs, 571 caps were granted to players based at clubs in Ulster and 11 to players based overseas.[1] It was countered that it was better to select Belfast players for matches held in Belfast and Dublin players for matches played in Dublin. However, when Dublin finally was offered a chance to host an international, against England on St. Patrick's Day 1900 (LFA 1900), there was just one player from a Dublin-based team selected, Dr George Sheehan from Bohemians. Eight of the players played for Ulster-based clubs, the other two were based in England (Briggs and Dodd 1993, 28). The capital would host just five internationals before the outbreak of the First World War.

Wales, in its adoption of soccer, was the country most similar to Ireland. This was reflected in the two countries results in the Home Championship compared to England and Scotland. Wales did not win a Home Championship outright until 1907 (Samuel 2003, 31). Like Ireland, the popularity of the game was concentrated in the north of Wales, the south choosing the ball carrying game of rugby as their football of first choice. The Welsh clubs were also considered weak and they, like the Irish clubs, haemorrhaged players to the more lucrative English and Scottish clubs (Taylor 2008, 104–105). The releasing of players from the English and Scottish clubs for international duty to Ireland and Wales was often not granted, leading to both countries fielding weaker teams than England and Scotland whose FAs did not encounter the same problems. This led to the IFA proposing, at the IFAB Annual Meeting of 1909 (IFAB 1909), held in the Great Northern Hotel, Bundoran, Co. Donegal, the following motion:

> That each Association, members of this Board, must arrange that any player or players (playing under their jurisdiction, and of a different nationality) selected to play in International matches be released for such matches. The motion was withdrawn on the understanding that each Association, when requested, would use its influence to have players allowed off when selected in International matches.

It would transpire that each Association, particularly the English and Scottish FAs, was ineffective in convincing clubs to release their players for international duty, a factor that almost derailed Ireland's efforts to win the Championship in 1914.

There were, however, grounds for some optimism as the gap between Ireland and the other nations shortened over the years. From a starting base of four clubs in 1880, the IFA had 124 affiliated clubs in 1890, 259 by 1901 and 420 by 1910 (IFA 1910). The formation of the Irish Football League in 1890 also increased the popularity of soccer and the quality of its players. This growth was facilitated by the increased wages and more leisure time available for workers, money and time that could be spent at soccer matches. The introduction of Factory and Workshop Acts during the late 1800s gave workers more free time to enjoy leisure activities. It became commonplace for workers to have their Saturday afternoons off. With increased industrialization, particularly in Belfast, more skilled workers were hired on higher wages (Garnham 2004 11). Greater urbanization allowed for more sports meetings to be attended by more spectators and the vast improvements in rail transport allowed for more events to be held in areas inaccessible previously (Garnham 2004, 8–11). Increased literacy levels and an expanding press, including media outlets dedicated solely to sport, helped to grow all sports including soccer. It is estimated that over 88% of the Irish population was literate by 1911 (Rouse 2005, 9).

The first decade of the twentieth century saw a huge upsurge in the popularity of football across the country, especially in Ulster and Leinster with more people attending matches. A total of 16,000 spectators attended a soccer match between England and Ireland on the same day as 5000 witnessed Ireland play Wales in a rugby match in Belfast in 1904 (Byrne 2012, 36). Irish Cup and League matches were also drawing larger crowds. The annual inter-provincial matches between Leinster and Ulster, first played in 1885 (*Belfast Newsletter*, November 8, 1884), were often used as trial matches to select the international teams and they also helped to improve the standard of soccer in Ireland. Of all regions, Leinster witnessed the most spectacular growth with 119 clubs affiliated to the IFA by 1910, just 15 shy of the largest region, the North-East (IFA 1910). The Leinster Football Association went on to overtake the North-East region as the largest region of the IFA in 1913.

Once professionalism was accepted by the IFA, it was soon decided to include players based at overseas clubs for international selection. As previously highlighted, just 11 of the 605 international caps awarded between 1882 and 1900 went to players based at clubs outside of Ireland. Of the 462 caps granted between 1901 and 1914, 207 went to overseas professionals who played against English and Scottish internationals on a weekly basis. And 204 caps went to players based at Ulster clubs with the remaining 51 going to players based at clubs in Dublin.[2]

The changed circumstances soccer in Ireland was experiencing saw the Irish soccer team become more competitive by the early 1900s. Instead of losing matches by margins of five goals or more, Ireland was now losing by one goal or two in most matches.[3] This improvement was echoed at an IFA Council Meeting in 1910 (IFA 1910):

> It is rarely that we are permitted to raise a jubilant note in connection with our International matches, but we can, without anything of undue egotism do so upon the present occasion. No one who has followed football in this country has ever seen an Irish team put up such displays as did the team which met the chosen representatives of England and Scotland this year. Never before has an Irish team succeeded in defeating the very cream of Scottish football upon Irish soil.

Soccer in Ireland was dealt a significant blow in 1912 when most of the senior clubs from the Irish Football League seceded from the IFA, Linfield and Bohemians being the only two clubs to remain with the parent body (*Freemans Journal*, February 23, 1912, 11). The dispute had nothing to do with the religious and political tensions that engulfed the nation with the introduction of the third Home Rule Bill that year. It arose over issues of governance and money primarily, with most of the senior clubs demanding more gate receipts from internationals than the 10% received from the IFA to date as well as more representation for the senior clubs on the IFA Council (*Irish Independent*, February 16, 1912, 7). The dispute led to the formation of a new association (simply called the New Irish Football Association) vying with the IFA for the public's support and money. The dispute lasted from February to September 1912, when it was resolved only as the 1912–1913 season was about to begin. The episode strained the finances of the IFA to almost breaking point. With the new association having most of the senior clubs in its fold (Linfield and Bohemians the only two remaining within the IFA), the IFA was deprived of significant income for most of 1912. The IFA received welcome support from the other British Home nations, who at the IFAB Annual Meeting of 1912 decided to 'play the International Matches with Ireland for the ensuing season in Ireland, and thus give the Irish FA valuable financial support' (IFAB 1912). As stated, the dispute finally did come to an end in the summer of 1912 with the seceding clubs welcomed back to the IFA fold whilst receiving many of the concessions they were looking for.[4]

Despite playing all of their games at home, Ireland finished bottom of the table in the 1913 Home Championship. Yet the championship witnessed Ireland's first ever victory over England in an international fixture. Ireland beat England by two goals to one on 15 February 1913 in Windsor Park, with debutant Billy Gillespie, who played for Sheffield United in England, being the hero of the day, scoring both Irish goals (Samuel 2003, 37). It was decided at the following meeting of the IFA's International Selection Committee to award the players with a memento of the victory, commemorative medals being granted to each player (IFA 1913). The win was lauded at the IFA's Annual Meeting the following May (IFA 1913):

> The year has been an epoch-marking one in Football. For the first time in history of the game four Internationals were played in this country, and for the first time similarly in the history of the game Ireland achieved the ambition of 32 years by securing a victory over England, and this is more creditable when it is taken into consideration that Ireland played the major portion of the game with only ten men.

The victory over England did give the team a much needed confidence boost going into the 1914 Championship, an optimism that would transpire to be well founded as the team achieved the status of Home Champions outright for the first time.

The 1914 championship

Ireland's first match of the 1914 Home Championship was against Wales held at the Wrexham Racecourse on Monday, 19 January, with a crowd of 5000 in attendance. It was reported in *Sport* on January 14 that 'the game was changed from a Saturday to a Monday in order to let both sides, the Welsh body especially, call on any Anglo players in the service of English or Scotch clubs'. Ireland won by two goals to one, Billy Gillespie being the hero once again scoring both goals (*Irish Times*, January 24, 1914, 19).

Commenting on the match, *The Irish Times* on 24 January, not known for its extensive coverage of soccer previously, was glowing in its praise for the team:

> Ireland gained a remarkable victory over Wales at Wrexham on Monday, the Principality being defeated by two goals to one ... It was a remarkable victory, inasmuch as the Irish team which was considered rather weak in defence and attack, had to play for a good part of the first half without Harris, who had to retire with a twisted ankle. The Welsh team was, on paper, a more formidable combination, but they failed to hold the fleet-footed Irishmen, who certainly rose to the occasion in a manner that did them great credit. It was a fine game, and, needless to say, the defeat of the Welshmen would have caused great jubilation among the small gathering of the Hibernian supporters.

Some of the British papers were less fulsome in their praise, saying the victory was more down to luck and bad shooting by the Welsh. The *Sportsman* wrote:

> The bad tactics of the Welsh forwards led to the team's defeat. They played effective football up to the goal and then were quite unable to push home their advantage ... it must be admitted that on occasions it appeared to be more by good luck than good management that the downfall of the Irish goal was averted. (*Irish Independent*, January 20, 1914, 6)

In the build-up to the second match against England played on Valentine's Day, 14 February, at Ayresome Park in Middlesborough, *The Freemans Journal* reported that

> the only occasion on which the [same] match was played at Middlesborough a drawn game was the outcome, and it is hoped that Ireland will improve on that record. The Irish team is not considered to be a strong side, owing to the changes that will have to be made.

As many of the players were based with English and Scottish clubs, the IFA was unable to field a full strength team. Val Harris was injured after the game against Wales. Laois born, Jim McAuley was not released by Preston North End. Bradford Park Avenue refused to release Jack McCandless, Glasgow Celtic refused to release William Crone and Brighton and Hove Albion refused to release Charlie Webb (*Freemans Journal*, February 14, 1914, 11). Regardless of being deprived of these players and perhaps emboldened by Ireland's victories over England the previous year and Wales a month earlier, the newspaper *Ireland's Saturday Night* 'raised hopes of a victory to an even chance' (Kerrigan 2005, 28).

If the first victory over England a year earlier was considered by some quarters to be a fluke, there was nothing lucky about the victory in Ayresome Park in 1914. Watched by 27,500 spectators with gate receipts of £1200, Ireland won by three goals to nil. It was reported that England's best players were the goalkeeper, Sam Hardy, and the two full-backs, Rob Crompton and Jessie Pennington, such was the dominance of the Irish team. Ireland's goal scorers were Billy Lacey with two and Billy Gillespie, continuing where he left off against Wales, scoring one (Kerrigan 2005, 28). Wexford born Billy Lacey would end up having a distinguished career in the game, playing with the likes of Shelbourne, Everton and Liverpool.

The result was lauded by the Irish press and also by many in the British Press who also condemned the English team, it being reported that the English fans were 'disgusted with' their team. The London *Times* stated that Ireland was the better side and deserved to win. *Athletics News* highlighted individuals from Ireland including Lacey, Galway-born 'Sandy' Craig, Mickey Hamill and Paddy O'Connell whilst also claiming Ireland played together as a unit and worked harder than England (Kerrigan 2005, 28–29). *Sport* (February 21, 1914, 2) was effusive in its praise of the Irish team:

> Ireland's first victory over England on English soil was a remarkable achievement. After many years of struggle, of shattered hopes and profound mortification, she has at length burst through in a veritable blaze of triumph. England had not the tiniest loophole of excuse for her failure on this occasion. It was a memorable victory insomuch as the sporting Press is unanimous in its verdict that the best possible talent was opposed to our lads, and the result was the complete supremacy in all departments of the Irish team. The game at Middlesbrough was a revelation, particularly as one of the Irish players selected could not turn out at the last moment, and Rollo, the Linfield full-back, had to be requisitioned, and had to play in an entirely new position for him – namely, outside right.

The *Irish Independent* (February 16, 1914, 4) claimed the victory over England was 'sensational' and showed 'the game has made great progress in recent years'. The *Freemans Journal* on the same day declared, 'the great achievement of Ireland at Middlesbrough on Saturday has been the solo topic for discussion ever since the result was declared'. It continued by claiming that the result:

> Makes it obvious to even the "man in the street" that the time has come when the representatives of the Shamrock can claim an equality with the representatives of the Rose ...
> The time has come when Ireland has to be reckoned with in International Association warfare.

Although declaring Ireland's win 'a remarkable victory' that beforehand 'no one, except a candidate for a lunatic asylum' would have 'prophesised', the *Irish Times* focused more on the Goliath slayed rather than the victorious David. The paper remarked that 'something is wrong with English football' and predicted 'a remarkable change of tactics on the part of the English team-builders' by bringing back a few of the first-class Amateurs from the famous amateur-only Corinthians team, a prediction that proved spectacularly wrong.[5]

The Irish team now had amassed four points out of four and should they beat Scotland on 14 March, at Windsor Park in Belfast, would not only win the Home Championship outright for the first time, they would win the Triple Crown too. The build-up to the match garnered significantly more interest than normal with the *Freemans Journal* (March 14, 1914, 10) declaring 'the sons of Erin have a chance of showing what they can do in the world of sport, and if they happen to succeed they will have conquered the football nations' of the world. Acknowledging the difficulty of the task ahead against a strong Scottish side, the *Irish Independent* (March 14, 1914, 8) believed that, 'with ordinary luck, Ireland will win the Triple Crown for the first time'.

Ireland was dealt a blow on the Thursday before the match when, due to his team, Sheffield United drawing against Manchester City in a FA Cup Quarter Final tie, Ireland's perilous forward, Billy Gillespie was not allowed to travel to Ireland to play against Scotland (*Sport,* March 21, 1914, 2).

On the same day as Ireland played Scotland in the Home Championship soccer match on 14 March, Ireland played Wales in rugby, both games held in Belfast, the former at Windsor Park, the latter at Balmoral Showgrounds. The Irish Rugby Football Union (IRFU) was not happy with this clash of fixtures, having scheduled the rugby match long before the soccer international against Scotland was set for 14 March. Attempts by the IRFU to have the date of the soccer match changed or even for the match to start at a later time than the rugby fixture were not realized, the match remained fixed to start at 3:30 pm (IFA 1914). Commenting on the continuing Home Rule crisis and on the potential of rugby and soccer matches as a unifying power, the *Manchester Guardian* (March 9, 1914, 1) remarked:

> At a time when the "two races" argument is being passed to breaking point the sporting passion of the common people should supply a not insignificant instance of the strength of the national sentiment. Next Saturday both teams will be drawn from the whole of Ireland, and the

native Ulsterman, who in all matters except political discussions will have you know that he is just as good an Irishman as they raise in Leinster or Munster or Connaught, is exulting in the hope of cheering a united Ireland to victory.

Due to the large interest both matches garnered, Great Northern Railway scheduled special trains from Amiens Street in Dublin to Belfast to facilitate the large crowds expected (*Freemans Journal*, March 11, 1914, 1). One of the 'special' trains broke a new record too that day by reaching Belfast from Dublin in two hours and one minute (Kerrigan 2005, 29).

In front of a crowd of over 30,000 (the highest ever attended Irish soccer international up to that point), the match itself was played under miserable weather conditions. The physique of the Scottish team also caused difficulties. Three of the Irish team's players got injured, the goalkeeper Fred McKee, Paddy O'Connell and full-back Bill McConnell. Whilst O'Connell and McConnell limped on, McKee was forced to retire and was replaced in goals by McConnell. With Ireland reduced to 10 men, Scotland took the lead halfway through the second half. The Irish responded strongly and with seven minutes to go Sam Young of Linfield scored the equalizer that ensured Ireland won the Championship outright for the first time (*Sport*, March 21, 1914, 2) (Table 2).

The press, in general, acclaimed the achievement of the Irish team. *Sport* on 21 March wrote:

> Ireland, International champions, Yes, that was the verdict of last Saturday. After thirty years' struggle in the face of extreme difficulty and in the face of adverse circumstances, few would begrudge old Ireland the success in this the greatest prize of the professional football nations.

In a follow-up article in the same paper, headlined THE WORLD'S CHAMPIONS, it was stated:

> The Irish Association team, which won the International Championship this season, has rightly been acclaimed the World's Association Football Champions, and the question has arisen how are the IFA to suitably recognise the fact. That recognition of a substantial character is due all the players who so nobly battled and won fame for Ireland is a matter that cannot be gainsaid.

At the following meeting of the IFA Council it was passed unanimously, 'that some recognition on the winning of the International Championship be made to the players, International Selection Committee, Chairman and Secretary' (IFA 1914). The Annual Meeting of the IFA IFA (1914) was a celebratory affair with the Council, stating:

> In submitting their Annual Report to the membership, the Council are able to sound a note never heretofore uttered in connection with Irish Football. It has never fallen to the lot of any previous Council to be able to record that the honour of champions had deservedly been won by Ireland. For 32 years succeeding Councils have striven for this honour and now it has at length been attained, and it was only ill-luck that prevented us from winning the still greater honour in International Football – the "Triple Crown", but this does not exceed the features that make the year unique. Never have the other three countries been placed in a position of having only the combined total of two goals to their credit.

Table 2. Final table of British Home Championship 1914.

Team	Played	Won	Drew	Lost	For	Against	±	Points
Ireland	3	2	1	0	6	2	+4	5
Scotland	3	1	2	0	4	1	+3	4
England	3	1	0	2	3	6	−3	2
Wales	3	0	1	2	1	4	−3	1

Source: Samuel, The British Home Football Championships 1884–1984, 38.

Commenting on the proceedings at the IFA Annual Meeting, *Sport* (May 9, 1914, 2) compared the status of soccer in Ireland in 1914 to just a few short years previously when the game was in turmoil:

> To-night the annual meeting of the IFA, Ltd., takes place in Belfast. When one thinks of the last Association meeting held in the Northern City and compare it with this one, there will be a marked difference. In the 1910 meeting we were in the throes of a revolution amongst the senior clubs as against what was termed the interference of the junior element in football, and it afterwards took place, and almost ruined the game. But for the staunch attitude of Linfield and Bohemians, who alone remained loyal to the governing body, dear knows what might have happened. The firm support of the other three countries, of course, counted. Then England played their annual match two successive years in Ireland and Scotland three. In the match this year, thanks to our victories over England and Wales, we met Scotland in a battle for either the triple crown or the championship. It is history now that we won the latter.

The paper continued by bemoaning one fact, the reliance of the International team on cross-channel players:

> Still, it is just a pity we have not more home players to call on for our Internationals. The all-power of the purse which is possessed by English or Scottish clubs is, of course, all against us. The day, however, is not far distant when it may be changed in this respect. Our clubs are able in most cases to give the maximum sum to players, and it is to be hoped they will for the future give preference to local lads. The latter are, to my mind, not encouraged as they should be, and is left to cross-Channel clubs to make the difference obvious. To-night's meeting shows progress in all departments, and I hope such a happy state of affairs may long continue.

As Table 3 illustrates, of a total of 15 players used by Ireland throughout the British Home Championship that season, only 5 played for local clubs, the other 10 representing English or Scottish clubs. An encouraging aside, though, was demonstrated by the truly all-Ireland nature of the team when birthplace was taken into account. Of the 15 players who played at least once that season, 5 were born in Belfast and Dublin, 2 in Galway, 1 in Wexford and 1, Louis Bookman, moved from his native Russia (present day Lithuania) at a young age to Dublin. The IFA had been accused on many occasions, with good justification, of having

Table 3. Irish players used during the British Home Championship of 1914.

Player	Club in 1914	Birthplace	Matches played in 1914 championship
Fred McKee	Belfast Celtic	Belfast	3
Bill McConnell	Bohemians	Dublin	3
Sandy Craig	Greenock Morton	Galway	3
Pat O'Connell	Hull City	Dublin	3
Sam Young	Linfield	Belfast	3
Billy Lacey	Liverpool	Wexford	3
Mickey Hamill	Manchester United	Belfast	2
Val Harris	Everton	Dublin	2
Dave Rollo	Linfield	Belfast	2
Frank Thompson	Clyde	Galway	2
Billy Gillespie	Sheffield United	Donegal	2
Ted Seymour	Bohemians	Dublin	1
Harry Hampton	Bradford City	Dublin	1
Rab Nixon	Linfield	Belfast	1
Louis Bookman	Bradford City	Present day Lithuania (Grew up in Dublin)	1

Source: For composition of Irish teams, see *Sport, The Irish Independent, Freemans Journal,* The *Irish Times,* D/4196/D/1 – Irish Football Association International Minutes – 1909–1966 and Northern Ireland Footballing Greats, available from http://nifootball.blogspot.ie/.

a clear bias towards Belfast players, selecting a token player or two from Dublin. This assertion could not be laid at the Association's door in 1914. The teams selected, represented a balance of players either based or from Belfast and Dublin, a team unified with one common goal, to win for Ireland the British Home Championship.

Conclusion

Compared to its neighbours in Britain, Ireland was a latecomer to soccer. The game took longer to take root and it was confined primarily to the North East of Ireland in its early years. Ireland's rural make-up meant fewer people could play or watch sports such as soccer. As England and Scotland started to accept and embrace professionalism in the mid-1880s, soccer was just beginning to gain a foothold in Ireland. This was demonstrated by results achieved by Ireland in the early years of the British Home Championship. As the competition progressed, the standards of soccer in Ireland also started to improve. Aside from sharing the Championship with Scotland and England in 1903, Ireland was still fighting with Wales on an almost annual basis to avoid the wooden spoon, albeit moving closer towards competitiveness against England and Scotland. Victories over Scotland in 1903 and 1910 and finally over England in 1913 were a sign of things to come. Ireland could now compete against the very best. That Ireland won the Championship in 1914, so soon after a bitter dispute in 1912 that led to the secession of most senior clubs from the IFA, was a remarkable achievement. Winning the Championship for the first time that year gave the Irish public and press great grounds for optimism for the future. It was felt this young team could dominate international fixtures for some years to come. Events outside of soccer's control, however, intervened. The world became immersed in war by late summer 1914, a war that would last for four years, a war that would change the nature of Ireland and the whole world irrevocably. Events that summer would lead to fundamental changes for soccer. The match against Scotland in March 1914 was the last International soccer match Ireland played until 1919. Many soccer players and supporters volunteered to serve in the war, many never to return (IFA 1917). The game suffered financially with many clubs forced to disband. Soccer became localized, consigned to regions throughout the war. The Dublin clubs seceded from the Irish Football League for the duration of the war. They would ultimately never re-join the League. After the war, divisions between the Leinster Football Association and the IFA increased and eventually led to the split of 1921, a split that remains today.

Disclosure statement

No potential conflict of interest was reported by the author.

Notes

1. For composition of Irish teams, see *Belfast Newsletter, Sport, The Irish Independent, Freemans Journal, The Irish Times,* IFA International Minutes – 1909–1966, D/4196/D/1, Brodie, *100 Years of Irish Football* and *Northern Ireland Footballing Greats,* available from http://nifootball.blogspot.ie/.
2. Ibid.
3. Of the 30 matches Ireland played between 1890 and 1899 and from 1900 to 1909, in both time periods, Ireland won five, drew four and lost 21. It is goal difference improved from −79 from 1890 to 1899 to −58 from 1900 to 1909. See Samuel, *The British Home Football Championships.*

4. D4196/A/3 – Minute Book of the Irish Football Association – 1909–1928, 3 September 1912. The major points agreed upon were representation on the IFA Council for all senior league clubs; the senior clubs to organize the Irish Cup except for Protests and Appeals and the finances for the final tie which would be under the remit of the whole council; reduced representation on the IFA Council for the regional associations; clubs from the second division to be eligible for the Intermediate Cup Competition; 10% could only be agreed to for 1912 for gate receipts to clubs; no punishment to be meted out to Linfield and Bohemians for siding with the IFA; and all suspensions to be automatically rescinded. The IFA also agreed to discharge the liabilities of the new association to the value of 70 pounds.
5. *The Irish Times,* February 21, 1914, 19. The Corinthians were an amateur English club comprising ex-pubic schoolboy and university players whose most successful period was in the last decade of the nineteenth century, long diminished as a footballing force by 1914. See Taylor, *The Association Game: A History of British Football,* 83–85.

References

Briggs, George, and Joe Dodd. 1993. *Leinster Football Association 100 Years Centenary Yearbook 1892–1992.* Dublin: Leinster Football Association.
Brodie, Malcolm. 1980. *100 Years of Irish Football.* Belfast: Blackstaff Press Ltd.
Byrne, Peter. 2012. *Green is the Colour: The Story of Irish Football.* London: Carlton Books Limited.
FA. 1879–86. "The Football Association Council Meeting and Annual General Meeting, 1879–1886.".
Garnham, Neal. 1999. *The Origins and Development of Football in Ireland: Being a Reprint of R.M. Peter's Irish Football Annual of 1880.* Belfast: Ulster Historical Foundation.
Garnham, Neal. 2004. *Association Football and Society in Pre-Partition Ireland.* Belfast: Ulster Historical Foundation.
IFA. 1880–86. "Irish Football Association Minute Book, 1880–1886, D4196/AA/1.".
IFA. 1909–28. "Irish Football Association Minute Book, 1909–1928, D4196/A/3.".
IFA. 1910–87. "Irish Football Association Annual General Meetings, 1910–1987, D4196/U/1.".
IFAB, International Football Association Board Meeting Minutes, 1886–1912.
Kerrigan, Colm. 2005. "Ireland's Greatest Football Team?" *History Ireland* 13 (3): 26–30.
LFA. 1899–02. "Leinster Football Association Minute Book, 1899–1902.".
Mason, Tony. 1980. *Association Football and English Society 1863–1915.* Brighton: The Harvester Press Limited.
Robinson, Richard. 1920. *History of the Queen's Park Football Club 1867–1917.* Glasgow: Hay Nisbet.
Rouse, Paul. 2005. "Sport and Ireland in 1881." In *Sport and the Irish: Histories, Identities, Issues,* edited by Alan Barnier. Dublin: University College Dublin Press.
Samuel, Richard. 2003. *The British Home Football Championships 1884–1984.* South Humberside: Soccer Books Ltd.
Taylor, Matthew. 2008. *The Association Game: A History of British Football.* Harlow: Pearson Education Limited.

The GAA and revolutionary Irish politics in late nineteenth- and early twentieth-century Ireland

David Hassan and Andrew McGuire

School of Sport, University of Ulster, Jordanstown, UK

>The argument outlined in this article builds on the recent detailed historiography of the role of the Gaelic Athletic Association (GAA) around the turn of the twentieth century in Ireland. In the minds of some persuasive authors, the organization exercised an important supportive role in the expression of physical force Irish Republicanism and was therefore a not insignificant player in the activities of bodies expressly committed to this course of action. Yet others, such as the scholar William Murphy, have claimed this interpretation of the GAA's role is wholly overstated and instead it contained within its ranks members who, entirely coincidentally, were also involved in a range of similar entities at that time and were therefore committed to the cause of Irish sovereignty in a relatively benign form. In other words, the GAA offered a useful setting in which prominent Irish nationalists could hone their organizational skills rather than operating as a body that, in any coherent fashion, constituted an active agent in the promotion of an aggressive form of Irish nationalism during this period. By profiling the lived experiences of a select number of prominent GAA personalities, it is possible to illustrate this important distinction and establish the precise role of the association in those seminal decades either side of the turn of the twentieth century.

Introduction

When the Gaelic Athletic Association (GAA) was founded in 1884 by Michael Cusack, he sought the patronage of three prominent Irishmen. The first was Archbishop of Cashel Thomas Croke, courted by Cusack because of the respect the population at large had for him and the central role of the Catholic Church in Irish life. Second was Charles Stuart Parnell, leader of the Irish Parliamentary Party (IPP), the face of constitutional politics at the time. The third was Michael Davitt, founder of the National Land League (NLL). Archbishop Croke was a strong supporter of the work of both Parnell and Davitt. The political views of the three original patrons of the GAA set the early tone for the leanings of the organization as a whole.

As the GAA grew in both numbers and reach, the Irish Republican Brotherhood (IRB) sought to influence the path the Association was to take and counter the influence of the IPP and NLL. Two of the seven men at the founding meeting of the GAA – John Wyse Power and J.K. Bracken – were known to be IRB members (de Búrca 2000). Wyse Power eventually would head up the Dublin County Board. Another member of the Brotherhood, P.T. Hoctor from Tipperary and an active organizer of the GAA in County Clare, would be elected Vice-President of the GAA at its general meeting in 1886. After his election, Hoctor extended an invitation to a fourth patron, this being the Fenian leader John O'Leary (de Búrca 2000).

The next general meeting held in 1887 saw the Fenian P.N. Fitzgerald elected Secretary of the GAA. A contingent of Catholic priests, led by Father Scanlan from

Nenagh, opposed the nomination of Fitzgerald on the grounds that he being an IRB Official would 'give a very questionable appearance to the outside public' (Mandle 1987, 50). For the next two years, the GAA operated with IRB members as high-ranking officials. During this period, the GAA came under intense scrutiny from the authorities, particularly the Royal Irish Constabulary (RIC), and a report entitled 'The Political Aspect of the Gaelic Athletic Association' was compiled. This same report concluded that two points of contention were deemed to show the 'true character' of the GAA as far as the British Government was concerned – the refusal of uniformed members of the RIC and Army to be allowed join the Association and the appearance of uniformed GAA members at demonstrations of the National League (Dublin Castle Records).

This period of IRB control and the subsequent invoking of the name of the GAA in Irish nationalist politics has been used by several historians, most prominently Marcus de Búrca in his publication *The Story of the GAA* and W.F. Mandle in *The Gaelic Athletic Association & Irish National Politics*, as apparent evidence of the active GAA contributions made towards the ultimate goal of Irish independence. Mandle went so far as to say that 'it is arguable that no organization had done more for Irish nationalism than the GAA – not the IRB ... not the Gaelic League ... not the Irish Parliamentary Party ... not even Sinn Féin' (Mandle 1987, 221).

Around the same time as Mandle and de Burca were advancing their views, David Fitzpatrick argued from a different perspective in his paper *'The Geography of Irish Nationalism, 1910–1921'*.

> Less overtly political bodies such as the Gaelic League, Volunteers, and GAA represented groups united in their professed enthusiasm for language, games or mock bloodsports. No Irish organisation outside of Ulster could win mass support without proclaiming it's nationalism; but it had also to defend or promote the interests of some clearly defined group or groups. (Fitzpatrick 1978, 134)

It was not the aim of the GAA to be actively revolutionary, but rather a product of the times that necessitated at least an outwardly nationalistic stance with which to court the Irish public and gain their acquiescence. With this view in mind, the GAAs seeming involvement in the Irish nationalist movement is not one of outward revolutionary fervor, but rather one of necessary self-preservation.

A new wave of scholarship, led by historians such as William Murphy, has built on Fitzpatrick's earlier work and placed the established view of the GAA during this period under scrutiny. Indeed Murphy has argued that 'the association's vulnerability and the limits of its influence in a period when nationalism realized revolutionary change are now evident' (Murphy 2009, 76). With a few test cases to illustrate its argument, this article will look to further explore and enhance Murphy's characterization of the GAA, not as an active player in the case for Irish independence, but rather merely constituting the 'playground of the revolution' where those who would go on to lead the rebellion could hone their skills.

Examples showing how revolutionary leaders were able to gain experience and training within the ranks of the GAA, which served them in their work towards gaining Ireland's independence, will therefore be considered. Some attention is paid to the actual events of Easter Week 1916 as it pertains to the GAA, but the uprising itself is not covered in great depth as this has formed the central tenet of many other excellent works and indeed falls outside the scope of this analysis. To begin with, in order to refute the historical point of view concerning the supposed revolutionary role of the GAA that remained dominant for a considerable period of time, it is necessary to understand how this belief first emerged then evolved. Thus, an appreciation of the origins of this viewpoint is necessary to properly refute its assertions, which are considered in more depth later in this essay.

A wider role for the GAA

By the early 1900s, the GAA had been through several attempts by various nationalist groups to co-opt its power structure for their own ends, with some attempts proving more successful than others. As John O'Beirne Ranelagh put it in his work *A Short History of Ireland*, 'from 1887 onwards, the GAA was regarded by the Special Branch of the RIC as an adjunct of the physical force national movement, and its activities were regularly reported (as such)' (Ranelagh 1983, 153). For the next 30 years, the RIC had informants inside GAA clubs and would follow members to and from its meetings. In 1910, Mr John O'Donnell, M. P. for Mayo South, questioned Augustine Birrell, Chief Secretary of Ireland, about the police allegedly following GAA members in County Galway. O'Donnell accused the police of having detectives pursue members at meetings in Athenry and 'to report to local police stations the names of persons who attend such meetings' (House of Commons 1910). Further, it was suggested, that the president of the county board, Tom Kenny, and other officials were even followed as they went to Dublin on GAA business. O'Donnell reiterated the position of the GAA as being non-political in nature. Birrell replied that 'no person is being shadowed or watched in County Galway or elsewhere because he is a member of the Gaelic Athletic Association' (House of Commons 1910).

Birrell's answer, upon first reading, appears short and perfunctory, quickly replying and indeed dismissing O'Donnell's latent concern. However, more can be made of Secretary Birrell's reply than is immediately apparent. Birrell does not say that Kenny and the others are not being followed *at all*; merely that membership in the GAA was *not grounds* for being followed. Police in County Galway could very well have been following Mr Kelly, or anyone else, because of the government's perception of the GAA as being an associated part of the IRB. As was stated in the Dublin Castle report after the IRB takeover in 1886–87, the GAA was thought to be part of the 'physical force movement' in Ireland, and would therefore be subject to police scrutiny (Dublin Castle Records). Birrell's answer implies that while the British government in Ireland might not have considered membership in the GAA to be of sufficient grounds for police interest in itself, there was still a level of distrust of the upper echelons of the GAA leadership.

Indeed the leadership of the GAA unquestionably struggled with how to handle it existing as a nationalist body without appearing to be political in nature. The police report to Dublin Castle admitted that Michael Cusack had been 'quite honest in his original idea, which was to initiate a purely non-political association of athletes', but this was doomed from the start because of 'the utter impossibility of establishing amongst the general body of the Irish people a society of any kind which could be kept free from politics' (Dublin Castle Records). In 1886, two years after the foundation of the GAA, the so-called 'political clause' was added to the constitution, saying,

> That the Gaelic Athletic Association shall not be used in any way to oppose any national movement, which has the confidence and support of the Irish people. (de Búrca 2000, 36)

The vague wording of the clause allowed both Home Rule and Fenian members to infer that the GAA supported their political views, which was subsequently used to great effect by Fitzgerald and other IRB sympathizers.

Nine years later, in 1905, on the occasion of his silver jubilee, Archbishop Croke wrote that, 'as far as he knew ... the Association was purely an athletic body and that alone. The members of the Association had taken sides in the recent political dispute, which was but natural' (de Búrca 2000, 104). At that year's convention, the 'first comprehensive constitution and rules of the GAA' were codified. In the constitution, Rule 2 clarified the apolitical nature of the GAA, reading:

> That the Gaelic Athletic Association shall be a strictly non-political and unsectarian [*sic*] association. No political questions of any kind shall be raised at any of its meetings, and no club shall take part as a club in any political movement. (de Búrca 2000, 105)

While this new constitution advanced the official position of the GAA with regard to its political stance, it did little to dissuade the police from keeping a watchful eye on the GAA as a whole. Indeed police scrutiny would again fall on the GAA as the Irish Volunteers emerged as a dominant nationalist body.

Upon the formation of the Irish Volunteers, the *Gaelic Athlete* was quite vocal in its support and assertion that GAA members should join. The *Gaelic Athlete* was a weekly newspaper that styled itself 'the only journal in Ireland entirely devoted to Gaelic pastimes'. During World War I, the editorial staff of the *Gaelic Athlete* was unapologetic in their anti-British views, indeed nearly appearing pro-German at times. In one such instance, an editorial decried what the author felt was a 'pronounced Imperial tinge which has developed in the Irish atmosphere since the outbreak of the war.' Continuing, the author went on to state that 'our whole constitution is sternly opposed to any Jingo or pro-British tendency' (Editorial 1914, 137). As de Búrca notes, the *Gaelic Athlete* was not officially endorsed by the GAA, but it did have the support of many prominent Association figures and seemed to 'accurately reflect the mood of average members' (de Búrca 2000, 130).

With further regard to the Irish Volunteers, the *Gaelic Athlete* was a vocal supporter of its readers supporting the nationalist cause. A weekly article called 'Jots and Tittles' ran small news items, usually of a similar theme or content. In one edition of 'Jots and Tittles', it was relayed to the reader that 'over the Channel the present European situation has brought forth expression of opinion that the football field ought to be used as a recruiting ground for the Army' (Jots and Tittles 1914, 138). In a display of support for the Irish Volunteers, the article went on to say that 'a similar remark applies to Ireland in regard to our own Volunteer force' (Jots and Tittles 1914, 138). A more explicit appeal to aid the Volunteers was to appear in the very next edition of the paper.

In it, a large advertisement was published announcing that the Irish Volunteer Aid Association had begun organizing the Volunteer Military Medical Corps, under the auspices of the Irish Volunteers. The aim of the Medical Corps was to supply the Volunteers with 'proper Medical and nursing staffs, and adequate hospital and ambulance equipment' (Appeal for Help and Money 1914, 139). By 1915, the *Gaelic Athlete* was reporting that GAA involvement in the Irish Volunteers in Co. Kildare was so extensive that 'nearly all the members of the GAA were identified with the "Volunteer movement" and that volunteer activities were interfering with the playing of Gaelic games' (Kildare 1915).

The most extreme position advocated by the *Gaelic Athlete* was that of the creation of rifle clubs, to be established, of course, under the auspices of the GAA. The idea for the rifle clubs emerged following a suggestion made by the Kerry County Board, the impetus for which was due 'to the growth of the military spirit in Ireland' (Editorial 1914, 142). The rifle clubs were to be organized in the same fashion as hurling and Gaelic football entities, with competition ranging from inter-club all the way to All-Ireland contests. The reason for the editorial staff believing the rifle clubs should be implemented under the organizational umbrella of the GAA was twofold. The first was that the rifle clubs would offer practical experience in the use of the rifle, and the 'material assistance' this in turn would present the Irish Volunteers. As such, this first reason was entirely a practical matter. Moreover, the newspaper's support for the Volunteers has been well established by this point. It only makes sense that the editorial staff would be in support of a programme to enhance the effectiveness of the Irish Volunteers. The second, more idealistic, reason was that the GAA was the only suitably 'nationalist' body capable of organizing such a competition. The logic was that if there was a demand for rifle clubs, that 'the GAA should be the body to cater for that demand, and not an alien body, or a body with no National motives' (Editorial 1914, 142). Again, the GAA is revealed as an organization with a firm nationalist orientation. The fear of the rifle clubs falling under the control of a body that was not nationalist in its outlook, or worse still a foreign one, required that the GAA be in control of any new development of the kind being discussed here. The GAA was founded on the grounds that it was to provide a means to promote and support Irish pastimes, in direct competition to those organizations that were British in origin, so no other body would do to run the proposed rifle clubs, which in turn would be effectively auxiliaries to the Irish Volunteers. Ultimately, of course, the rifle clubs never came into being.

In the direct aftermath of the Easter Uprising in 1916, the government of Great Britain held an official inquiry, the Royal Commission on the Rebellion in Ireland. A few choice quotes from high-ranking officials in the RIC and British Army reveal the attitude of those in power towards the Association. Sir Matthew Nathan, Under-Secretary for Ireland under Augustine Birrell, testified that he believed that the GAA had 'always been anti-British. They would not allow soldiers in uniform to attend their games' (Lieutenant-Colonel The Right Honourable Sir Matthew Hill, 3). Sir Neville Chamberlain, then Inspector General of the Royal Irish Constabulary, joined in with Nathan in condemning the GAA and its policy of refusing 'soldiers or sailors or police in joining in their games' (Sir Neville Chamberlain, Inspector General of the Royal Irish Constabulary, 3). Major Ivan Price, Director of Military Intelligence for Irish Command, believed that the Irish Volunteers had gained 'practically full control' of the GAA and Gaelic League (Major Ivan Price, 3). The connection between the GAA and Irish Volunteers had been well established and quite public. However, the GAA was not under the control of the Volunteers. Rather, as de Búrca suggests, the two bodies shared an 'informal but effective alliance' (de Búrca 2000, 133). Most of the information related to the commission regarding the GAA fell into two categories – displeasure with the ban on police and military and the belief that the GAA was controlled by the IRB, Sinn Féin or Irish Volunteers.

Throughout the earliest days of its creation, during one of the most pivotal moments in the move towards independence, the GAA had been characterized by the powers-that-be as an organization that was full of seditious IRB members, who worked hand in hand with the GAA to further the cause of independence. From here, it follows that if later historians accept the perspective put forward by the British government, but from the position that the GAA was a force for good in Irish society, that during this time the Association would have been an influential player in Irish life and its actions an essential part of the march towards independence.

However, this characterization is undoubtedly flawed. While it is indisputable that there was indeed overlap between the memberships of the two organizations, correlation does not imply causation. Rather, by drawing upon a few mere examples, it is possible to illustrate instead that the GAA provided a forum in which to gain experience in leading a complex group of individuals. It is this experience that served the men of the IRB, not the GAA itself. It is for this reason Murphy somewhat accurately characterized the GAA as 'the playground of the revolution' (Murphy 2009, 76).

Michael Collins

When Michael Collins emigrated to London as a young man, he 'threw himself with all the enthusiasm of a healthy and vigorous youth' into the Geraldines Football Club (Béaslai 1926). Before long, Collins was elected secretary of the club at the tender age of 18 (Béaslai 1926). The effectiveness of Collins's diplomacy in sensitive matters can be seen with the handling of the payment of a debt to the proprietor of a pitch that was used by the Geraldines Club for its football matches. The incident began when the treasurer of the club, Mr Sullivan, mislaid the money for the rental of the pitch and neglected to tell anyone else in the club about this, presumably in an attempt to recover the money on his own without admitting to his error. The owner of the pitch, Mr A. Toley, threatened to no longer allow the Geraldines use of the grounds until the rent had been paid, a sum of £3-16-6. Collins then turned his attention to O'Sullivan, the club treasurer, in an attempt to resolve the matter. It was at this point that O'Sullivan finally admitted to having lost the money at the pitch. O'Sullivan worked to repay the club the lost funds. The careful handling of the situation by Collins led to a resolution satisfactory to almost all involved.

As secretary of the Geraldines, Collins had a responsibility to act in the best interests of the club. In the conflict with Mr Toley, Collins was at risk of losing the use of the pitch, which was so necessary to the continued survival of the club. However, Collins was able to assuage any slight perceived by Mr Toley to the point where Toley offered the club the use of a winter pitch. Without Collins's intervention, the club could have been faced with the loss of the pitch, or even legal action from Mr Toley as he sought compensation for his rent owed. However, the situation with the issue of pitch rentals would ultimately pale in comparison to the upheaval the London GAA would undergo at the end of the year, specifically in regard to the issue of the playing of foreign games.

Many of the London GAA members wished to play association football in addition to Gaelic football and hurling. However, the GAA had, since its inception, been adamantly against members playing or patronizing such so-called 'foreign' games, with those found to have done so subject to expulsion. Collins was steadfast in his refusal to allow the men of the Geraldines Club to partake in what he termed 'garrison games' (Coogan 1990, 16). Collins's report to his club at the end of the year was scathing in its indictment of the actions of the club:

> An eventful half year has followed a somewhat riotous general meeting. Great hopes instead of being fulfilled have been rudely shattered ... Our internal troubles were saddening but our efforts in football and hurling were perfectly heartbreaking. In no single contest have our colours been crowned with success ... In hurling ... we were drawn to play five matches but, disgraceful to say, in only one did we field a full team. If members are not prepared to act more harmoniously together and more self-sacrificing together ... the club will soon have faced into inglorious and well-deserved oblivion. (Coogan 1990, 16)

Michael Collins was uncompromising in his view that foreign games were one of Britain's most effective agents in the 'peaceful penetration' of Irish society, and that under all circumstances there should be 'no soccer for Gaels' (Béaslai 1926, 16). By the end of the rift, only three clubs remained, one of them Collins's Geraldines (Coogan 1990). For Collins, the GAA was an important organization in the movement for Irish independence (Coogan 1990).

The commitment of the leadership of the Geraldine club to the ideals of Irish nationalism can be seen by a resolution passed by the team regarding the use of the Irish language. By a vote of 12 to 4 in favour, the club resolved for each member to obtain a copy of *The Gaelic Athletic Annual* so that they might 'learn the different terms in Irish used in Gaelic Football and Hurling thereby to carry into practice the ideal of our club – our national language on the field of play' (Michael Collins Collection: Geraldine Club Note).

The passion Collins carried for Gaelic games is readily evident from the dramatic speech he gave to his fellow Geraldines. His address also shows the general lackadaisical attitude of the other members of the club. Of the club's five hurling matches, only once did they manage to get enough players to field a team. Many members of the club were not nearly as emphatic in their support of it as was Collins. Collins' obvious belief in the GAA's role in supporting Irish nationalism is not reflected in the attitudes of the general membership. Even the ballot on the use of Irish language was not unanimous, and the amount of men who voted on the motion was just one more person than is needed to field a hurling team. Coming from a club with such strong beliefs in the tenets of Irish nationalism, Collins was a prime candidate to join more openly nationalistic and political bodies. Another member of the London GAA, Sam Maguire, would recognize this in Collins and recruit him into the IRB.

Sam Maguire

Maguire was a Corkman who had emigrated to London, where he played football for the Hibernian football club (Cronin 2005). As well as being a member of the London GAA, he also joined the Gaelic League and eventually the Irish Republican Brotherhood (Cronin 2005). Maguire remained at his job in the postal service in England until after the Irish War of Independence, working to intercept documents that may have been of interest to the military planners within the IRB. Maguire eventually returned to Ireland after the Irish Civil War, but could not keep his employment in the postal service after the government removed all former IRB members from civil service posts. Maguire eventually returned home to Cork where he died of tuberculosis in 1926 (Cronin 2005). However, Maguire is best remembered today as the namesake of the trophy given to the All-Ireland Gaelic football champions each year. Upon his return from London, Maguire saw himself as both an IRB and GAA member, adhering to neither pro- nor anti-treaty political parties. This left him to a position of being embraced by neither side, which resulted in turn to his dismissal from the civil service (Cronin 2005). However, as the GAA had always placed itself as a nationalist, but non-political, entity, Maguire was a perfect man to be honoured by a championship trophy.

J.J. Walsh

In addition to the GAA giving opportunities for direct leadership, it also gave leaders a chance to implement and test logistical measures designed to best run and organize large groups. The most appropriate example of using the GAA to implement such ideas is apparent in the work undertaken by J.J. Walsh, while a member of the Cork County Board. Walsh was a post office employee in Cork, as well as an influential GAA member. In his memoirs, *Recollections of a Rebel*, Walsh recounts that around 1902 the GAA was in decline in Cork, after 'all the educated and influential classes were switching over to alien games' (Walsh 1944, 16–17). Walsh and his cohorts saw an opportunity to bolster the falling ranks of the Cork GAA. 'In a short time', wrote Walsh,

> we had organized hurling and football leagues, not only in the country, but also in the lanes and streets of the City and towns ... With this intensely organized instrument, war was declared on foreign games, which were made to absorb the shock so heavily that, one by one, soccer and rugby clubs began to disappear. (1944, 17)

However, Walsh's grassroots organization of GAA clubs in Cork was still subject to oversight from the county board. Walsh felt that the board at the time was using methods that were 'out of date' and that his approach would be better if he and his men took 'on the whole responsibility for the GAA in the county' (1944, 17–18).

In 1909, Walsh was elected as chairman of the county board by a margin of 15 votes. Walsh divided his time between his job at the post office and his responsibilities with the county board. He wrote that he would often work on GAA matters until 'one or two a.m. and find myself at the Post Office counter at seven' (1944, 19). Walsh's experiences from working in the civil service allowed him to revolutionize the efficiency of the Cork GAA to the point that the county board had generated sufficient income to buy shares in the Great Southern Railway, which gave Walsh and the county board 'the necessary pull where travel facilities counted for a great deal' (1944, 18). The railways were a vital link for inter-county games, so the ability of the county board to influence the railways as shareholders, in addition to the clout exercised by the GAA, was a major boost to Cork. As would be seen after the Easter Uprising, restrictions on the use of the railways were to prove very detrimental to the abilities of the county boards to schedule matches against each other. In his book, Walsh wrote that soon county boards across the country, such as the Dublin County Board led by Harry Boland and Mick Crow, were emulating the techniques pioneered in Cork (1944).

However, unsurprisingly the British authorities in Ireland were not keen on Walsh's activities in Cork. After five years as chairman of the county board, Walsh was transferred to the post office in Bradford, England. The *Gaelic Athlete* immediately took up the issue of Walsh's transfer, decrying it as the 'first shot' in a 'campaign of terrorism' aimed at the Cork GAA (Editorial, 149). Its editorial described the chain of events that befell Walsh. First, he was subject to a compulsory transfer to the Bradford post office, for what they claimed was 'on account of that gentleman's National activities'. Walsh tendered his letter of resignation to the Cork County Board, which the board refused to accept. Instead, the county board adopted a resolution to petition the Postmaster-General to reinstate Walsh to his previous position in Cork. This resolution was presented to the Cork Corporation, of which Walsh was also a member. However, the Cork Corporation voted against the resolution. The *Gaelic Athlete* quoted the Corporation's decision as being 'a protest against [Walsh's] politics.' The editorial condemned Cork Corporation for what it called the 'intrusion upon the right of a free man in an alleged free country to hold what political views he wills'. GAA boards around the country passed resolutions in support of Walsh, but all to no avail (Editorial, 149).

Seven months on, in June 1915, J.J. Walsh had moved to Dublin and opened a shop at the corner of Blessington and Berkeley Streets on Dublin's north side. The *Gaelic Athlete* carried the news in an article entitled 'Rally Round, Boys!' (Rally Round, Boys, 182), urging its readers to show its support of 'his great services to the GAA' by purchasing goods from Walsh's new store. The article called for Walsh to receive a 'welcome from the Gaels of Dublin' by way of business for his new establishment. 'In patronizing that establishment,' the article continued, 'you are helping your own' (Rally Round, Boys, 182).

Dick Fitzgerald

Many people know Dick Fitzgerald as the famed footballer from Kerry, a man who won five All-Ireland medals and many more honours with his club side. Less well known is Fitzgerald's political involvement. Beginning as a member of the Gaelic League, Fitzgerald would become progressively more involved in the Kerry political scene as he aged. During the War of Independence and following the Civil War, Fitzgerald served on the Killarney urban council. At times, his political and sporting lives intertwined as he served on various GAA councils, from the board of his local club all the way to hearings of the organization's Central Council in Dublin.

Fitzgerald would assume his first leadership role with Dr Crokes when becoming club secretary in 1908 (Looney 2008). That year, Kerry won the Munster championship, but lost to Dublin in the All-Ireland Home Final. In 1911, Fitzgerald resigned his role as club secretary for Dr Crokes for an elevated role as a member of the club committee (Looney 2008). That year, during a particularly contentious match against Dr Crokes' main Kerry rivals, Tralee Mitchells, Fitzgerald and the rest of Dr Crokes left the pitch in protest. Because of a newly enacted rule that made any such walk-off a mandatory suspension – in an effort to curtail a growing number of such protests – Kerry were without the services of Fitzgerald and other Dr Crokes players for the county team. That year, Cork would go on to claim the All-Ireland title (Looney 2008). Despite these on-going problems, 1913 would be a banner year for Dick Fitzgerald. At a meeting of the Kerry County Board over which he presided, Fitzgerald moved that Kerry finally change their playing kits and formally adopt what would become their iconic green and gold hoops. Later in 1913, Kerry would defeat Wexford in the All-Ireland Final. Thanks in part to the small world of Irish politics and smaller world of the GAA, Harry Boland, the Dublin GAA leader and prominent IRB figure, refereed the final.

On 28 November 1913, Pádraig Ó Siochfradha, sometimes known by his *nom de plume* An Seabhac (The Hawk), formed a company of Irish Volunteers in Killarney. This formation of the Killarney Company took place at a meeting of the local Gaelic League, wherein the men in attendance, numbering approximately 40, unanimously voted to form the company (Bureau of Military History). Dick Fitzgerald was among the men in attendance, and would later be elected 2nd Lieutenant of the company (Bureau of Military History). Less than a month later, on 13 December 1913, Austin Stack, Chairman of the Kerry GAA Board, joined the Irish Volunteers at a meeting in Tralee.

Easter 1916

No coverage on the politics of Ireland in the movement towards independence would be complete without at least some considered mention of the happenings of Easter Sunday, 1916. The details of the exact goings on of the day, such as troop movements or buildings held by either side, do not fall within the scope of this article. Rather, brief note will be made about various roles played by GAA members during that pivotal week. Among those GAA members who were active throughout the Easter Rising were a handful of men who held key positions in the insurgency. The aforementioned Harry Boland was chairman of the Dublin GAA County Board at the time of the Easter Rising (Nolan 2000). In fact, Boland would find himself among the hundreds imprisoned after Easter Week. Other members of the GAA would also find themselves in pivotal roles in the fighting that took place, among them Frank Burke and Peadar Boyle. Frank Burke, who would go on to win two All-Ireland Senior Hurling and three All-Ireland Senior Football championships for Dublin, was a 2nd Lieutenant in the Irish Volunteers (Nolan 2000). Peadar Boyle, who served as quartermaster of the South Dublin Union Garrison, would go on to hold several important governmental positions, serving on Dublin Corporation, as Lord Mayor of Dublin, and as Fine Gael T.D (Nolan 2000).

The response of the British government after the Easter Uprising was swift. The rebellion was quelled within a week, many hundreds arrested, and its main leaders executed.

As William Nolan notes, 'four of the executed leaders of the Easter Rising – Patrick Pearse, Con Colbert, Michael O'Hanrahan and Eamon Ceannt – were associated either in a players or administrative capacity within the GAA in Dublin' (Murphy 2009, 67).

Up until this point, this article has presented only a very small, purposive sample of evidence in support of its primary thesis concerning the comparatively modest role played by the GAA in the cause of forceful expressions of Irish nationalism. Such evidence could easily have been cherry-picked for its seeming ability to bolster the arguments presented here, where in actuality the small size of the sample is not, in truth, sufficient to reinforce any claims made either way. Seeking to augment these stories, this essay will delve briefly into some statistical work previously undertaken on the matter.

In fact, the figures on the number of members actively taking part in the Uprising further underpin Murphy's interpretation of the role of the GAA as a training ground, rather than active player, for Irish revolutionary politics. In *The Gaelic Athletic Association in Dublin 1844–2000*, William Nolan wrote that 'it was not so much membership of the GAA that motivated men and women to take up arms but rather membership of the Gaelic League' (Nolan 2000, 125). Figures in that same work show that many of the GAA clubs in Dublin had few or no members who partook in the Uprising. Murphy, citing figures from Walsh, figured that of the seventy GAA clubs in Dublin, thirty-two clubs had three or fewer members taking part, while 17 had no members involved in the Uprising (Murphy 2009). The actions of the few have influenced perceptions of the GAA as a major force in the events of Easter Week 1916. The high profile members of the GAA who did take up arms invited the attention of the British authorities upon the organization, even though, as has been made clear, a majority of clubs in Dublin had few or no members who took part in the Uprising. This attention has passed on to the histories of the GAA, where a disproportionate amount of responsibility has been placed on the GAA for the events of Easter Week.

Peter Hart produces similar figures for the lack of involvement of the GAA in Irish Republican Army activities. In his publication '*The Geography of Revolution in Ireland*', Hart compares incidences of IRA violence and membership in the GAA and concludes that 'there is little other evidence to suggest a strong link between [the GAA and IRB]'. The correlation coefficient of such a relationship stands at only 0.06, suggesting no correlation at all between the two otherwise independent factors. Hart then cites J.J. O'Connell's assertion that 'it was a fact that the Volunteers did not receive from the GAA the help they expected' (Hart 1997, 169).

Conclusion

Dominant historiography has treated the GAA as a major force in Irish independence. Authors like Mandle and de Búrca have equated the particular nationalism of the GAA with the movement for Ireland's campaign for sovereignty. High-profile GAA members who also were involved in revolutionary activities have reinforced this perception still further, both in popular thought and academic research. Gaelic games provided men like Michael Collins with practical experience in leadership and organizational skills, which has erroneously been extrapolated into the belief that the GAA was an active organ for independence. Merely having revolutionaries in its ranks does not itself make the GAA a revolutionary body. While the GAA contained a small number of men who would fight and indeed die for Ireland, the association and its members were not taking up arms on any grand, coordinated scale. The decision to participate in the events of Easter Week, for example, was an entirely personal one, not one dictated by the GAA and it is the important distinction that must continue to be highlighted in any examination of the association either side of the dawn of the twentieth century.

Disclosure statement
No potential conflict of interest was reported by the authors.

References
"Appeal for Help and Money". *Gaelic Athlete*, vi, no. 139. August 29, 1914.
Béaslaí, P. 1926. *Michael Collins and the Making of a New Ireland*. Vol. 2. London: Harrap.
Bureau of Military History. *Witness Statement of Michael Spillane and Michael J. O'Sullivan*, WS 132.
Coogan, T. 1990. *Michael Collins: A Biography*. London: Hutchison.
Cronin, M. 2005. "Sam Maguire: Forgotten Hero and National Icon." *Sport in History* 25 (2): 189–205. doi:10.1080/17460260500186744.
de Búrca, M. 2000. *The GAA: A History*. Dublin: Gill & Macmillan.
Dublin Castle Records. *The Political Aspect of the Gaelic Athletic Association*, CO904/16. National Archives, London.
Fitzpatrick, D. 1978. "The Geography of Irish Nationalism 1910–1921." *Past & Present* 78 (1): 113–144. doi:10.1093/past/78.1.113.
"Editorial". *Gaelic Athlete*, iv, 137. August 15, 1914.
"Editorial". *Gaelic Athlete*, v, 142. September 19, 1914.
"Editorial". *Gaelic Athlete*, vi, 149. November 7, 1914.
Hart, P. 1997. "The Geography of Revolution in Ireland 1917–1923." *Past & Present* 155 (1): 142–176. doi:10.1093/past/155.1.142.
House of Commons. 1910. "Gaelic Athletic Association Meetings (County Galway)." *Sessional Papers: Oral Answers to Questions* 16: 1699–1700.
"Jots and Tittles". *Gaelic Athlete*, iv 138. August 22, 1914.
"Kildare". *Gaelic Athlete*, vii, no. 158. January 9, 1915.
"Lieutenant-Colonel The Right Honourable Sir Matthew Hill". *Minutes of Evidence Given before the Royal Commission on the Rebellion in Ireland*, 3, [Cd. 8311], H.C. 1916, xi.
Looney, T. 2008. *Dick Fitzgerald: King in a Kingdom of Kings*. Dublin: Currach Press.
"Major Ivan Price". *Minutes of Evidence Given before the Royal Commission on the Rebellion in Ireland*, p. 3, [Cd. 8114], H.C. 1916, xi, 242.
Mandle, W. F. 1987. *The Gaelic Athletic Association and Irish National Politics 1884–1924*. Dublin: Gill and Macmillan.
Michael Collins Collection. "Geraldine Club Note (undated)." P123/36 UCD Archives.
Murphy, W. 2009. "The GAA During the Irish Revolution 1913–23." In *The Gaelic Athletic Association 1884–2009*, edited by M. Cronin, W. Murphy, and P. Rouse, 61–76. Dublin: Irish Academic Press.
Nolan, W., ed. 2000. *The Gaelic Athletic Association in Dublin 1884–2000*. Dublin: Geography Publications.
"Rally Round, Boys!". *Gaelic Athlete*, vii, 182. June 26, 1915.
Ranelagh, J. 1983. *A Short History of Ireland*. Cambridge: Cambridge University Press.
"Sir Neville Chamberlain, Inspector General of the Royal Irish Constabulary". *Minutes of Evidence Given Before the Royal Commission on the Rebellion in Ireland*, 3, [Cd. 8311], H.C. 1916, xi.
Walsh, J. J. 1944. *Recollections of a Rebel*. Tralee: The Kerryman.

The emergence of hurling in Australia 1877–1917

Patrick Bracken

International Centre for Sports History and Culture, De Montfort University, Leciester, UK

> Hurling was an early example of transnational sport, in the context of Irish sport. It was a means by which Irish emigrants maintained a cultural bond with their homeland. Hurling in Australia, as popularised by the emerging Irish communities, was an instrument of identity. If these new, colonial Irish were playing hurling in the antipodean lands, then it follows that the game was not in total freefall in Ireland. Yet, the story of hurling among the Australian Irish is akin to that of a reclusive ancestor. Hurling narratives have not countenanced the potential of its worth. Hurling in Australia, in the era before the foundation of the Gaelic Athletic Association, in Thurles in 1884, had codification, structure and competition, however limited the player base was. The untold story of hurling in Australia has a historic significance for both the nascent Gaelic association and the transnational appeal of sport across two continents.

Introduction

In the aftermath of the Great Famine, thousands of Irish people fled the country to start a new life in Great Britain, the United States of America, Canada, Australia and New Zealand (Fitzpatrick 1980, 138–139). Along with their personal belongings they took aspects of their culture. This paper explores one such aspect, the sport of hurling. The men who founded and established new hurling clubs in the latter half of the 1870s, in Australia, were newly arrived immigrants as a means of facilitating recreation and playing a game native to their homeland. Hurling clubs were formed in Victoria and in the process the Victorian Hurling Association established of code of rules for the regulation of the game in the colony, a code which preceded the Gaelic Athletic Association (GAA) code of 1884 (*The Argus*, April 17, 1878).

Hurling was an example of the diffusion of sport among migrant communities. The diffusion of sport in Australia was not a new feature of transnational sport. Both cricket and rugby union had been diffused throughout the colonies by emigrant English settlers previous to the emergence of hurling in the Irish communities. In the context of the transnational spread of sport, the emergence of hurling in 1870s Australia is very important in presenting an argument for its presence in Ireland in the era before the foundation of the GAA in Thurles, County Tipperary, in 1884. Hurling was unique to Ireland and that the migrants established a hurling association to support the development of the game in Victoria suggests that they brought with them a great knowledge of the game and by extension this demonstrates that hurling was not on the cusp of oblivion in 1870s Ireland.

This paper adds to the transnational appeal of sport, not only from an Irish context, but an international one, in that it demonstrates that a minority sport, from a predominantly rural-based society, could cross continents and become an important part of the life of the emigrant Irish. It also received support from Ireland as hurleys were shipped out to Australia to meet the demand of the players.

Hurling takes off

Hurling in Australia, after 1872, was principally a sideshow event connected with celebrations of St Patrick's Day often organized by the Hibernian Australasian Catholic Benefit Society (*The Mercury*, March 29, 1872; March 18, 1875; February 26, 1876). Yet, what these occasions instilled was a desire among the newly arrived Irish to create, in some format, an identity for themselves. Over the next 5 years the game appeared as an important element of these celebratory events, from where it emerged as the focal event of St. Patrick's Day festivities. From being a sideshow event in 1872, hurling had, by 1877, become an important recreational activity for the emigrant Irish. By that time men living and working in the emigrant Irish communities established several hurling clubs in Victoria (O'Farrell 1988, 178). Clubs such as Brighton, Collingwood and Heidelberg emerged in Melbourne and in the mining communities, in the south of the state, were found the Geelong, Kyneton and Warrnambool clubs. Between 1877 and 1917, there were a minimum of 97 hurling teams in Australia, the majority of which were in Victoria and New South Wales (Table 1). However, hurling also spread to Queensland, Western Australia and Tasmania, where it enjoyed periods of popularity while only infrequent references to the sport in South Australia were made (*South Australian Register*, May 17, 1877; March 15, 1879). The year 1906 featured the most number of clubs in press reports, with a total of 17 recorded. There is no way of knowing, and there likely may never be, how many ephemeral clubs were in existence, whose activities went unrecorded in the press. For those clubs which featured in the press they played matches on a frequent basis, which was often weekly, with a three o'clock throw-in on a Saturday afternoon. They provided a meeting place for Irish men and women, with attendance figures at matches ranging from a few hundred up to 5000 recorded.

During 1877, reports of hurling matches appeared with greater regularity in the Australian press. Most of the adult Irish who emigrated during and in the immediate aftermath of the Famine would have been too old to participate in such fixtures. The names of those participating in these matches show that the names, save for a rare few, were predominantly of Irish origin. Purcell, Cody, O'Meara, Ryan and O'Brien are typical of the range of names found on team lists, often with sets of brothers competing. The Irish were also attracted to other sports inclusive of cricket, Australian Rules football, and rugby union, while boxing and rugby league especially appealed to the working classes, now filling the suburbs which were springing up around the developing cities. A. J. Rose, in his study of migration to eastern Australia found that:

> the age structure at this time indicates that the major influx of Irish had probably eased before 1875. The deep impress made upon Australian society by Irishmen resulted from the relatively and absolutely greater immigration prior to about 1860. (1959, 79)

That the Australian newspapers were a medium for transmitting leisure and sporting news to club members is evident from the frequency with which fixtures and times for challenge matches appeared in the press. Local meeting places, such as Cody's Abbotsford

Table 1. The number of hurling clubs in Australia, 1877–1917.

1877–81	1882–86	1887–91	1892–96	1897–01	1902–06	1907–11	1912–16
44	37	2	18	46	50	15	27

Sources: The Advocate; The Argus; Australian Town and Country Journal; Bendigo Advertiser; The Brisbane Courier; The Colac Herald; Evening News; Freeman's Journal; Kalgoorlie Miner; Kyneton Guardian; Mercury and Weekly Courier; Referee, Sydney Morning Herald.

Hotel and Kavanagh's Star and Garter Hotel, South Melbourne, were regularly frequented by hurling clubs. The hotel owner was a key agent in the development of hurling clubs (*The Argus*, April 18, 1863; May 16, 1877; *Bendigo Advertiser*, July 30, 1877; *Mercury and Weekly Courier*, January 19, 1878). Typical of such an association was evident at a meeting, held at the Carlton Club Hotel, Grattan-street, Melbourne for the purpose of forming a hurling club:

> The chair was occupied by Mr. John W. Howard, who explained that sixty persons had already agreed to join the club, and that about thirty had been playing during the past few weeks. It was intended, when the club was fairly started, to play the game according to the strict rules, and as there were many good players in the colony, they would be able to teach young men who might be desirous of learning the game. The promoters of the club had received such promises of support that there was no doubt of its success, and of the introduction of the game as one of the permanent sports of the colony. (*The Argus*, May 16, 1877)

For the match between the Melbourne and Richmond clubs, to mark St. Patrick's Day, in 1878, 60 best players were picked, with 2 teams of 25 players aside chosen. The players used 'imported hurlies (*sic*) from the old sod' (*The Argus*, March 22, 1878). Evidently there was either still a demand for hurleys in Ireland or that the knowledge of making them was still alive. When Michael Cusack got involved in hurling in Dublin, one of the greatest challenges facing him was that there was no one in the city who could make hurleys (De Búrca 1989, 63).

Codification and Michael Cusack

By 1878 hurling was a very popular recreation in the Irish communities of Melbourne, and other towns in Victoria. On Monday, 15 April 1878, a meeting took place with 'delegates from the various hurling clubs' attending at Dillon's Hotel, Melbourne:

> for the purpose of adopting one code of laws for the regulation of the game for the whole of the colony, and also for the formation of a Hurling Club Association. Representatives from Melbourne, Kyneton, Collingwood, Brighton, Prahran, and Richmond clubs were present. It was decided to form an association, to be called the Victorian Hurling Club Association and a provisional committee was appointed to carry out the revision of the laws, and submit them to the various clubs for approval. (*The Argus*, April 17, 1878).

One could assume that word of this did, at some stage, reached Ireland. Did it filter back so much that the news of a Hurling Club Association in Australia ultimately prompted Michael Cusack to switch to hurling? In his study of Cusack, Marcus de Búrca, offered some valid arguments as to why Cusack decided to revive hurling in Ireland noting that in the early months of 1884, through his column in the *Shamrock*, he referred to hurling and football regularly (De Búrca 1989, 71). Cusack was initially an anglophile in sport. He was an advocate of the rugby code. His subsequent change to the promotion of Gaelic recreations and pastimes was a complete u-turn in his sporting direction. Prior to the foundation of the GAA, there is evidence of at least 22 teams that played hurling between 1877 and 1884 in Australia (Table 1), among which 20 were in Victoria, and 1 each in New South Wales and South Australia.

While it is quite possible that word of hurling in Australia went unnoticed in Ireland, it is argued here that news of Australian hurling did filter through to Ireland and that the Victorian Hurling Association was a critical development in the enduring legacy of hurling, not only in Australia – mindful that it would experience periods of growth and decline – but also in Ireland. This new hurling association was potentially a key stepping-stone in the revival of hurling in Ireland. Little evidence has come to light to connect hurling in Ireland and Australia previously, neither in contemporary reports or subsequent research. Seamus King has outlined the emergence of the game in some parts of Australia in the pre-GAA era, but the majority of his account dealt with twentieth century hurling (King 1998, 139–146). It is improbable that this new association went unnoticed in Ireland mindful that Australian newspapers were received in Dublin on a regular basis. It is not improbable that accounts of hurling in Australia were sent to Ireland, and came to the notice of Michael Cusack. Letters home were informative and it is possible that information about hurling matches was included in some of those letters. There are many instances of family members writing home to inform people about life in Australia (Fitzpatrick 1994). Many of those letters were private, but other accounts of life in the colonies appeared in the local press. For example, the success of three D'Alton brothers on the cricket fields in Australian was reported in the Tipperary press. They had emigrated to Victoria from Nenagh, County Tipperary, where they had previously played cricket. (*The Pleasant Creek News and Wimmera Advertiser*, January 27, 1879; March 10, 1879; March 24, 1879; May 5, 1879; *Nenagh Guardian*, June 11, 1879).

The rules of hurling, as adopted in 1878, were published in the Australian press in 1887 (*Bendigo Advertiser*, September 7, 1887). Henry Ives, who was secretary of the Lauriston Hurling Club, had no reason to publish the rules apart from the fact that he wished to impress on those attempting to revive the game, in 1887, that a series of laws were adopted by the Victorian Association some years previously. The Australian hurling code contained 16 rules. These were very specific in the use of terminology and in all matters relating to play. Rules pertaining to the field layout, the number of players, umpires, goals, frees, and others were clearly outlined. In Ireland, examples of pre-GAA rules included those promoted by the Killimor club, dating to 1869, which contained 10 rules. In 1870, the laws of hurley, as defined by students of Trinity College, contained 16 rules while the rules of the Dublin Hurling Club, in 1883, contained 20 rules (Lennon 1997, 1–5).

There were elements of the game which were common to Ireland and Australia. The Killimor rules appeared to have no cross-bar on the goals. The Australian rules also had goal posts which had no horizontal bar. Their rules did contain side-posts, which were a feature of Australian Rules football. Side-posts were also introduced into the GAA's 1886 hurling rules, which Maurice Davin had devised following the foundation of the GAA (Ó Riain 1994, 64–65; Lennon 1997, 20). The inter-changeability of rules infers that elements of codification were borrowed from similar stick and ball games. In the Australian hurling rules, rule 15 was very specific in the terminology used as it specifically stated that 'chopping hurleys' was strictly prohibited. The term 'chopping' is not defined in the current GAA rule book, though it is a term widely used by hurling followers and is as evident in the game of hurling in 2015 as it was in 1878. In rule 5.15, it is a foul 'to strike an opponent's hurley unless both players are in the act of playing the ball' (Gaelic Athletic Association 2014, 48).

The Australian hurling rules are very important in the context of hurling in Ireland, as they not only infer continuity but are clear evidence of the transnational spread of sport in the Victorian era. Cricket was transnational in its appeal. The first test match between England and Australia took place in 1877 (*The Argus*, March 15, 1877; *The Brisbane Courier*, March 24, 1877; *The Australasian*, March 24, 1877). By that date rugby football had spread to Ireland (Diffley 1973, 20–21). Association football was also about to embark on a transnational journey which would ultimately propel it to the forefront of sporting recreation in many countries. It arrived in Ireland in 1878 (Garnham 2004, 4). Hurling is another sport that may be added to this brief list.

The style of hurling, and indications as to the pitch layout at this time in Australia are worthy of consideration. At an early meeting of the Melbourne club, in June 1877, 'a new ball of a peculiar make' was tried on the occasion, and it was 'a great improvement upon any one yet used' (*The Argus*, June 16, 1877). In June 1878, a report on the Collingwood Hurling Club concluded with

> a few words now as to the game of hurling, which is now getting so very popular. It is a grand old national Irish game, and is now in its second season in this colony, the Melbourne Club having started first, closely followed by Collingwood, Heidelberg, Kyneton, Brighton, Warrnambool, Prahran and Geelong. (*Mercury and Weekly Courier*, July 6, 1878)

Dight's Paddock, Melbourne, was one of the common playing areas for the Collingwood club and it later became known as Victoria Park, home of Collingwood FC. The Arden Street reserve, in Hotham, played host to the Melbourne and Young Victorian clubs, among others. In July 1878, a match between Kyneton and a club which took the name of the 'Bohemians' commenced:

> at about three o'clock [when] both teams formed in procession, each team wearing their caps, and with their hurleys on their shoulders. When the racecourse was reached the ground was found well marked out by the usual number of boundary flags, and the goal posts fixed east and west. The playing ground was 250 yards by 150 yards. (*Mercury and Weekly Courier*, July 13, 1878)

The first set of playing rules for hurling, as adopted by the GAA at its convention, in December 1884, had specifications in relation to ground size as its first rule. The ground 'shall, when convenient, be at least 200 yards long by 150 yards broad, or as near to that size as can be got' (Lennon 1997, 11). Furthermore, Rule 5 stated that 'there shall not be less than fourteen or more than twenty-one players aside in regular matches' (Lennon 1997, 11). The Australian rules, of 1878, noted that teams must not number more than 21 players (*Bendigo Advertiser*, September 7, 1887). In this match, several thousands of miles away in Australia, and 6 years before the foundation of the GAA, are features of the game remarkably similar to the rules constituted in 1884. Once more this evidence demonstrates common elements of codification, and also knowledge of hurling, continuity and tradition.

Hurling's popularity continued. *The Mercury*, in an account of hurling on St. Patrick's Day 1879, commented that as soon as:

> the hurling commenced, this gentle soothing pastime so dear to all true sons of Erin's Isle, was plied with nimble step and tortuous measure with impetuous zest. What scene can equal it? The wild disarray, the tumultuous exciting onslaught, like Sioux Indians in full war cry; the hand to hand encounter, the hoarse shouts rising above the din of the fast and furious fray – this game of hurling, this war of clubs, with the Celtic blood hot with the, dash and courage of the race. What can equal it? Football was feebly introduced, but it was insipid, tame, and effeminate beside the fascination of hurling. (*The Mercury*, March 18, 1879)

The appeal of the game in the state of Victoria soon spread to New South Wales. One of the first clubs established abroad, after the GAA was founded, was in Sydney, in May 1885. A local press announcement stated that:

> a hurling club has been formed at Parramatta by the Gaelic Athletic Association of that town. At an adjourned meeting of that club, held at the Currency Lass Hotel on Saturday night, fourteen members were elected, and it was stated that a large number of persons were prepared to join as soon as the club became fairly started. A committee was formed to draw up a code of rules for the guidance of the club and Mr. P. Long was elected secretary. The rules of the game adopted are those observed by the Thurles, Tipperary Club. (*The Sydney Morning Herald*, May 19, 1885)

Patrick Long was a native of Tuam, County Galway. Not only was word of the GAA spreading quickly throughout Ireland, word was also spreading globally. Here the rules adopted were those as outlined by the founders of the GAA, in Thurles, as opposed to a specific set of Thurles rules. The foundation of the GAA gave renewed impetus to the game in Australia. Hurling clubs in Lismore, Coraki and Brisbane also emerged in 1885, but the player base was limited.

Ongoing problems

Hurling in Australia, in spite of intermittent periods of success, was beset by two principle problems. Hurling clubs had no fixed location. Parkland was often used by various clubs, not just hurling teams. Second, the nature of employment meant that many men and their families had to move to places where there was work. This resulted in the rise and fall of several clubs over a relatively short period of time, as the vagaries of life impacted on recreational sport.

For most of the early to mid-1890s, there were intermittent hurling reports in the Australian press. This was symptomatic of the malaise which had engulfed the continent. By the middle of the decade signs of improvement were evident. In 1895, the first hurling match ever played in Colac took place in the Agricultural Reserve under the auspices of the newly formed club. A large number, many of whom were described as old players, had joined as members. Though the match was only a practice one, the novelty of the game, as far as Colac was concerned, was expected to attract a large attendance with hurleys provided for the players (*The Colac Herald*, August 30, 1895).

In 1896, a match, under the rules of the Gaelic Athletic Association, was played in Sydney, between the Michael Davitt and Volunteer Hurling Clubs, on the Volunteer Football Club Ground, Pyrmont, Mr. M. Furlong captained the Michael Davitt team, and Mr. B. Martin acted in a similar capacity for the Volunteers (*Australian Town and Country Journal*, September 19, 1896). In the latter half of the 1890s, in New South Wales, there was evidence that the game was structured and organized. Mirroring developments in Ireland, a GAA Central Council was established in the state to oversee development and growth of the game in the state. At this juncture, there was no evidence to suggest that the council also took initiatives to promote Gaelic football. Australian Rules football, rugby union and association football were the codes most commonly played. It was a hard enough struggle for hurling to gain a foothold in urban and rural communities without the Sydney association having to try to introduce a recently invented football game, when there were already established football codes in existence.

In 1897, at a meeting of the central council of the Gaelic Athletic Association of Sydney, the council decided to offer a cup and a set of medals for a competition to be known as the GAA Cup and Medals (*Evening News*, June 25, 1897). The competition between the Michael Davitt, Tempe and Robert Emmett clubs kept the respective members busy during 1898. The Robert Emmet Club was under the presidency of Mr. Eugene Ryan, a native of Turraheen, Rossmore, County Tipperary and a prominent Irish speaker and supporter of the Gaelic revival movement. Initiatives to promote and revive interest in the Irish language and Irish Gaelic culture – including folklore, sports, the arts and music – were a feature of late nineteenth century Ireland. Supporters of such initiatives were referred to as being part of the Gaelic revival movement (*Freemans Journal*, July 23, 1898; O'Farrell 1988, 178). In 1898, the newly formed Tempe Hurling Club was established under GAA rules (*Evening News*, June 25, 1898). The president of the club was Tom Malone, an acclaimed athlete from County Clare, who emigrated to Australia in the 1882 (Sheedy 2000, 54, 57). Malone became a champion sprinter in Australia, but dislocated his ankle while playing a hurling match, in 1885, which led a Darwin newspaper to remark that they 'thought you could only get your skull dislocated at hurling' *North Australian*, September 11, 1885). For almost 20 years, from 1885 to 1904, Malone played an important role in the promotion of hurling, not only in Sydney and New South Wales, but also in Victoria and Western Australia. Between 1898 and 1904, Malone worked as an administrator with the New South Wales board and as a referee/umpire. He was an important figurehead for hurling in Australia and it was later stated that the game of hurling would never die out while Tom Malone lived (*Freemans Journal*, July 2, 1898).

In June 1898, in a match between the Tempe and Michael Davitt teams, the press report noted that:

> to many the game was hurling, while to others it brought back pleasant recollections of the days of their youth, when in the far distant plains of Ould Ireland, the home of the hurly, they saw the game played for all it was worth. Amongst those who were on the ground was Mr. William Walsh, one of chief founders of hurling, some years back; and now president of the Davitt Club. (*Referee*, June 29, 1898)

Hurling spreads to Western Australia

In 1893, in Western Australia, the committee entrusted with the work of carrying out celebrations for St. Patrick's Day at Fremantle drew up a code of rules for a hurling match. The game was new to Western Australians, though the press stated that

> we may inform our readers that it is the national pastime of Irishmen, played with sticks and a ball. Goal posts similar to football are used, and considering the number of athletic Irishmen at present in Fremantle who have entered for the match it should prove an interesting display. (*The Inquirer and Commercial News*, March 10, 1893)

In 1898, in Western Australia clubs were formed on foot of a gold rush. In September 1892, two prospectors, Arthur Bayley and Bill Ford, found gold in a place that became known as Coolgardie described as an area 'where one half of the population was engaged every day in burying the other half. In the three hot months of the year the temperature rose above 100°F (Clark 1988, 108–109). One might expect that it was a climate that was not conducive to hurling.

By 1898, the arrival of more than 16,000 people made it the third-largest town in West Australia.

In 1893, gold was found by an Irishman, Paddy Hannan, at nearby Kalgoorlie (Clark 1988, 111). The influx of people on foot of gold fever inevitably brought with them a large contingent of Irish emigrants, who bought with them hurling. Word of hurling on the west coast was soon brought to the attention of Tom Malone, when the secretary of the Coolgardie Club, W. E. Nolan, wrote to him noting that he had:

> read with great pleasure the reports of the various matches played by your club, which from time to time have appeared in the Sydney Freeman, and we are greatly pleased to see the Irish-Australian game of hurling has developed into one of the leading athletic pastimes at the mother city ... I am writing from Coolgardie. We have a fine club here which numbers over 80 playing members, whilst our books show some 200 names of the most prominent citizens who are patrons, etc., to our club. We have formed a Goldfields Hurling Association, in which four teams compete, viz., the Coolgardie, Kanowna, Boulder City, and Kalgoorlie Hurling Clubs ... If you could favour us with a code of your rules I would esteem it a special favour. (*Freemans Journal*, August 27, 1898)

The provision of hurleys was a constant concern. While there were good quality hurleys available in Ireland, getting them to Australia was another matter. In April 1899, two dozen were supplied by Malone and shipped to Kalgoorlie. Malone had acquired them from C. G. Hatte, of Newtown, a suburb of Sydney (*Referee*, April 26, 1899). It was Hatte, who supplied hurleys around Australia, with the newspapers noting that he had a splendid supply of hurleys in all shapes and bends, and, as he was at one time an adept at the game in the 'ould sod,' he knew exactly the best material to get. It was also remarked that Hatte was president of several clubs (*Referee*, May 31, 1899). In Australia itself, John Quain was the principal hurley maker. Though the hurleys imported from Ireland were made from ash, Quain had no such luxury at his disposal. The hurleys he made were fashioned from wattle, a timber derived from the acacia tree, which was common in New South Wales (*Kyneton Guardian*, January 15, 1914; February 3, 1914).

Though there was a Central Council established for Sydney, delegates from the Davitt, Emmett, and Tempe clubs, met at Eugene Ryan's Hotel, in July 1899 where the Gaelic Association of New South Wales was founded and Eugene Ryan, M. P. Furlong, and Tom Malone were appointed to draw up and submit rules for the guidance of the new body. A proposal was made to send a representative team of hurlers to Western Australia to play a match between Ireland and Australia. The representatives were chosen from players of the clubs from Coolgardie to Kanowna (*Kalgoorlie Miner*, July 25, 1899). The match took place with the Irish team playing in green jackets, which were supplied by the Kalgoorlie Club and the Australians played in white singlets with blue sashes. The match was the first of its kind in Australasia. It was remarked in the press report that

> never in the history of Ireland was hurley more popular than today, as is proved by the thousands who witness the Gaelic Athletic Association's meeting, where the game is the principal attraction; in olden times it was the custom to pit village against village, and the ball being thrown off at the boundary line the contestants took the leather over hedges and ditches until the covetous ground of the victorious villagers was reached. (*Kalgoorlie Miner*, August 2, 1899)

In 1899, there were at least 13 clubs in existence across the colonies, while Maitland, West Wyalong, and Parramatta also formed clubs. Press reports stated that the ball used in hurling was nearly twice the size of a cricket ball (*Sunday Times*, September 18, 1904). In Western Australia, at a meeting of the Coolgardie club, in October 1900, it was resolved that a letter should be sent to Mr. M. Cusack, of the Gaelic Athletic Association, Dublin, to thank him for his efforts in the establishment of the club (*Kalgoorlie Miner*, October 18, 1900). At this time in Dublin, Cusack had given his support to plans to rebuild the GAA starting with provincial councils (De Búrca 1989, 169–170). This letter from Coolgardie also demonstrates that he was in contact with individuals in Australia with a view to establishing a club there. Cusack was supportive of clubs abroad. A delegate from the London clubs had given him his backing for the position of secretary at the 1901 GAA convention (De Búrca 1989, 169).

At the start of the 1900s, there were indications that the game in Australia was about to experience another period of decline. Many of the men who led the charge for the promotion of the game were advancing in years and there was not the same impetus emerging to maintain any momentum. There was no regeneration of new blood into the sport as the influence of key individuals declined. Even on the goldfields of Western Australia the game came to a halt. Though clubs at Kalgoorlie, Coolgardie, Kanowna and Boulder had formed a Goldfields Hurling Association in Western Australia (*Freemans Journal*, August 27, 1898), it too suffered from a lack of momentum and declined. Still, there remained optimism for the future. With the formation of state teams in Victoria and New South Wales, it was anticipated that a healthy rivalry would result, as interstate contests were organized. The ultimate aim was to send a team of Irish-Australian hurlers to Ireland and defeat an Irish team, similar to the success which Australian cricketers had in

England (*Freemans Journal*, October 1, 1904). This, however, was a dream too fanciful for the Australian hurling followers.

However, it was likely that the arrangement of interstate contests provided the necessary fillip for the game to re-commence once more. Interest grew and more clubs emerged. In 1904 there were at least 15 clubs in existence in all of Australia, which was a healthy increase on a minimum of three for the previous year. Interstate contests did take place, and in 1904, the members of the Victorian hurling team travelled to Sydney to take on the New South Wales team. Eugene Ryan, the manager of the Victorians and president of the Victorian Hurling Association, expressed the hope that the players in Australia would in time become sufficiently proficient, so that a team could be sent to Ireland (*Evening News*, September 24, 1904). By this stage, as has been noted, hurling was a popular game in Victoria, and, in Melbourne it was reported that there were about 20 clubs playing the game (*The Catholic Press*, September 22, 1904).

Also in September 1904, Eugene Ryan received an endorsement of the association's objects from Archbishop Carr, in a letter of patronage that was very reminiscent of the one which Archbishop Croke sent to Cusack, Davin and Davitt, in 1884. In his letter the archbishop, a native of Moylough, County Galway, remarked that

> some of the happiest recollections of my boyhood are connected with hurling. I could write a great deal on this theme if the occasion permitted. But it is sufficient for the present to say that you may use my name in support of the inspiring game. (*Freemans Journal*, September 24, 1904)

Later that month, at a match between the states of Victoria and New South Wales, members of the Victorian team were presented to Cardinal Moran. It was his intention, he said, to give a prize of £25 for the next contest. Moran, a native of Leighlinbridge, County Carlow, informed the players that he had played the game himself in the fields of Tipperary and Kilkenny, and knew 'what a splendid and manly exercise it was'. He told the players that 'occasionally they hit at the ball, but missed it and hit someone's head' (*Australian Town and Country Journal*, September 28, 1904).

Though the New South Wales team emerged comfortable winners, the losing Victorians complained that the ground was rather short, and they also objected to the cross-bar, which was unknown among their rules. However, a compromise was agreed and the cross-bar was allowed to remain. The rule concerning the cross-bar is worthy of note. Though indicative of its use in one state and not another, the issue of importance relates to the absence of a cross-bar in Australian Rules football and the use of side point posts in that football code. These posts were a feature of hurling in both Ireland and Australia. In hurling, points scored to the side of the goals were counted as forfeit points in Ireland but were known as behinds in Australia, a term still used in Australian Rules. The use of point posts and the absence of a cross-bar in the Victorian hurling rules indicate that some of its rules were borrowed from the Australian Rules football code. In Ireland, the forfeit or side posts were removed from the GAA rule book in 1910 (Lennon 1997, 87).

In Sydney, in June 1910, a challenge match between Redfern and the Glebe took place for a set of hurleys imported by Victor Trumper. The hurleys were described as far superior to any yet seen in Australia and were procured in the 'old country' by Trumper (*Evening News*, June 2, 1910). Trumper, one of the leading Australian cricketers of all time, visited Ireland with the Australian cricket team in 1909, after they had won the Ashes in England (*The Register*, October 18 1909; *Clarence and Richmond Examiner*, October 23, 1909. His maternal Connors line emigrated to Australia from Cork, though prior to this the family had been living in County Offaly. Also on that Ashes winning tour was Bill

Whitty, and he was scheduled to take to the field with the Redfern team in that match against Glebe. Though international cricketers in their own right, the association of Trumper and Whitty with hurling was indicative that the game still had an appeal, however limited it was.

After 1909 another dormant period occurred, which was only broken in 1912, when another revival saw the game once more in good working condition. This effort was inaugurated by a few individual members of the Gaelic League, who reformed the old Emerald Hill team under the name 'Erin-go-Bragh' and established a new club at North Melbourne, which was called the 'Brian Boru' team (*The Advocate*, December 1, 1917). The emergence of Gaelic League in Australia had, yet again, its parallel in Ireland. Centenary celebrations for the 1798 Rising, the Gaelic League and hurling were indicative of the transnational spread of ideologies and sport. Meanwhile, hurling was kept alive by the Bungaree and Trentham clubs, and these teams visited Melbourne to contest some matches on the Ascot racecourse. Return matches took place and this epitomized the state of hurling until August 1914, when war broke out in Europe. The Brian Boru team was broken up after their ground was commandeered for military purposes, necessitating the club to amalgamate with Erin-go-Bragh. The newly formed club then adopted the original name of Emerald Hill (*The Advocate*, December 1, 1917).

At the start of 1914 Allen Doone, a popular actor, donated a handsome silver cup, to be competed for by the various Victorian teams. Though he never played hurling himself, his father was a prominent player and supporter of the Yonkers (USA) hurling team (*The Advocate*, August 22, 1914. A central executive was formed, composed of delegates from all the teams. This was once more known as the Victorian Hurling Association (*The Advocate*, December 1, 1917). Further north, in July 1914, a match took place in Brisbane, between Ipswich and the St. Finbarr's team (Brisbane) as a curtain raiser to the All Black v Queensland Rugby Union match at Woolloongabba (*The Brisbane Courier*, July 20, 1914). The game had returned to what it had been in the early 1870s, an event on the programme of sports, which may, or may not, have greater appeal to the Australian sporting public. The advent of the war hampered the operations of the executive, who wisely decided to hold the competition over until more peaceful times. This state of affairs typified the condition of hurling in Victoria in 1917, with only four teams in the state at that time.

Conclusion

There can be no doubt that hurling was very popular within the Irish communities of Victoria, New South Wales, and to a lesser extent in Queensland and Western Australia. It was the Irish emigrants who brought the game with them. From the 1840s, it had a chequered history but it developed as a meaningful recreation for recent Irish migrants and some first generation Irish-Australians in the 1870s. This coincided with the emergence of the Hibernian Australasian Catholic Benefit Society. This Irish identity became prevalent in Melbourne and south Victoria as clubs were founded in developing mining communities. The input of hotel owners as club administrators was a common theme with all clubs. With no specific community centre in existence where Irishmen could meet, the hotelier filled the void. This arrangement benefitted all parties as there was a focal point where men could meet, there was food and drink, and there was hurling.

With the formation of the Victorian Hurling Association, in 1878, and a code of rules consistent to those that would form the basis for the GAA hurling rules of 1884 in place the initial prosperity of hurling appeared to be well founded. These factors suggest that the game was not dead in 1870s Ireland. There were periods in which the game ebbed and flowed in its formative years, much as it did in Ireland, but for entirely different reasons. Second generation Irishmen supported the game, but it was the impetus given to it by established hurlers and athletes, from Ireland, which supported it in the colonies.

However, in spite of the heat in Western Australia, one of the main stumbling blocks to the clubs there and throughout the colonies was that they had no fixed or owned ground. Though hotels were the principal meeting places for clubs, with the owner quite often the treasurer or chairman, there is no evidence to suggest that he made moves to make permanent any ground for the club. Similar problems faced GAA clubs all over Ireland as playing grounds were not owned by clubs here either.

How does hurling, as a leisure activity in Australia fit into the hurling analysis of the nineteenth century, prior to the foundation of the GAA? Where does it fit into the broader scheme of trying to understand the reasons why Michael Cusack took up the cause of hurling? If news of the nascent GAA spread quickly to Australia, as it obviously did, what was there to stop news of hurling in Australia from spreading to Ireland prior to Michael Cusack calling his historic meeting in Thurles, in 1884? As this paper demonstrates there was so much interaction between the hurlers of Ireland and Australia from the 1870s, a case can be made that Cusack was knowledgeable of hurling in Australia. It is not implausible that the formation of a hurling association in Australia was the missing link between Cusack and a revival of hurling in Ireland. Whatever one's interpretations of the various documentary sources and evidence are, the possibility is that news of the emergence of hurling did reach Ireland and hence to Cusack, considering his journalistic connections.

Cusack was very much in touch with Irish sporting society in the late 1870s. He was familiar with rugby football, athletics and cricket. That developments in relation to hurling in Australia and elsewhere escaped his attention was not unlikely. But his switch to hurling in 1882 suggests that he was aware of developments in the codification and establishment of various sporting bodies. In this respect, he happened to be the correct man to lay the building blocks for the renewal of hurling and the invention of Gaelic football. However, no definitive answer has been arrived on which to pin the career change of Cusack from athletics and rugby to hurling. Though personal animosities with the athletics establishment in Dublin were a factor in his distaste for pot-hunters, it was likely that some indication of a hurling awareness abroad came to his attention. One cannot discount the fact that he never made mention of this, but if Cusack was going to be the saviour of hurling he was not going to lay credit elsewhere.

Hurling, as a leisure activity in Australia, was anything but a game of the past. Its origins were in Ireland, the Ireland of the mid-nineteenth century. The documentary evidence from far away shores suggests that hurling was not forgotten. It needed a spark to bring it to flame. That spark was the foundation of the GAA.

Centenary hurling matches were played on the goldfields of Western Australia to commemorate the 1798 Rebellion and there were marches and celebrations to lament Robert Emmett, Michael Davitt and Wolfe Tone. Teams incorporated the names of these men into the name of the hurling club. There was the Robert Emmett Hurling Club, the Michael Davitt Hurling Club (*Sunday Times*, July 11, 1897) and the Boulder Wolfe Tone Hurling Club (*Kalgoorlie Miner*, February 4, 1899). But it was to a handful of emigrant Irishmen that hurling owed much of its initial success. Men of the calibre of Eugene Ryan, Tom Malone, M. P. Furlong and Patrick Long were instrumental in the promotion and success of hurling, albeit among a percentage of the population that was not reflective of Australian society as a whole.

These men maintained contact with Ireland. Through their initiatives, hurleys and sliotars were imported. That they tried to make hurling another sporting recreation available to all was of merit. But, as Patrick O'Farrell has demonstrated, they were fighting a lost cause. Not only did many of the newly arrived Irish try to build a new life for themselves in Australia, which did not include hurling, Catholic schools too had to assess the direction that they were going to take. Going out on a limb in support of an ideology, in terms of heritage and sport, which was not consistent with other educational institutions was not in their best interests (O'Farrell 1988, 187). Consequently, the school sector did not embrace hurling as a recreational pastime. With only a limited number of emigrant Irishmen supporting the game, it was little wonder that there were periods of high activity that were offset by periods of low activity. Hurling was, after all, an Irish sport, but one that owed much of its revival to the impetus given to it by the emigrant Irish community of the 1870s, and the Victorian Hurling Association of 1878.

Acknowledgements

This paper would not have been possible without the fantastic resource which is the National Library of Australia's online resource Trove. Newspaper quotations have been sourced from this outstanding online initiative. I wish to thank Dr. Tom Hunt for insightful comments that he gave in terms of my research. I also thank Terence J. O'Connor, Essendon, Victoria for information on hurling clubs in the state, especially those at Lauriston and Kyneton.

Disclosure statement

No potential conflict of interest was reported by the author.

References

Clark, Charles Manning Hope. 1988. *A History of Australia V: The People Make Laws 1888–1915*. Reprint. Carlton, VIC: Melbourne University Press.
De Búrca, Marcus. 1989. *Michael Cusack and the GAA*. Dublin: Anvil Books.
Diffley, Sean. 1973. *The Men in Green: the Story of Irish Rugby*. London: Pelham Books.
Fitzpatrick, David. 1980. "Irish Emigration in the Later Nineteenth Century." *Irish Historical Studies* 22 (86): 126–143.
Fitzpatrick, David. 1994. *Oceans of Consolation: Personal Accounts of Irish Migration to Australia*. Cork: Cork University Press.
Gaelic Athletic Association. 2014. *Official Guide – Part 2*. Dublin: Central Council of the Association.
Garnham, Neal. 2004. *Association Football and Society in Pre-partition Ireland*. Belfast: Ulster Historical Foundation.
King, Seamus J. 1998. *The Clash of the Ash on Foreign Fields: Hurling Abroad*. Cashel: Seamus J. King.
Lennon, Joseph. 1997. *The Playing Rules of Football and Hurling 1884–1979*. Gormanstown: The Northern Recreation Committee.
O'Farrell, Patrick. 1988. *The Irish in Australia*. Kensington: New South Wales University Press.
Ó Riain, Seamus. 1994. *Maurice Davin (1842–1927): First President of the GAA*. Dublin: Geography Publications.
Rose, A. J. 1959. "Irish Migration to Australia in the Twentieth Century." *Irish Geography* 4 (1): 79–84. doi:10.1080/00750775909555529.
Sheedy, Kieran. 2000. *Peerless Tom Malone: the Life and Times of an Irish-Australian Sprinter and All-round Athlete*. Ennis: Bauroe Publications.

Irish-born players in England's Football Leagues, 1945–2010: an historical and geographical assessment

Conor Curran

History Department, Dublin City University, Dublin, Ireland

> Studies on the places of origin of Irish footballing migrants have been scarce. During the period from 1945 to 2010, 500 Republic of Ireland-born footballers and 417 players born in Northern Ireland played league football in England. This article will illustrate that while the majority of Irish footballers who migrated to England in this period were born in Dublin and Belfast, there were a number of reasons why rates of production were significantly lower outside these cities. The lack of street football in more rural areas, the role of schools, the slow establishment of local leagues and strong competition from other football codes help explain this disparity. An outline of scouting networks across Ireland will be given and the recent emergence of players from more peripheral regions will also be discussed. It will determine which English clubs were initially favoured by these players and the most significant Irish source clubs will be identified. Using interviews conducted with players and biographical information gathered, an assessment of their schoolboy-playing experiences will be offered while the migration of young players from more peripheral counties to clubs on the east coast of Ireland will also be examined.

1. Introduction

Outside the work of Patrick McGovern (1999) and Jonathan Magee and John Sugden (1998, 2002), the migration of Irish footballers to Britain has received scarce academic interest. The majority of work on migration within Irish sporting historiography has instead focused on the Irish diaspora in America and Gaelic games (Darby 2010; Darby and Moore 2011). While McGovern is correct to state that 'association football [in Ireland] has traditionally been a game of two cities, namely Dublin and Belfast' and has discussed their professional clubs' role in producing English league footballers, little has been written about the migrational patterns of players from regional areas in both the Republic and Northern Ireland in the post-war period (McGovern 1999, 7). In examining the movements of 68 Irish internationals in the period from 1900 until 1925, Robin Peake has established that the north-west of England, London and Central Scotland were common destinations for these players (Peake 2010, 37).

Despite Irish migration to non-European countries, during the twentieth century Britain was the primary destination for Irish emigrants with a lack of restrictions on employment access, the availability of work, a similar language and culture and close geographical proximity significant factors in this (Delaney 2002, 9–11). However, while Enda Delaney has shown that 'emigrants came from every county in Ireland' and emigration's 'impact was greatest on those areas with a predominantly rural population, small farm holdings and an absence of industrial or manufacturing employment', how Irish football migrants reflected this trend has not been sufficiently addressed (2002, 13). This article will therefore examine the geography of Irish-born football migrants who played at various levels in the English Premier and Football Leagues from the end of the Second World War until 2010.[1] This is significant not only for the study of football migration but also for the more mainstream history of Irish migration, and for the geography of Irish history itself. In particular, the work of Ruth Dudley Edwards on the latter subject gives scarce attention to sports migration from Ireland or the places of origin of Irish men entering the British work force as professional footballers (Dudley Edwards 2005, 234–239). In providing a statistical account of these players' birthplaces, this article adds to the growing international studies of the origins of professional athletes, and to that of football migrants themselves (see for example, Bale and Maguire 1994; Lanfranchi and Taylor 2001). Irish-born players have, most notably in the late twentieth century, played a key role in the success of English clubs within European and domestic football, but despite this, they have largely been ignored as a quantitative research group.[2]

In using oral sources as well as secondary material, this research is unique within Irish academic historiography in that it provides an account of the experiences of Irish football migrants who played league football in England in the post-war period and it illustrates the views of a number of these players on the reasons why certain areas have produced more professional footballers than others. For this research, 30 Irish footballers who migrated and played at various levels in the English football leagues and Premiership in the period between 1945 and 2010 were interviewed. It is important to state here that those interviewed will remain anonymous. Only players who actually appeared in the Football League or Premiership were considered as the volume of trainees and trial players who did not reach this level would have been too great and, unlike Barry J. Hugman's data on those who played league football in England, no complete record of these players exists (Hugman 2005a, 2005b, 2006, 2007, 2008, 2009, 2010). 917 players – 500 from the Republic and 417 from Northern Ireland – were analysed for this study, which identifies their places of birth along with their migrational patterns.

It will be shown that while the majority of Irish footballing migrants were born in Ireland's cities, there are a number of reasons why those from more rural locations have struggled to break into English first team league football. It will also illustrate that leagues at schoolboy and junior club level were slower to be developed in a number of more peripheral Irish counties than in cities such as Dublin, while the strength of the Gaelic Athletic Association, and its role within rural Irish society, has also impacted on rates of player production. In addition, the Christian Brothers Schools and their policies that prevented the playing of soccer will be addressed along with the slow development of scouting networks in the Irish countryside. The reasons why Manchester United, Arsenal, Millwall and Newcastle have initially recruited, and given league football to, more Irish-born players than any other English clubs since the war will be outlined.

2. The birthplaces of Irish Football migrants in the English Premier and Football Leagues

The geography of sport in Ireland still lacks the type of analysis carried out by John Bale in his article, 'Sport and National Identity: A Geographical View'. Through his construction of 'images or mental maps of the regional geography of certain sports', Bale has highlighted areas within Britain which are perceived to be associated with cricket, rugby, golf and soccer and has looked at the media's role in the formation of 'sport-place images' as well as examining continental patterns (Bale 1986, 25–40). In regard to association football, he states that 'in England and Wales professional league clubs are, in a relative sense, concentrated in the north with relative deprivation in the south' and 'a similar pattern exists in player "production", counties in the north and midlands being relative over-producers, though since 1950 there had been a tendency for regional convergence in this respect' (1986, 32–33). In Ireland, centres of industry have differed geographically from those in England with the majority of Irish cities, and professional football clubs, located on the east coast. While Bale has linked the strength of football to 'the English industrial heartland' with Scotland playing a significant yet lesser role, Ireland has lacked this type of concentrated industrial infrastructure. Industrially, only Belfast and Dublin resembled English cities such as Manchester, Liverpool, Preston and Sheffield in the late nineteenth and early twentieth centuries (Rouse 2005, 8).

Table 1 and Figure 1 establish the birthplaces of the 500 Republic of Ireland-born footballers who played in the English football leagues between 1945 and 2010 on a county-by-county basis. While care must be taken in acknowledging that some players, such as Shane Long, may have been born in hospitals outside their own counties, this illustrates that the majority, just over 64%, were born in the capital and Ireland's largest city, Dublin. Areas of soccer migration in Ireland have been very clustered and traditionally associated with the country's cities (Curran 2014, 17). Players born in Cork city made up over one-tenth of the total number, while those born in Limerick (4.20%), Waterford (3.20%), Galway (1.60%) and Kilkenny (0.60%) did not feature as prominently. This highlights Dublin's position as the powerhouse of Irish football

Table 1. Birthplaces of players who migrated from the Republic of Ireland to England, 1945–2010.

Republic of Ireland players by county	Number	Percentage
Dublin	322	64.40
Meath	1	0.20
Wicklow	5	1
Westmeath	5	1
Kilkenny	3	0.60
Carlow	1	0.20
Offaly	3	0.60
Laois	2	0.40
Kildare	0	0
Wexford	5	1
Louth	23	4.60
Longford	1	0.20
Mayo	5	1
Galway	8	1.60
Roscommon	0	0
Sligo	4	0.80
Leitrim	0	0
Donegal	9	1.80
Monaghan	2	0.40
Cavan	1	0.20
Kerry	6	1.20
Cork	54	10.80
Waterford	16	3.20
Tipperary	2	0.40
Limerick	21	4.20
Clare	1	0.20
Total	500	100

Source: Hugman (2005a, 2005b, 2006, 2007, 2008, 2009, 2010).

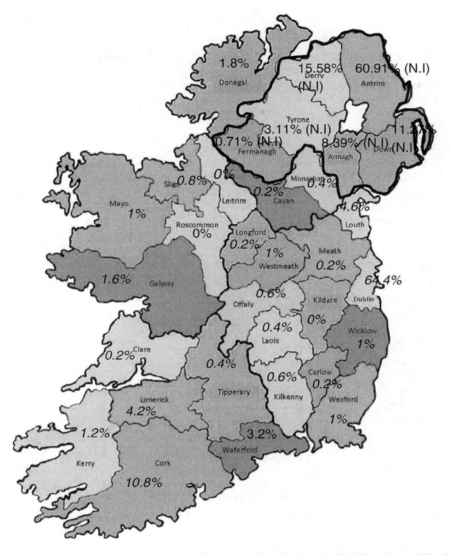

Figure 1. Birthplaces of Irish-born footballers who played in the English Premier and Football Leagues, 1945–2010. Note: Shown by percentage of each country's number of football migrants (ROI = 500, NI = 417). Source: Hugman (2005a, 2005b, 2006, 2007, 2008, 2009, 2010).

migration and is unsurprising given its east coast location, with shipping links with British sea ports and, later in the twentieth century, air links between cross-channel cities easing transport difficulties and indeed strengthening support bases of clubs such as Manchester United, Liverpool and Glasgow Celtic (Hannigan 1998, 17–18).

In addition, conditions in cities meant that street football was more prominent and this undoubtedly helped players' development. One ex-Republic of Ireland international interviewed, on 13 August 2013, has noted the impact of street football in his local area in Dublin on his early development as he played 'day in, day out, mostly all day long' and felt that 'it was great to grow up in the inner city like that'. According to another former Republic of Ireland international, interviewed on 17 October 2013, 'soccer [as opposed to

Gaelic football] was the common game, in the cities, on the streets'. A former First Division player interviewed on 11 November 2013 felt that his skills were developed playing a game known locally as 'combo' with older players, where under informal rules, players were prohibited from letting the ball touch the ground.

Player production rates from 'peripheral' Irish counties have been minimal. An assessment of counties along the west coast has indicated that along with Donegal (1.8%), Kerry (1.2%), Mayo (1%), Sligo (0.8%) and Clare (0.2%) have failed to produce significant numbers of professional footballers appearing in the English football leagues. Donegal has produced only nine players since the war, while only one Clare-born footballer has played English league football with Willie Boland joining Coventry in 1992. Midland counties have fared no better, with Westmeath (1%), Offaly (0.6%), Laois (0.4%) and Longford (0.2%) producing only 11 players in total. Three counties – Roscommon, Leitrim and Kildare – have failed to produce any players during the period studied and factors behind these low rates will later be addressed.

3. The birthplaces of Republic of Ireland-born football migrants, decade by decade

Table 2 illustrates the overall figures of player production per city in the Republic of Ireland and more rural areas as well as providing a breakdown of how these figures have changed on a decade by decade basis. Soccer has attracted much support in Belfast and Dublin as well as having 'a strong following in Cork, Limerick, Waterford, Sligo and Dundalk' (Keogh 2005, 36), but player production outside the island's capital cities has been less significant. As shown here, despite a small decrease in the 2006–2010 period, there was no major change in Dublin's dominance as the leading birthplace of Republic of Ireland-born football migrants over the entire period covered here. Per decade, it was Dublin which consistently produced the most players who broke into English first team league football.[3] The country's other cities have failed to challenge Dublin in terms of player production, with Cork's total of 17% in the decade immediately following the war the highest total produced in any other city. Limerick has similarly consistently struggled to produce English league players on anywhere near the same scale as Dublin, while in some decades Waterford has not produced any, although the total lack of players in the 1966–1975 period may be at least partially explained by Waterford's domestic success in winning the League of Ireland six times in this period.[4] In producing only three players, all in the 1996–2005 period, Kilkenny's general failure to contribute significantly to the overall total can be attributed to the county's strength in hurling, while Galway's rate of player production (1.6% overall) can be linked to its west coast location, and the competition with hurling and Gaelic football. The remainder of players not born in the Republic of Ireland's cities came from smaller urban areas such as Dundalk, Drogheda, Sligo and Athlone and were placed in the 'other' category along with those in other less urbanized areas and made up just over 15% of the overall total. Rates of player production from areas in this category have also been quite low but recently have risen to just over 21%, reaching a peak in the 2006–2010 period, and this will later be addressed.

4. Republic of Ireland Source Clubs: the strength of Dublin

As McGovern has noted in his earlier study of Irish football migrants, the majority of players came from clubs located in or relatively near to Ireland's cities, with Shamrock Rovers, Shelbourne, Dundalk, Home Farm and Bohemians being identified as the top five Republic of Ireland selling clubs in the period from 1946 to 1995 (McGovern 1999, 7).

Table 2. Birthplaces by decade of players who migrated from the Republic of Ireland to England, 1945–2010.

City	1945–1955	1956–1965	1966–1975	1976–1985	1986–1995	1996–2005	2006–2010	Total
Dublin	58 (61%)	31 (75%)	29 (70.73%)	24 (72.7%)	55 (61.11%)	94 (63.51%)	31 (59.61%)	322 (64.4%)
Cork	16 (16.90%)	2 (4.87)	2 (4.87%)	2 (6.06%)	9 (10%)	16 (10.81%)	7 (13.46%)	54 (10.8%)
Limerick	6 (6.31%)	1 (2.43%)	5 (12.19%)	0	4 (4.44%)	4 (2.70%)	1 (1.92%)	21 (4.20%)
Waterford	3 (3.15%)	3 (7.31%)	0	2 (6.06%)	0	8 (5.40%)	0	16 (3.2%)
Galway	0	0	1 (2.43%)	1 (3.03%)	4 (4.44%)	0	2 (3.84%)	8 (1.60%)
Kilkenny	0	0	0	0	0	3 (2.02%)	0	3 (0.60%)
Other	12 (12.60%)	4 (9.75%)	4 (9.75%)	4 (12.12%)	18 (20%)	23 (15.54%)	11 (21.15%)	76 (15.2%)
Total	95	41	41	33	90	148	52	100%

Source: Hugman (2005a, 2005b, 2006, 2007, 2008, 2009, 2010).

Shelbourne has now replaced Shamrock Rovers as the leading transferring club although in terms of overall suppliers, i.e. taking into account source clubs as trainee and transfer suppliers, schoolboy clubs have supplied more players than these League of Ireland clubs. As shown below, Home Farm (7%) have supplied the greatest number of players per club since the Second World War, while other Dublin clubs – Cherry Orchard (6.8%) and Belvedere (6.2%) – follow behind. Only one non-Dublin club, Dundalk, of nearby County Louth (3.40%), features in the top 10 (see Table 3).[5]

As Paul Rowan stated in a *Sunday Times* article on 28 April 2013, Dublin-based clubs have been guilty of poaching the best young schoolboy players and this has affected the development of clubs in external leagues such as in Kildare and in the Midlands. This strengthens the idea that Dublin is considered the best location for Irish schoolboys wishing to migrate to English clubs, despite the recent transfers of Irish internationals and regionally born players such as Kevin Doyle, Shane Long, Seamus Coleman and Noel Hunt (via Scotland) without serving trainee terms in England or Scotland (Hugman 2010, 89, 124, 208 and 257–258). As well as being home to the Republic of Ireland's top schoolboy clubs, and having a higher density of soccer clubs than many regional counties, Dublin is also where the strongest League of Ireland clubs have been based, with 7 of the 19 clubs that have won this championship located there.[6] The presence of a professional football club in a regional county, however, does not necessarily mean that rates of player production will be that much higher there than in counties where there are no such clubs. While rates of production in Louth (4.6%) have been boosted by its east coast location, the presence of two professional clubs, Dundalk and Drogheda, and the county's close proximity to Dublin, other counties with professional clubs such as Donegal (Finn Harps), Sligo (Sligo Rovers) Longford (Longford United) and Westmeath (Athlone Town) could hardly be said to be high producers of players who break into English league football. This further illustrates the strength of Dublin soccer with its concentration of League of Ireland clubs and coaches. Regional Irish professional clubs have struggled to create a type of identity similar to the county identity fostered by the GAA in many Irish counties (Cronin, Duncan, and Rouse 2011). This role of these soccer clubs within their counties has differed significantly to industrialized parts of England, where Gavin Mellor (2003) has illustrated how they were significant in fostering local and regional identities in Lancashire in the post-war period, while the work of Alan Metcalfe on East Northumberland (1988) has shown how the presence of Newcastle United helped strengthen the identity of miners in this area in the early twentieth century.

Table 3. Top 10 Republic of Ireland migrational transfer source clubs, 1945–2010.

Club	Number	Percentage of overall total (500)
Home Farm	35	7.00%
Cherry Orchard	34	6.80%
Belvedere	31	6.20%
Shelbourne	30	6.00%
Bohemians	21	4.20%
Shamrock Rovers	21	4.20%
Stella Maris	21	4.20%
Dundalk	17	3.40%
St Joseph's	14	2.80%
Drumcondra	8	1.60%

Source: Hugman (2005a, 2005b, 2006, 2007, 2008, 2009, 2010).

5. Northern Ireland-born footballing migrants

Of the 417 players born in Northern Ireland who migrated between 1945 and 2010, 197 players (47.24%) were born in Belfast, while 47 (11.27%) were born in Derry City, again illustrating the advantages of growing up in a large urbanized area for those aspiring to become professional footballers. A number of players have linked this to environmental conditions within these cities, which may have helped their development as teenage footballers. One former English Third Division player, interviewed on 26 September 2013, stated that growing up in Belfast gave him a toughness which helped him in his later playing career and as a youth player facing regional selections from 'country' areas, he felt that Belfast teams had a certain hardness which 'country' teams lacked. A Derry city-born player, interviewed on 16 January 2014, stated that soccer was the most popular game there, with the county's Gaelic football selection mainly drawing their support from areas outside the city for its home matches. While overall, as shown in Figure 2, a total of 254 footballers (61%) were born in Belfast and County Antrim and 65 players (15.58%) were born inside the city and county of Derry, other western counties in Ulster have produced fewer players, with only 13 players born in counties Tyrone (3.11%) and three born in Fermanagh (0.71%). This highlights the footballing benefits of growing up in East Ulster for aspiring Northern Ireland footballers. Fermanagh's three players who went on to play in England in the timeframe covered here earned professional contracts over a period of 44 years, with Pat Corr turning professional at Burnley in 1951 and Roy Carroll successfully completing his trainee period and signing for Hull City in 1995. This was followed by Kyle Lafferty who joined Burnley in 2005. Similarly, Tyrone's first football migrant to play English league football in the 1945–2010 period did not break through at this level until 1962, when Cookstown-born Bert McGonigal appeared for Brighton and Hove Albion in the English Third Division. The 1996–2005 period saw the number of Tyrone-born players to make their debuts in English league football peaking at just five, while previously there had also been sporadic breakthroughs by Billy Johnston (1966), Allan Hunter (1967), Patrick Sharkey (1973), Noel Ward (1976), Stephen Devine (1982) and Rodney McAree (1991).

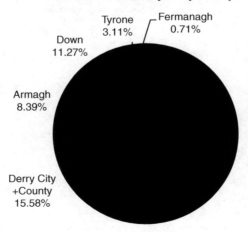

Figure 2. Birthplaces of players who migrated from Northern Ireland to England, 1945–2010. Source: Hugman (2005a, 2005b, 2006, 2007, 2008, 2009, 2010).

As will be discussed in more detail later, scouting networks have been stronger along the east coast of Ireland, although competition from rugby union and Gaelic football, to some degree, must also be considered. In particular, one former Northern Ireland international, interviewed on 13 January 2014, felt that Gaelic football was more prominent than soccer in Fermanagh and Tyrone. Indeed, a number of Irish-born migrants have toyed with both codes in the early stages of their careers, including Derry-born Gerry McElhinney, who won an All-Star for his Gaelic football performances in 1975.[7] In the East Ulster county of Down, 47 players or 11.27% players migrated and played league football while in Armagh, 35 players or 8.39% experienced English league football in the period covered here.

One County Down-born interviewee whom I spoke with on 14 January 2014, and had grown up in the 1980s, felt that

> a lot of the city areas can produce more players as a whole but the networking system ... sometimes you thought that it didn't go outside a fifteen mile radius of Belfast... most of the [Northern Ireland born Football League] players came from that area.

There is also some evidence of internal migration to stronger underage clubs in Northern Ireland. A fellow Down-born player I interviewed on 21 January 2014 felt that 'it's well known that the highest quality leagues are always in Belfast' and 'all the best players played in the one league as such ... usually it was the Lisburn Youth League and South Belfast League that were the best leagues' as aspiring players 'knew that was where they had to be playing'. As a result of this Lisburn/Belfast concentration, he felt that the best players were produced in these areas, and cites the example of Northern Ireland's Aaron Hughes who was born in Cookstown, County Tyrone but played his youth football with Antrim club Lisburn Youth, a team for whom David Healy, Jonny Evans, Gareth McAuley, Marc Wilson and Sammy Clingan also starred before migrating to England.[8] One former League One player, interviewed on 8 October 2013, felt that playing in this concentrated area was fundamental to getting noticed by scouts, although he admitted distance and transport to clubs located there was probably a problem for young players in more outlying counties. A former Northern Ireland international, interviewed on 29 January 2014, also felt that scouts were more likely to stick to areas with a higher density of quality players rather than attend matches in more regional areas where there was less talent on show. According to the Northern Ireland football historian John Duffy, clubs such as Linfield and Portadown have also looked to recruit schoolboy footballers from Fermanagh and Tyrone to their youth teams, while smaller clubs would have struggled to pay these players' travel allowances and this would also have affected their chances of attracting them.[9]

Most players interviewed felt that the 'Troubles' of 1968–1998, which saw the deaths of over 3000 people, did not have a major impact on player production. It is difficult, however, to quantify how many aspiring players may have missed out in their early development because of the social dislocation, which came with the violent conflict between the provisional Irish Republican Army, the British security forces and loyalist paramilitaries within Northern Ireland during this time.[10] One player, interviewed on 26 September 2013, felt that he had consciously decided to stay away from anything that would have affected his football and stated that 'the Troubles were on my doorstep-most of my friends that I grew up with-are now either in jail or dead. I was fortunate-I know people say, "oh, you were lucky, you got away"; I knew what I wanted to do'.

Like the League of Ireland with its heavy concentration of clubs around Dublin, the strength of the Irish League lies in and around the capital city, with its most successful clubs located in the north-east of Ireland. Glentoran (6.71%), Linfield (6.23%) and Coleraine (5.27%) were found to have supplied the most players transferred to England. Of the 12 clubs that have won the championship, the majority have been from Belfast with teams from Lurgan, Portadown and Newtownards also enjoying success while only two clubs from outside this region, Coleraine and Derry City, have won titles.[11] Although former junior clubs such as Dungannon Swifts (Tyrone) and Ballinamallard United (Fermanagh) now appear in the Danske Bank Premier League, these clubs have only recently been affiliated to this competition.[12]

6. Competition with other sports and a lack of schools' football

A lack of schools' soccer has probably impeded the development of young players in some areas of Ireland. Twenty-one players or 5% of the Northern Ireland total of 417 footballers who played league football in England were born in the East Ulster town of Lurgan, County Armagh, with Norman Uprichard claiming in his autobiography (Uprichard 2011, 13) that it has produced more international footballers than any other town in Ireland. Although he was unsure why, he stated that 'there were some very good footballers around' when he was at school, which would indicate the value of schools' football in a young player's development. This may sound obvious, but some players have expressed a need to attend a school which provided soccer for them, the most famous case being George Best who switched schools partially because of this (Best 2001, 25), while Terry Neill (Neill 1985, 29) also changed to a soccer-playing technical college after getting into trouble with the headmaster for not playing rugby at grammar school. Willie Irvine, who joined Burnley in 1960, was grateful to his former sports master, described as 'a tremendous football fan', for his early input (*Buchan's Football Monthly*, May 1966, 10). A lack of soccer at secondary school could certainly have a damaging effect on a young player's morale, with one former Northern Ireland player, interviewed on 9 October 2013, stating that the failure of his Belfast rugby-playing school to organize an association football team left him very frustrated as a teenager and had an impact on his attitude to education at the time.

Opportunities for aspiring soccer players were also hindered by the presence of the Gaelic Athletic Association's 'Ban' on 'foreign' games, enforced until 1971. The image of association football within Irish society was not helped by some of those running educational establishments, while social pressure was also exerted on GAA players to stay away from soccer with vigilance committees in operation throughout Ireland. As noted in the *Anglo-Celt* newspaper on 14 January 1905, under the 'Ban', initiated that year, GAA players who participated in rugby, soccer, hockey and cricket could be suspended from Gaelic games although this rule was often ignored by GAA clubs in many counties. Admittedly, the inconsistency of monitoring by these vigilance committees, set up to assess players' non-GAA playing movements in the 1920s, was often a key factor in this failure in areas such as Donegal, but there were many areas where it was rigidly enforced (Curran 2012, 426–452).

Although, as noted by one player I interviewed on 27 September 2013, many GAA players covertly participated in soccer both as spectators and players, they were reluctant to publicize this and this may have hindered some players' chances of a career in England, particularly those from more rural areas. Some schools operated a strict policy of playing Gaelic games only. Peter McParland has written that during his time at the Christian Brothers School in Newry in the 1940s, 'you played Gaelic football whether you liked it or not and soccer was a forbidden word' although he admits that this lack of sporting choice was not unique to Irish-born schoolboys, with rugby-only playing schools common in England (McParland 1960, 10). According to one player interviewed on 14 January 2014, soccer was still not on the curriculum at his Newry school in the 1980s and he also felt that it was 'a bit of a bad word' there.

While there were some exceptions in the Christian Brothers' education system, such as at the former school of one former Republic of Ireland international, interviewed on 27 September 2013, where 'they were of course GAA orientated, but a lot of them had a soft spot for soccer and you were allowed play it in the schoolyard', a lack of variety in sporting codes was also a problem in the Republic of Ireland with a number of Republic of Ireland internationals stating that there was no soccer allowed in their schools. Some members of the Catholic clergy resorted to physical abuse to ensure soccer was not played, according to one ex-Irish Republic international, interviewed on 11 November 2013. In addition, pressure was put on young players to play Gaelic football for their school selections.[13]

Despite the lifting of the 'Ban' in 1971, many Irish schools in the Republic of Ireland were still slow to set up association football teams, with students in Mount Sion CBS of Waterford going on strike to get the Christian Brothers there to recognize their soccer team. One former Second Division player, interviewed on 22 August 2013, who migrated from the midlands of Ireland in the 1990s has stated that soccer was not played at his secondary school, and he did not appear in a soccer match until he was 17.

Traditionally, some second-level educational establishments on the island are rugby-based, such as Methodist and Campbell College in Northern Ireland and Blackrock College in Dublin.[14] Similarly, Gaelic football has been the dominant sport in numerous secondary schools including St Patrick's of Maghera and St Jarlath's of Tuam. As one Northern Ireland-born player, interviewed on 26 September 2013, has stated, some school principals will point to the fact that students know these sporting policies before enrolling, and he has noted the loss of talented soccer players in his local area as a result of this lack of choice. Although the education systems in Northern Ireland and the Republic are obviously different, a lack of schools' soccer has probably hindered levels of player production in both countries in the period covered here. Despite this, a 2002 study undertaken by Anne Bourke on the recruitment of 90 Irish-born players who had professional contracts in England has shown that the presence of a local soccer club in Ireland played a more significant part in these players' development than association football at school as 'many attended schools where soccer was not an option' (Bourke 2002, 378). However, it must be noted that structures for junior and schoolboys' soccer were slow to be developed in many parts of Ireland and her study mainly uses players from the larger urban settlements of Dublin, Cork, Galway and Limerick and County Louth (which has two professional clubs) with only 11 players from outside these areas assessed.

7. The slow development of schools' soccer and schoolboy leagues in Provincial Ireland

As well as distance from Dublin and Belfast and schools' policies on the playing of soccer, factors such as the slowness of Irish soccer's governing bodies to develop significant infrastructures at provincial and county level must be taken into consideration in assessing the geographical distribution of players' origins. While it is difficult to be precise about the chronology of the formation of these competitions throughout Ireland, some assertions can be clearly made at a macro level. Early structures for schools' football in the Republic were centred mainly in Dublin, with a Leinster Schools' Easter Vacation League in operation by the middle of the 1950s. They were joined in competition for the Irish Schools' Senior Cup by the winners of the Connacht Schools' Cup in 1966 and the Football Association of Irish Schools was formed in 1970.[15] Club structures for schoolboys were similarly slow to spread around the Republic of Ireland and would help explain the low rates of player production from more westerly counties. Although the Schoolboys Football Association of Ireland was founded in 1943, some regional developments did not get underway until much later, with the Clare Schoolboys and Girls Soccer league not formed until 1985, the Meath and District schoolboy section first organized in 1986, the South Donegal Schoolboys' League founded in 1988 and the Midlands Schoolboys/Girls League formed only in 1996.[16] This differed significantly to more urban areas with an under 15 league competition in operation in Waterford city by the late 1940s, according to one Republic of Ireland international interviewed on 27 September 2013, who grew up there.

The Kennedy Cup, traditionally the Republic's top under 13 soccer competition, was not held until 1976 and has been won by schoolboy selections representing Dublin and its districts, Cork, Limerick and Waterford only, again illustrating the strength of soccer in these areas.[17] After a Donegal selection was easily defeated by Dublin in 1976 in the quarter final of the O'Kennedy Cup, a competition for older boys, one reporter in a *Derry People and Donegal News* article, published on 20 March of that year, felt that the Donegal League 'must realize it is pointless for Donegal teams to take on city teams at this level. Invariably the opposition is always bigger, stronger and much more mature'. Despite this slow regional development, there are now 32 district schoolboy leagues in operation in the Republic of Ireland's 26 counties. In particular, one former Republic of Ireland player who migrated in the immediate post-war era and was interviewed on 17 October 2013, felt that it would have been difficult for anyone trying to organize soccer leagues in rural Ireland in the 1940s and 1950s as the support would not have been there for it and this idea would not have been welcome within Irish society at the time.

Early developments for schoolboy players within Northern Ireland also appear to have been focused mainly in soccer's heartland in the north-east of Ulster. Although the Northern Ireland Schools Football Association was founded in 1931, early district associations were mainly centred in the east of the province, and the slower rate of development in other areas may partially account for low production rates in Tyrone and Fermanagh mentioned above. Amongst the initial schools' football associations founded in Northern Ireland were the Belfast SFA in 1924, the Coleraine (Derry) SFA and the Northern Ireland Day Tech. SSA in 1928, the East Antrim SFA in 1932, the Mid-Ulster SFA and the Lisburn (Antrim) SFA in 1936.[18] There are presently 19 district schoolboy associations registered with the Northern Ireland Schools' Football Association and while the Northern Ireland Boys Football Association was not founded until 1976, by 2012 it catered for 1070 teams within 240 clubs.[19] In 1971, a coaching scheme was implemented by the IFA to cater for 2000 schoolboys at 50 centres in Northern Ireland, as noted in the *Irish Independent* on 23 March that year, although it is unclear how successful this was in terms of player production.

Two prominent competitions, in particular, have helped give young Irish footballers the opportunity to illustrate their talents on an international stage. The Milk Cup, founded in 1983 and held annually in Derry and Antrim, is now a renowned international competition, which attracts clubs such as Manchester United and Glasgow Rangers, as well as the interest of football scouts.[20] The Foyle Cup, first held in 1992 and organized by the Derry and District Youth FA, provides competition for under 10s to under 19s and in 2011 had a record 144 entries, and the development of these international competitions means that young players can showcase their skills and gain the attention of English clubs.[21] Along with participation in the Milk and Foyle cups, some Northern Ireland football migrants, including Norman Whiteside (Whiteside 2007, 32–35), have also benefited from their involvement in Boys' Brigade football clubs.[22] Centres of excellence are also now in operation although problems remain, with an enrolment fee of £100 noted on the IFA's website (http://www.irishfa.com/kit/model/11/playerdevelopment-programme/, accessed October 12, 2013) likely to hinder some less well-off families from sending their children, according to one former player, interviewed on 26 September 2013.

8. The recent growth of scouting networks and regional structures for Football

The recruitment of players from regional Irish counties has been hampered by a failure of scouts to branch out into these areas, although this improved over the past number of decades and soccer's popularity grew with the success of the Republic of Ireland's national team in the late twentieth century. Although major clubs such as Manchester United and Arsenal have used Irish scouts since the 1960s (McGovern 1999, 14), English scouts were slow to pay attention to players in other more rural counties with Roscommon not being visited until 1995 (Hannigan 1998, 24). Since 1993, the GAA stronghold of Kerry, traditionally known as the bedrock of Gaelic football with a record number of All-Ireland championship wins in this code, has produced six players who migrated and played in the English football leagues, which would suggest a widening in scouting networks and an improvement in local structures for association football in the past 20 years.[23] As noted in *The Kerryman* on 29 January 1972, Kerry did not get its first soccer league until then with the removal of the GAA's ban on foreign games the previous year, and 18 teams were initially affiliated. Like those in Kerry, Donegal's soccer players struggled to get noticed until the 1990s. For those playing schoolboy football in the north-west of Ireland in the 1980s, there were few scouts attending matches, as stated by a former Second Division player who migrated in this decade, when interviewed on 29 October 2013.

In 2009, there were 47 legitimate scouts based in the Republic of Ireland working for 35 clubs outside the FAI's jurisdiction, while the number of registered FAI scouts is now 52 according to their website.[24] Despite this growth in scouting numbers, three Irish counties – Leitrim, Roscommon and Kildare-have, as noted earlier, failed to produce any footballers who played in the English Leagues between 1945 and 2010. There are only six soccer clubs in Leitrim and no soccer league in this county.[25] In addition, population rates in this county have consistently been amongst the lowest in Ireland in the period covered here.[26]

An increase in soccer's popularity within the Irish countryside can be traced to the latter decades of the twentieth century. Diarmaid Ferriter has noted the effect of the 1966 World Cup, which was shown on Irish television, as having an impact on soccer's popularity in Ireland (Ferriter 2004, 606). *Irish Independent* journalist Seán Ryan was able to state in his newspaper column on 9 February 1971 that 'English soccer is getting a grip on rural areas which have for long been considered strongholds of Gaelic games'. Dave Hannigan has highlighted the impact of the Jack Charlton era and satellite transmissions of live English matches on the popularization of association football throughout the country in the 1990s (Hannigan 1998, 20–27). Along with events in Kerry previously mentioned, there is some evidence that county league structures for soccer became more firmly implemented early in the 1970s, although not every county managed to achieve this. While the current Roscommon and District League was formed in 1971, the Kildare and District Football League was not founded until 1994.[27] In general, league structures for soccer in rural Ireland have been slow to gain permanency. Although a league was founded in Mayo in 1953, it was slow to develop while as noted in the *Donegal Democrat* on 6 June 1996, Donegal did not get its first sustained structure for junior soccer until 1971, perhaps illustrating an increase in organizational freedom and movement which came with the removal of the Ban.[28] County and district leagues were operational in Cavan by the summer of 1967, as noted in the *Anglo-Celt* on 25 August of that year, and the *Longford Leader* highlighted the presence of a league in that county on 26 January 1973, but some more eastern areas were slower to develop. The Meath and District League was not founded until 1980, illustrating their sporadic growth throughout Ireland.[29] One former Republic of Ireland international, interviewed on 27 October 2013, believes that previously the lack of structures in Irish rural society for the development of young players was a 'huge factor' as

> if you take somebody ... say a kid in Clare. I mean, if he had the will or desire to want to play, he couldn't. Society would have been against him, never mind the actual availability of a club to play with.

In turn, some junior soccer clubs, such as the West Donegal Gweedore Celtic club in 1977, have had their property vandalized, such was the opposition to the playing of soccer from some sections of society, as noted in the *Derry People and Donegal News* on 7 May that year.[30]

Other more inland counties have also struggled to produce top-flight players. As mentioned to me in an interview with former Belvedere FC Director of Football Gerard Mooney on 4 May 2013, the first Cavan-born player to feature in the English Football Leagues during these years, Cillian Sheridan, did not sign professionally with Plymouth Argyle until 2009 (on loan), and he had initially come to the Dublin club for trials. One former Second Division footballer who grew up in the Midlands in the 1980s has stated, when interviewed on 22 August 2013, that during his youth,

> there was no formal coaching, there was no progression or path, for most fellas who weren't in Cork, Dublin, Galway, Limerick, at that time, there was nothing, absolutely nothing. So it was up to you, if you wanted to make it, you had to go [to Dublin].

He also acknowledges that this has now changed through the work of the FAI with Tullamore now having an academy, an FAI coach and a Centre of Excellence along with regional development and elite squads in place and that nowadays, if 'there's a young fella who's fifteen, who wants to play soccer, there's a pathway'. In addition, Irish international schoolboy squads have now become more diverse. As one former Republic of Ireland player, interviewed on 17 October 2013, has stated, 'there's now hardly any chance really that a youngster who's good won't be recognised and won't be known about ... with modern society, the communication is hugely different whereas before, the scouting only existed in cities'.

Some players, such as Roy Keane, have previously complained of a Dublin-bias in the selection of Republic of Ireland schoolboy squads (Keane 2002, 8–9), although this was not unique to Ireland with Steven Gerrard claiming that international selection for England was difficult at underage level for those not part of the Lilleshall set-up (Gerrard 2006, 44–45). One football migrant, interviewed on 29 October 2013, who grew up in a peripheral county, felt that the FAI only became aware of his presence in England in the early 1990s after Billy Bingham, then Northern Ireland manager, enquired if he was eligible for Northern Ireland.[31] A former Republic of Ireland international, interviewed on 13 August 2013, has stated that a lack of experience of consistent quality opposition for those living outside Dublin has probably impeded their development as players, as many provincial schoolboy clubs lack the quality found in such a concentrated area amongst clubs in the capital. As noted elsewhere, leading Irish clubs have also acted as nurseries for English clubs in recent times, while some Dublin-based clubs such as St Kevin's Boys and Home Farm also host international tournaments as noted on the St Kevin's Boys (http://www.skbfc.com/2013-tournament-the-best-yet/, accessed October 25, 2013) and FAI websites (http://www.fai.ie/domestic-a-grassroots/17-district-leagues/103629-home-farm-fc-hosts-u16-tournamentthis-weekend.html, accessed October 25, 2013) (McGovern 1999, 13; Bourke 2002, 381, 389).

9. Initial recruiting clubs

While this study covers only players who migrated from 1945 onwards, it is possible to establish the English cities which were most prominent amongst Irish-born footballers who played English league football during this particular period. An examination of initial recruiting clubs indicates a correlation with Taylor and Lanfranchi's assessment that Irish footballers 'seem to have been drawn to cities or regions with high migrant populations' (Lanfranchi and Taylor, 42). Manchester United (5.2%), Arsenal (3.2%) and Millwall of London (3.2%) have emerged as the top three recruiting clubs for players born in the Republic of Ireland. These players do appear to have therefore favoured cities with an Irish emigrant population as places of settlement, with 91 players or 18.2% opting to initially play their English league football in London while 38 players or 7.6% initially joined Manchester clubs City and United. Merseyside clubs Everton, Tranmere Rovers and Liverpool made up 6.2% of this total with 31 players initially being recruited in this area. Admittedly, there is a greater range of London-based clubs, but this still partially reflects the English capital's strength as an Irish emigrant base as well as its other advantages. Despite these cultural links, it would be incorrect to assume that Irish-born players consciously decide to settle in a particular city with strong Irish links. One former Republic of Ireland international, interviewed on 17 October 2013, believes that the recruiting strength of Manchester United and London clubs is because of their scouting systems and has noted Manchester United's Irish scout Billy Behan as being initially fundamental to his club's dominance in that regard as 'at that time [the 1960s], there wasn't that many English clubs that were looking to recruit from Ireland'.

Other interviewees support this assessment with a number of footballers stating that most players usually go to the club that offers them a contract rather than considering geographical locations. One former Second Division player, interviewed on 22 August 2013, stated that 'you don't go to a club because it's in a nice area, like say Southampton, you go because the manager wants you and he's going to pay enough'. A former Northern Ireland player, interviewed on 7 January 2014, felt that it was more to do with the city itself and its number of clubs available than any relationship as an Irish emigrant centre. First team football is clearly a major factor with one former Second Division player, interviewed on 12 July 2013, admitting that he chose a less prominent Premier League club over Manchester United because he felt he would have a better chance of playing Premier League football there. In addition, Peake's study of earlier Irish football migrants has illustrated that 'while many of these footballers were following an established migration route, it was not necessarily due to the appeal of congregating in areas where first and second generation Irish lived' (Peake 2010, 37). Similarly, Manchester United was found to be the top recruiting club of Northern Ireland-born players (6.71%) with Arsenal (3.59%) and Newcastle United (3.59%) following behind. Sixty players or 14.38% initially joined London clubs, while 39 players or 9.35% opted to settle initially in Manchester at City or United.

As Seamus Kelly has written, 'English soccer clubs have a long history of recruiting young Irish players which constitutes a form of "demonstration effect" in which the success (or failure) of previous Irish migrant players influences future recruitment

Table 4. Leading initial recruiting clubs by decade of Republic of Ireland and Northern Ireland born football migrants, 1945–2010, with number of players per decade in brackets.

Period	1945–1955	1956–1965	1966–1975	1976–1985	1986–1995	1996–2005	2006–2010
Rep. of Ireland-born players	Everton (9)	Man. Utd. (5)	Man. Utd. (6)	Arsenal (4), Liverpool (4), Man. Utd. (4), Wolves (4) Man. Utd. (5)	Brighton & Hove Albion (7) Man. Utd., Man. City (4)	Wolves (10)	Nottm. For. (4)
Northern Ireland-born players	Burnley (6)	Sunderland (10)	Oldham Athletic (7)			Blackburn Rovs. (4)	Everton (2), Man. Utd (2)

Source: Hugman (2005a, 2005b, 2006, 2007, 2008, 2009, 2010).

decisions' (Kelly 2014, 77). Some Irish managers in England, such as Damien Richardson, Roddy Collins and Mick McCarthy, have shown a tendency to sign Irish players, as shown in *Soccer Magazine*, no. 56 (1990) and in the *Irish Times* on 2 December 2002, 8 March 2004 and 24 March 2008. As one former Second Division player has stated when interviewed on 22 August 2013, 'managers pick players to fit the system, but also to fit the culture of the team that they want... [they] pick players that they trust to do the job, and trust that they're not going to be bad eggs'. During his time as manager of Gillingham in 1990, Richardson was said to have had five Irish internationals at the club, according to *Soccer Magazine* (no. 56). Some players, such as Timothy Dalton, clearly availed of Irish connections and at times moved to clubs where Irish managers were in charge. The presence of an Irish manager could improve the chances of an Irish-born player signing for a club (although breaking into the first team was still difficult) with Millwall earning a reputation as an Irish player-friendly club in some sections of the media as highlighted in *Soccer Magazine* (no. 92) in 1994.

As shown in Table 4, Manchester United have been replaced as the leading recruitment club of Republic of Ireland-born Premier and Football League players who have signed professionally per decade since the 1980s, while Arsenal have similarly declined in signing and giving first team opportunities to these migrants. In the 1996–2005 period, Wolves (10 players), Coventry City (9) and Blackburn Rovers (9) have been more willing to give these footballers a chance in their first teams, illustrating the elite clubs' interest in signing foreign players and a switch in their recruitment policies since the 1980s. Similarly, Manchester United have not always been the club which initially recruited the highest number of Northern Ireland-born players per decade, although they have consistently higher figures than any other Premiership or Football League club. Initially, Burnley, Sunderland and Oldham have shown a strong interest in offering professional terms, and first team appearances, to these players, with United becoming the leading recruiting club per decade only in the 1976–1985 period. As mentioned by a former First Division player interviewed on 10 January 2014, Burnley's prominence in the 1945–1955 period can be explained by the presence of a club scout, Tommy Coulter, in the Belfast area. Since the late 1970s and early 1980s, per decade, Manchester City, Blackburn Rovers and Everton have also been more willing than others to give Northern Irish-born players a chance, although not in the same numbers as Manchester United over the 65 year period covered here. This shift in the top English clubs' recruiting policies is reflected in the advice given to aspiring football migrants by schoolboy clubs in choosing their English club by Gerard Mooney, with players being advised 'to go to teams they like and are comfortable with' as mentioned in an interview with me on 4 May 2013.

10. Conclusion

It can clearly be stated that Dublin is the powerhouse of football migration in the Republic of Ireland, with, north of the border, Belfast supplying the greatest number of players who have migrated to play in the English Premier and Football Leagues since World War II. Affiliation with a city-based Irish club has been shown to be a major help to Irish youngsters aspiring to play in England at a professional level, and despite improvements in structures in many rural counties, schoolboy players are still eager to move to Dublin-based clubs. In Northern Ireland, there is certainly some evidence that the movement of regional schoolboy players to more successful clubs in the east of the province exists. Unsurprisingly, Dublin and Belfast were also identified as being the leading cities of birth, and source clubs, of footballing migrants to Scotland (Curran 2014, 16).

Statistically, Irish players have favoured moves to English cities with large Irish emigrant bases, while some players are keen to migrate to a club with an Irish presence. Some Irish managers have accommodated this by signing Irish players in greater numbers, although the option of joining a preferred club is not available to all players. Despite this, first team football at an internationally competitive level is obviously more important than location and Robbie Keane's move to LA Galaxy, when he could still be playing English league football, is generally an exceptional case amongst current Irish-born players. Post-career, most Irish players have stayed relatively near home, and have generally looked to take up positions related to football (Curran 2013).

As John Bale has stated, 'despite its fundamentally geographical character, sport was not traditionally thought of as a subject worthy of serious geographic enquiry' (Bale 1989, 2). While this article has outlined the geography of Irish-born footballing migrants and professional player production per county, more work needs to be undertaken on the geography of sport in Ireland and how this has shifted since the late Victorian era. Despite a small number of works of note such as Kevin Whelan's 1993 article on the geography of hurling and Cronin, Duncan and Rouse's *The GAA: County by County* (2011), the question remains, how does one judge the strength of a county in any particular code? Is it by national or provincial titles, number of clubs per population and size of county or individual club success? Should it be defined by international caps or provincial team selection? Can a comparison of the number of registered players and pitches per sport in each county be made? Success in sport can be consistent, cyclical or simply disappear in some cases. Until more work has been undertaken on sport's role within Irish society and its relationship with particular areas and national identity, the difficulties of making straightforward connections between geographical regions and the various codes available to Irish sportspeople will remain.

Acknowledgements

I am grateful to CIES and FIFA for providing me with funding to undertake this research. I am also indebted to Prof. Matthew Taylor, Prof. Mike Cronin, Dr Tom Hunt, John Duffy, Seán Ryan, Gerard Mooney and Vincent Butler for their suggestions and assistance and also to the 30 players who took part in the interviews.

Disclosure statement

No potential conflict of interest was reported by the author.

Notes

1. Until 1958, along with the First and Second Divisions, there were two Third Divisions, north and south, with one club from each gaining promotion. These were amalgamated into the Third Division that year and a Fourth Division was put in place. After the 1991–1992 season, the First Division became known as the Premier League, with the new First Division being replaced by the Championship in the 2004–2005 season. At a lower level to the Premier League, the Football League now contains the Championship, League One and League Two.
2. See, for example, the role of Steve Heighway, Ronnie Whelan, Steve Finnan (Liverpool), Tony Dunne, George Best, Denis Irwin, Roy Keane and John O'Shea (Manchester United) and Martin O'Neill (Nottingham Forest) in their clubs' European Cup/Champions League successes.
3. These figures have been calculated in relation to when the players actually made their debuts in English league football; cup-ties and European matches have not been included in the data.
4. See 'Waterford United: Club Information' (http://www.waterford-united.ie/club-info/, accessed October 18, 2014). I am grateful to David Toms for drawing my attention to this.

5. The Irish Football Association was formed in Belfast on 18 November 1880 but after relations between a number of Dublin clubs and the IFA in Belfast deteriorated, the Football Association of Ireland was founded in Dublin on 2 September 1921. This was renamed the Football Association of the Irish Free State in September 1923 but is today again known as the FAI. See Garnham, *Association Football and Society*, 177–196. Governed by the FAI and its clubs, the League of Ireland is the Republic of Ireland's highest level of professional football, while the Irish League, for clubs in Northern Ireland, is controlled by the Northern Ireland Football League.
6. Shamrock Rovers have won the trophy a record number of 17 times with other Dublin-based clubs Shelbourne (12), Bohemians (11), St Patrick's Athletic (7), Drumcondra (5), St James's Gate (2) and Dolphin (1) also claiming victories.
7. 'Gerry McElhinney' (http://nifootball.blogspot.ie/2007/01/gerrymcelhinney.html, accessed 30 October, 2014). An All-Star is an award given annually to those deemed to have been the best players in their positions over the All-Ireland Gaelic football and hurling championship season. Other football migrants who have played both codes include Bud Aherne, Niall Quinn, Shane Long (hurling) Norman Uprichard, Gerry Armstrong, Mal Donaghy, Pat McGibbon, Neil Lennon, Anton Rogan, Con Martin and Kevin Moran (Gaelic football).
8. 'Lisburn Youth Football Club' (http://www.lisburnyouth.co.uk/about-us/, accessed January 22, 2013).
9. I am grateful to John Duffy for this information.
10. For an assessment of the impact of theTroubles on other sports see Ferriter (2004, 650).
11. 'NIFL Premiership' (http://en.wikipedia.org/wiki/NIFL_Premiership, accessed August 7, 2013).
12. 'The Official Website of the Danske Bank Premiership' (http://premiership.nifootballleague.com/, accessed September 29, 2013).
13. See also Brady, *So Far So Good*, 11–13. Brady was expelled from his Christian Brothers school for captaining the Republic of Ireland international schoolboy team in a match versus Wales instead of playing in a Gaelic football schools' game.
14. See for example, the playing activities at Methodist College, Belfast-'Sport and Games' (http://www.methody.org/School-Activities/Sport—Games.aspx, accessed September 29, 2013). While rugby teams are selected at a variety of levels, competitive association football is only available to Sixth Form boys.
15. 'FAI Schools: About Us' (http://www.fais.ie/about-us/, accessed October 20, 2013).
16. 'Schoolboys Football Association of Ireland'; 'Clare Schoolboys/Girls Soccer League' (http://www.cssleague.ie/, accessed October 14, 2013); 'Meath and District League' (http://www.yellowtom.ie/155446, accessed October 25, 2013); *Sunday Independent*, 13 February 2011 and 'Midlands Schoolboys/Girls League' (http://www.msleague.ie/, accessed October 14, 2013). The SFAI claims to cater 'for close on 100,000 players from more than 1000 clubs'.
17. 'Schoolboys Football Association of Ireland: Kennedy Cup: Past Winners' (http://www.sfai.ie/index.php?option=com_content&view=article&id=161&Itemid=144, accessed October 12, 2013).
18. 'NI Schools FA' (http://www.irishfa.com/grassroots/ni-schools-fa/, accessed October 12, 2013).
19. 'NI Schools FA' and 'History of NIBFA' (http://www.nibfa.org/?tabindex=5&tabid=913, accessed October 12, 2013).
20. 'History of the Milk Cup' (http://www.nimilkcup.org/index.php?option=com_k2&view=item&layout=item&id=27&Itemid=90, accessed October 12, 2013).
21. 'Hughes Insurance Foyle Cup: About' (http://www.foylecup.com/About.aspx, accessed October 12, 2013).
22. The Boys' Brigade was a movement founded in Belfast in 1888 for the development of young men. See Garnham, *Association Football and Society*, 17.
23. 'Rolls of Honour' (http://www.gaa.ie/about-the-gaa/gaa-history/rolls-ofhonour/, accessed August 7, 2013).
24. 'Eoin Hand welcomes new regulations for scouts and trials' (http://www.fai.ie/football-services-a-education/player-a-club-services/100500-eoin-hand-welcomes-newregulations-for-scouts-and-trials.html, accessed May 5, 2013).

25. 'Soccer Clubs Leagues in Leitrim' (http://www.leitrimcoco.ie/eng/Services_A-Z/Community_and_Enterprise/Community-Soccer-Programme/Soccer-Clubs-Leagues-in-Leitrim.html, accessed September 11, 2013).
26. 'Leitrim Genealogy Centre' (http://www.leitrimroots.com/, accessed December 27, 2013).
27. 'Kildare and District Football League' (http://www.kdfl.ie/about.htm, accessed September 11, 2013) and 'History of the Roscommon and District League' (http://www.sportsmanager.ie/uploaded/8525/History_from_Begining_up_to_2006.pd, accessed September 11, 2013).
28. 'Men's League History' (http://inform.fai.ie/League/Clubs/portals/MAFL/mayomensleague-history.aspx?ClubID=1283, accessed September 12, 2013).
29. 'Meath and District League'.
30. This report stated that the pitch had been vandalised for the seventh time, with glass broken on the playing surface, goalposts smashed and cars used to cut up the playing surface.
31. See also *Derry People and Donegal News*, 9 December 1978. The reporter lamented the fact that only one Donegal player had been selected for the national youth squad and questioned whether 'the Dublin mafia was back in control'.

References

Bale, John. 1986. "Sport and National Identity: A Geographical View." *The British Journal of Sports History* 3 (1): 18–41.
Bale, John. 1989. *Sports Geography*. London/New York: E & F.N. Spon.
Bale, John, and Joseph Maguire, eds. 1994. *The Global Sports Arena: Athletic Talent Migration in an Interdependent World*. London: Frank Cass.
Best, George (with Roy Collins). 2001. *Blessed: The Autobiography*. London: Ebury Press.
Bourke, Anne. 2002. "Road to Fame and Fortune: Insights on the Career Paths of Young Irish Professional Footballers in England." *Journal of Youth Studies* 5 (4): 375–389.
Brady, Liam. 1980. *So Far so Good: A Decade in Football*. London: Stanley Paul.
Charles Buchan's Football Monthly, May 1966, p. 10.
Cronin, Mike, Mark Duncan, and Paul Rouse. 2011. *The GAA: County by County*. Cork: Collins Press.
Curran, Conor. 2012. "The Development of Gaelic football and Soccer Zones in County Donegal, 1884–1934." *Sport in History* 32 (3): 426–452.
Curran, Conor. 2013. "The Post-Career 'Choices' of Irish born Footballers in Britain, 1945–2010." Paper presented at the British Society of Sports History Annual Conference, September 6.
Curran, Conor. 2014. "Professionals on the Move: Irish Born Footballers in Britain, 1945–2010: An Historical and Contemporary Assessment." Unpublished FIFA Havelange Scholarship, Dublin City University.
Darby, Paul. 2010. *Gaelic Games, Nationalism and the Irish Diaspora in the United States*. Dublin: UCD Press.
Darby, Paul, and Stephen Moore. 2011. "Gaelic Games, Irish Nationalist Politics and the Irish Diaspora in London, 1895–1915." *Sport in History* 31 (3): 257–282.
Delaney, Enda. 2002. *Irish Emigration since 1921*. Dundalk: The Economic and Social History Society of Ireland.
Dudley Edwards, Ruth, with Hourican, Bridget. 2005. *An Atlas of Irish History*. 3rd ed. London: Routledge.
Ferriter, Diarmaid. 2004. *The Transformation of Ireland 1900–2000*. London: Profile Books.
Garnham, Neal. 2004. *Association Football and Society in Pre-Partition Ireland*. Belfast: Ulster Historical Foundation.
Gerrard, Steven. 2006. *Gerrard: My Autobiography*. London: Bantam.
Hannigan, Dave. 1998. *The Garrison Game: The State of Irish Football*. Edinburgh: Mainstream.
Hugman, Barry J., ed. 2005a. *The PFA Premier League & Football League Players' Records 1946–2005*. Harpenden: Queen Anne Press.
Hugman, Barry J., ed. 2005b. *The PFA Footballers' Who's Who 2005–2006*. Harpenden: Queen Anne Press.
Hugman, Barry J., ed. 2006. *The PFA Footballers' Who's Who 2006–2007*. Edinburgh: Mainstream.
Hugman, Barry J., ed. 2007. *The PFA Footballers' Who's Who 2007–2008*. Edinburgh: Mainstream.
Hugman, Barry J., ed. 2008. *The PFA Footballers' Who's Who 2008–2009*. Edinburgh: Mainstream.
Hugman, Barry J., ed. 2009. *The PFA Footballers' Who's Who 2009–2010*. Edinburgh: Mainstream.

Hugman, Barry J., ed. 2010. *The PFA Footballers' Who's Who 2010–2011*. Edinburgh: Mainstream.
Keane, Roy (with Eamon Dunphy). 2002. *Keane: The Autobiography*. London: Penguin.
Kelly, Seamus. 2014. "The Migration of Irish Professional Footballers: The Good, the Bad and the Ugly." In *Football and Migration: Perspectives, Places, Players*, edited by Richard Elliott and John Harris, 76–92. London: Routledge.
Keogh, Dermot. 2005. *Twentieth Century Ireland: Revolution and State Building* [Revised Edition]. Dublin: Gill & Macmillan.
Lanfranchi, Pierre, and Matthew Taylor. 2001. *Moving with the Ball: The Migration of Professional Footballers*. Oxford: Berg.
Magee, Jonathan, and John Sudgen. 2002. "'The World at their Feet': Professional Football and International Labour Migration." *Journal of Sport and Social Issues* 26 (4): 421–437.
Magee, Jonathan, and John Sugden. 1998. "Simply the Best; Patterns and Early Career Experiences of Migrant Northern Ireland Soccer Players." *Scottish Centre for Research Papers in Sport, Leisure and Society* 3: 57–69.
McGovern, Patrick. 1999. "The Brawn Drain: English League Clubs and Irish Footballers 1946–1995." Centre for Employee Relations and Organisational Performance Business Research Programme, no. 28, Dublin: UCD Graduate School of Business.
McParland, Peter. 1960. *Going for Goal: My Life in Football by Aston Villa's Flying Irishman*. London: Souvenir Press.
Mellor, Gavin. 2003. "Professional Football and its supporters in Lancashire, circa 1946–1985." PhD diss., University of Lancashire. Accessed October 18, 2014. http://clok.uclan.ac.uk/1744/.
Metcalfe, Alan. 1988. "Football in the Mining Communities of East Northumberland, 1882–1914." *International Journal of the History of Sport* 5 (3): 269–291.
Neill, Terry. 1985. *Revelations of a Football Manager*. London: Sidgwick and Jackson.
Peake, Robin. 2010. "The Migrant, the Match Fixer and the Manager: Patrick O'Connell: A Typical Professional Footballer of his time?" Unpublished Masters of Research, University of Ulster.
Rouse, Paul. 2005. "*Sport* and Ireland in 1881." In *Sport and the Irish: Histories, Identities, Issues*, edited by Alan Bairner, 7–21. Dublin: UCD Press.
Soccer Magazine, no. 56 (1990).
Soccer Magazine, no. 92 (1994).
Uprichard, Norman (with Chris Westcott). 2011. *Norman 'Black Jake' Uprichard*. Stroud: Amberley.
Whelan, Kevin. 1993. "The Geography of Hurling." *History Ireland* 1 (1): 27–31.
Whiteside, Norman. 2007. *Determined: The Autobiography*. London: Headline.

Irish rugby and the First World War

Liam O'Callaghan

School of Health Sciences, Liverpool Hope University, Liverpool, UK

This article explores the relationship between Irish rugby and the First World War. When the war initially broke out, the response of the Irish Rugby Football Union (IRFU) was much in keeping with that of their English counterpart: fixtures were cancelled and clubs were encouraged to urge enlistment among players and members. The IRFU set up a Volunteer Corps from which a 'pals' regiment fought at Gallipoli. Yet for all this ostensibly selfless support, the game of rugby in Ireland, collectively, had a complex relationship with the War. Though rugby players in significant numbers signed up, the motivations for enlistment were complex and contingent upon multiple factors, many of which may not have been rugby-related. Nevertheless, the rugby establishment in Ireland attempted to carve out a special claim for the game of rugby union and its contribution to war effort. This was done mainly through sympathetic newspaper editorials highlighting the sacrifice of individual clubs and players, and making favourable comparisons between the war record of rugby union and other less 'loyal' sports. It is argued, ultimately, that the sport may have made exaggerated claims for itself and that these, in turn, were inspired by a hostile political context that threatened the position of southern Irish protestants, the group from which the rugby establishment was largely drawn.

1. Introduction

Men who were prominent in the football field, and whose prowess was admired every Saturday at Lansdowne Road and other football centres, have thrown aside their interest in sport and devoted themselves purely to the affairs of war, in order that Ireland and other parts of the Empire may be kept free from the horrors of war. (*Irish Times*, August 6, 1914, 5)

The collective sacrifice made by rugby union was one of the most popular contemporary rhetorical links made in Britain between sport and the First World War. Tony Collins has pointed out that in an English context, and of all sports, rugby union was the most enthusiastic supporter of the war effort. Its openly ideological stance, often framed in contradistinction to other sports, saw the game cultivate for itself an identity based upon ideas of manliness, patriotism and selflessness. The game of rugby union, and the qualities its supporters claimed that it inculcated, became directly analogous to the virtues needed in the effective soldier. Much of this stemmed from the game's links with elite education institutions. As Collins concluded: 'Rugby Union saw itself as the very embodiment of the late Victorian and Edwardian ideal as practised in the Public Schools – vigorous, masculine, militaristic, and patriotic' (Collins 2002, 797). It was a game that shunned individualism, the prioritisation of winning and professionalism. These were phenomena that undermined the intrinsic values of sport. In Ireland, these links between rugby football and the war were also in evidence. Giving a speech at the annual prize-giving at St Andrew's College, Dublin, in 1915, Mr Justice Barton asserted that

> It was a marvellous thing to see what a narrow space divided the football field from the battle field. Many glorious deeds would have been done before this campaign was over by those who had learned the lessons of courage and how to obey and command upon the football field at St Andrew's College. (*Irish Times*, December 1, 1915, 5)

Similar rhetoric was used by the Primate of All Ireland speaking at the Portora School prize-giving ceremony the same year. Asserting that working in 'union and cooperation with other people' was one of the 'great objects of education', the Primate claimed that this

> was what had made the men they were of the soldiers and sailors who had been educated at public schools. They had learned to cooperate with others. And what had taught them that? More than anything else, he ventured to day as an old Rugby captain, it was Rugby football. (*Irish Times*, December 23, 1915, 3)

Much of this phraseology would have been familiar to contemporary British middle-class observers and elite protestant schools such as Portora and St Andrews eagerly promoted ideological links between sport, civilisation and empire common in the British public school system (Seldon and Walsh 2013).

A cursory examination of the wartime efforts of the Irish Rugby Football Union and coverage of this in the Union's principal press advocate, the *Irish Times*, could have one believe that Irish rugby's war experience faithfully mirrored that of England, where rugby was a self-appointed agency of recruitment and where players displayed their unyielding 'spirit of sacrifice, their willingness to die for their country' (Collins 2002, 810). While such a conclusion would not be without merit, the rhetoric obfuscates, to some extent, the complexities of the relationship between sport and the First World War in Ireland.

In the first instance, the war took place against a back drop of political instability in Ireland. By the time the conflict broke out, a degree of self-government for most of the island looked certain as the finer details of the third Home Rule Bill were being torturously teased out. The country also hosted two private armies, the Irish Volunteers and the Ulster Volunteer Force, divided bitterly along political and sectarian lines.[1] By the time the war had ended, Ireland was in chaos politically. The 1916 Easter Rising was followed by the radicalisation of Irish politics and outright separation had replaced devolution as the key demand of popular Irish nationalism. Meanwhile, political alignments in the House of Commons not to mention Ulster unionist bellicosity and military strength, made it likely that any devolved state would not include some counties in the northeast (Fanning 2013).

All of this had clear implications for the Irish rugby establishment.[2] As a body predominantly made up of middle-class protestants (most of whom, in turn, would have been, unionists), its members were of a community whose disproportionate access to power and networks of patronage, particularly outside of Ulster, was already under threat before the real possibility of 'native' rule had arisen (Campbell 2009). Moreover, in purely sporting terms, it had an ideological counterpoint in the form of the Gaelic Athletic Association (GAA), an institution whose war record would be subject to considerable criticism from unionist commentators. These are the circumstances in which we must seek to understand the wartime experience of Irish rugby, and the posture adopted by the game's administrators and promoters. This article, then, examines rugby in Ireland during the First World War and sets it against the context of the country's broader experience of the war, the key social and political changes that were occurring in Ireland at the time, and the broader links between rugby union and the war in the British Isles. The principal source for this paper is editorial commentaries and letters published in the main unionist newspaper, the *Irish Times*.[3] This was the only newspaper that commented with any regularity on the links between sport and war and can be taken as giving voice to the 'establishment' rugby position.

2. Irish rugby and the outbreak of War

When the war initially broke out, few envisaged the conflict lasting as long as it did and sporting organisations, in general, adopted a 'wait and see' attitude to the potential cancellation of events. Already by September, however, the rugby authorities across the British Isles decided to cancel fixtures for the remainder of the season and from then until the end of the war, only schools and regimental teams played with any regularity (O'Callaghan 2011). In Ireland, in late September, the Leinster Branch 'bearing in mind the decision of the other three countries' recommended the cessation of rugby with the exception of charity and schools matches (*Irish Times*, September 24, 1914, 7). Club fixtures continued for a period, however, and as late as December, matches in Dublin, Cork and Limerick were still being played.

The Irish Rugby Football Union (IRFU), in keeping with its English counterpart, was quick to signal its moral and practical support for the war effort. The *Irish Times* took a predictable stance, campaigning for the discontinuation of sports and for the enlistment of athletes in the forces. The efforts, or predicted efforts, of rugby players were held up as an example to the followers of other sports and leisure pursuits:

> Our sturdy young "forwards" and clever young "backs" are just the right men for that supreme game – in which is at stake our national existence – that we are now playing against Germany. We are quite sure that a very large number of Rugby footballers will answer the call. In doing so they will furnish a salutary precedent for many young devotees of less robust pastimes, such as golf and lawn tennis. (*Irish Times*, September 5, 1914, 5)

They also endorsed the IRFU's position that any footballer up to the age of 35 years was fit enough to enlist.

On the ground, clubs were quick to adopt the IRFU's September recommendation. In early October, Wanderers and Old Wesley cancelled all fixtures for the season and Palmerstown, with 'over half the club's playing members ... at present serving in His Majesty's forces' did likewise (*Irish Times*, August 24, 1914, 4). Some rugby clubs appear to have been impressive agents of recruitment. An extensive study of press reports for the season 1913–1914 was conducted in order to compile lists of men who played for selected Dublin rugby clubs that season. Of the 60 players who lined out for Wanderers FC in 1913–1914, 35 (58%) served in the War. Of the 39 players who played for Dublin University, 30 (77%) served. Of 46 men who played for Clontarf in the final pre-war season, 24 (52%) joined up.[4]

The IRFU were responsible for more direct initiatives. As early as the first week of August, FH Browning, under the auspices of the IRFU, had a letter published in the *Irish Times* seeking details from club secretaries as to how many of their members would be willing to join a (yet to be properly constituted) rugby volunteer movement (*Irish Times*, August 6, 1914, 5). Palmerstown RFC immediately responded by placing their own advert in same paper directing members wishing to join an 'Irish Rugby Football Volunteer Corps' to contact Browning (*Irish Times*, August 8, 1914, 4). A meeting of clubs was subsequently called and the Irish Rugby Football Union Volunteer Corps officially came into being (*Irish Times*, August 10, 1914, 8). Similar circulars to that issued by Palmerstown quickly followed from the Old Wesley and Monkstown clubs (*Irish Times*, August 15, 1914, 7; August 24, 1914, 4). On 25 August, it was reported that over 100 members turned out for the Corps' 'opening muster,' with the Union eager to advertise the fact that 'members of other athletic clubs are eligible to join' (*Irish Times*, August 25, 1914, 5). By the beginning of September, membership had increased to 250 and the corps was inspected by General Sir Bryan Mahon, later the commander of the 10th Irish Division at Gallipoli (*Irish Times*, September 1, 1914, 3). The corps quickly evolved from a purely defensive, home-based outfit to one which would provide recruits for active service and by mid-September the first contingent of army enlistments left for the Curragh to join the 7th Battalion of the Royal Dublin Fusiliers (RDF) (Hanna 1916) This came after Lieutenant Colonel Downing, commander of the battalion and himself a former rugby player, addressed the corps at Lansdowne Road and immediately convinced 89 of its number to enlist (*Irish Times*, September 14, 1914, 4).

The departure of the Rugby Union Volunteers (hereunder the rugby 'pals') for the Curragh was an event accorded considerable pomp. After gathering in the parade ground at Trinity College Dublin, they marched through Dublin to Kingsbridge Station headed by the Royal Irish Constabulary band and before boarding carriages bearing the Union Jack, sang the national anthem. The *Irish Times* noted that the contingent included five Dublin barristers, and they were 'well set up and hardy fellows, well-educated and athletic and include in their ranks a majority of professional men' (*Irish Times*, September 17, 1914, 2; September 19, 1914, 5). The rugby volunteer corps eventually, then, separated into two outfits: D Company of the 7th RDF, who served in Gallipoli with the 10th Irish Division; and a group of older men who stayed behind in Dublin as a home defence corps. D Company departed Ireland in the summer of 1915. The rugby pals, 239 men in strength, arrived at Suvla Bay in the first week of August and took enormous losses before departing again in September with their numbers reduced to 79 (Hanna 1916, 129). The conflation of rugby with military endeavour was evident in the recollection of the Company's efforts. An officer from the 7th RDF summarised the early contribution of the rugby pals to the attack on Chocolate Hill as follows: 'In a few minutes "D" Company came into our ditch with a dash for all the world like a wild forward rush at Lansdowne Road' (Hanna 1916, 76).

In one particularly disastrous manoeuvre on 16 August, the company lost three commanding officers in succession and twenty-one men were killed after attempting to dislodge a group of Turkish bombers with a bayonet charge on a well-entrenched position in broad daylight at Kireçtepe. Two of the dead commanders were the high-profile rugby players, Poole Hickman and Richard Tobin (Hanna 1916, 108). Some stories of extraordinary courage emerged. Private Albert Wilkin, a protestant shop manager and Clontarf FC rugby player, was blown up when his tactic of catching enemy bombs and throwing them back at the Turkish position went fatally wrong (Cooper 1918, 176). This was the end of the rugby pals as a coherent military unit. Many of those who survived were redeployed to the Balkans with the rest of the 10th Irish Division, while many also took up commissions in different regiments and were scattered across different theatres of conflict.

Elsewhere, we have evidence of significant enlistments of rugby players in different regiments around the country. In Ulster, rugby had become militarised ever before the threat of European War appeared on the horizon. In late 1913, the North of Ireland Football Club declared its loyalty to the Ulster Volunteer Force and abandoned rugby in preference to drilling. A similar move quickly followed from Queens University Belfast (Bowman 2007). In December 1913, Edward Carson, leader of the Ulster Unionists paid a fulsome tribute to NIFC:

> I need hardly tell you how gratified I am at the action taken by the North of Ireland Football Club in cancelling their engagements for football matches, and making the sacrifices involved ... should it become necessary to the Home Rule conspiracy. (*Irish Times*, December 23, 1913, 5)

Many Ulster rugby players, through UVF membership or otherwise, joined the 36th Ulster Division in France.

It is difficult to estimate the numbers of rugby players from other parts of the island who enlisted. The explicit links between rugby and recruitment efforts seen in Ulster and Dublin do not seem to have been replicated elsewhere. That is not to say that rugby players did not join in significant numbers. In March 1915, Sir Frederick Moore, the Trinity College botanist and future president of the IRFU claimed that 'over 1,000 Rugby footballers were now doing their duty in the Dublin Fusiliers, the Munster Fusiliers and the Connaught Rangers,' and that at his club (Dublin University) 'it would not, at the present moment, be possible to put a team of fifteen men on the field' (*Irish Times*, March 26, 1915, 6). This was replicated elsewhere. University College Cork rugby club saw 73 members join up. While 9 of the 22 men who won Munster Senior Cup medals with the College in 1912 and 1913 also enlisted (O'Callaghan 2011, 48). Catholic rugby-playing schools also saw considerable numbers of ex-pupils join the colours. Christian Brothers College in Cork had 295 ex-pupils enlist whereas the equivalent figures for Clongowes Wood College in Kildare was 604. Blackrock College in Dublin lost 51 former pupils in the war. The number of enlistments from the College was not known (Seldon and Walsh 2013, 67, 68, 296). By the law of averages, it was certain that a proportion of these men were rugby players.

On the home front, the IRFU supported the War through various initiatives. In 1915, Justice Henry Hanna gave a lecture in which he claimed that the 'Irish Rugby Football Union had given a great number of its best members to His Majesty's forces.' Of the remaining members of the IRFU Volunteer Corps, he said 'There were ... a number of people full of enthusiasm who were, unfortunately, past the age at which active service would be required' (*Irish Times*, November 23, 1915, 6). This enthusiasm ensured that the Corps remained very active on the home front. In the summer of 1915, the IRFU Corps affiliated with the Irish Association of Volunteer Corps and regularly trained and drilled with similar organisations. By late 1915, the IRFU contingent stood at 170 members. It was the fifth largest corps in the Association, accounting for roughly 7% of its total strength. Although, if the Belfast Defence Corps' large share of 917 members is temporarily removed from the total, the contribution of the rugby group looks even more impressive (*Irish Times*, November 6, 1915, 7). The IRFU also attempted to recruit a detachment of stretcher-bearers to work with the Red Cross at the front (Irish Rugby Football Union Volunteer Corps minutes, 15th May 1915 M/065 [Hereunder 'IRFU M/065 VC minutes']).

Rugby clubs enthusiastically supported wounded soldiers' clubs. In one series of events in June 1916, Wanderers, Bective Rangers, Lansdowne, Old Wesley and Clontarf catered for an aggregate of 400 soldiers (*Irish Times*, June 3, 1916, 6). Several benefit matches were held throughout the course of the war to aid organisations treating injured and disabled soldiers. The charity effort was also supported by ex-internationals who arranged a series of 'crocks' (retired rugby players) matches to raise funds for different war-related causes, usually concerned with wounded soldiers. The build-up to one such match drew the following tribute in the press: 'Those gallant "crocks" will be "doing their bit" today in a way that should shame a good many men of half their years into action. Now, as ever, they stand for the best spirit of Rugby football' (*Irish Times*, April 22, 1916, 4). As well as initial recruitment efforts, the IRFU quickly set about coordinating a financial contribution on behalf of the sport in Ireland. In a letter to the *Irish Times*, the Union's secretary, Cecil Ruxton, called for the 'hearty cooperation of all Rugby football clubs and players to make their contributions' to a 'collection for the Prince of Wales's Relief Fund worthy of the noble game and distinguished patron' (*Irish Times*, August 10, 1914, 3). Within a week, the Union had raised more than £200 (*Irish Times*, August 18, 1914, 5).

Charity matches, while honourable, needed to be kept in check lest the wrong impression was created. A correspondent to the *Irish Times*, having complained about the apparent failure of soccer to contribute to the war effort asserted that it was

> pleasing to see, on the other hand, that players and followers of the Rugby code have responded splendidly to the call of their King and country ... Here in Dublin we are deservedly proud of the large number of Rugby men who have volunteered for service.

The writer went on to warn, however, the continued staging of fixtures for charity was being overdone and that 'accounts of these engagements ... look singularly out of place ... side by side with a Roll of Honour of the brave men who are playing a sterner game on the Continent and elsewhere' (*Irish Times*, November 28, 1914, 3).

Participation in the 'sterner game', of course, came at a considerable human cost. Twenty-four members of Clontarf Football Club died in the war. The equivalent figure for Wanderers was 29, whereas Trinity College Dublin FC lost 46 members (West 2003, 28). Yet death allowed commentators, to reaffirm, with pride, the sacrifice made by rugby union. In 1915, the *Irish Times*, with regret, reported the death of Irish international player RA Lloyd. Though his reported death subsequently proved to be a mistake on the part of the War Office, the *Times* took the opportunity to pay tribute to the broader sacrifice made by rugby as a sport, and its international players in particular:

> These men had earned a certain responsibility as a result of their celebrity; they were, more than others, charged with the duty of maintaining the high traditions of the game, both on the playing field and off it. They did not fail when the moment of trial came. They showed to the very utmost of their ability that Rugby football trains men to discharge their obligations in the sterner business of life ... If ever a sport justified its existence when the country required manliness and courage, it is Rugby football. (*Irish Times*, May 11, 1915, 4)

When Lt Gerald Bradstreet, a former captain of the Trinity rugby team was killed in Gallipoli, he was hailed as having 'played the sterner game of war as well as his numerous football admirers would expect, and died ... a soldier and an Irish gentleman' (*Irish Times*, December 15, 1915, 5). Similar rhetoric greeted the death of international Robert Burgess who was killed in France and described as 'Fearless, high-hearted, gay, yet with a strong sense of duty ... an Irish soldier and gentleman of the best type' (*Irish Times*, December 14, 1915, 5).

In all, nine Irish internationals died as a result of the war. Seven died on active service. The ninth casualty revealed something of the deep human tragedy caused by war that the pomposity about rugby tended to conceal. Jasper Brett of the rugby pals, an international with Ireland in the season before war broke out, was deeply traumatised by his war experience and committed suicide in Dublin in 1917. Brett's father, giving evidence at the subsequent inquest, said that his son has 'lost nearly all his friends in action' at Suvla Bay (*Irish Times*, April 4, 1917, 5).

3. Cultural conflict: rugby, the Gaelic Athletic Association and the War

The rhetoric extolling rugby union's sacrifice was often accompanied by a rueful indictment of other sports and their apparent failure to rally behind the war effort. If rugby was the sporting embodiment of selfless duty, soccer and Gaelic games were guilty of institutionalised slacking. In England, soccer and rugby league bore the brunt of the rhetorical attacks from the rugby union establishment. As professional sports with working class constituencies, soccer and league were targeted by rugby union as much for their class profile and accompanying values as for any objective shirking of their wartime responsibilities (Collins 2009). In Ireland, wartime conflict between sporting organisations also occurred, but on the grounds of culture as well as class. Much of this bombast emanated from the editorial and letter pages of the *Irish Times*, the readership of whom would largely have been hostile to Gaelic games.

The GAA, in turn, was never likely to be an enthusiastic supporter of the British war effort. As the sporting expression of cultural nationalism, the Association was, by definition, anti-British. Not that loyalty to Britain was a psychological prerequisite for enlistment, especially given the stance of the Irish Parliamentary Party. Yet with its disdain for the British state institutionalised in the form of bans on members of the police and army from joining the Association, there was little prospect of the GAA being a fruitful agency of recruitment for Kitchener's Army. In that context, efforts to recruit GAA players by appealing to that fact amounted to wishful thinking. The Lord Lieutenant, addressing a recruitment conference in Limerick in 1915, put forward the idea that the captains of hurling and football teams should be approached with a view to raising 'pals regiments among GAA players' (*Irish Times*, November 29, 1915, 5). At a recruitment meeting at Ballinasloe, a Lieutenant Patterson appealed to young Irishmen to forgo 'their football and hurley when the interests of Ireland demand the united efforts of every one of its sons to crush the brutality of the profane Prussian anti-Christ' (*Irish Times*, October 11, 1915, 6).

In reality, the determined continuation of Gaelic games for the duration of the war was the GAA's priority, one which provided ample ammunition for the Dublin rugby establishment through its principle mouthpiece, the *Irish Times*, to attack the Association for withholding men from war duty. The staging of the All Ireland football final in November 1914, 2 months after the IRFU had decided to cancel all fixtures of any import, gave rise to the initial criticism of the GAA:

> Was not an All-Ireland final football match being played at Croke Park under GAA rules? Fifteen lithe, athletic young men from County Wexford were to meet a similar number of stalwarts from County Kerry, and it was apparently a matter of momentous importance that these sturdy young athletes should receive the support and encouragement of a crowd of upwards of 20,000 football enthusiasts ... As I watched the game, noted the keen zest of the players, their fine stamina and their capable, manly bearing ... I could not help wondering what it was kept these young men from joining their brothers in maintaining and enhancing the honour of Ireland in the trenches in Northern France and Belgium. (*Irish Times*, November 30, 1914, 5)

Critiques of the GAA were frequently embedded in general broadsides against other groups that the *Irish Times* felt were shirking such as farmer's sons, shop assistants and the National Volunteers.[5] These attacks became more pronounced as the war dragged on and as recruitment from Ireland slowed. At a recruitment rally in Rush, county Dublin in 1915, the parish priest of Donabate, Father Magill, complained that 'Irishmen were at the front for over a year, and they were calling for relief, but that relief could not be given as long as people went to football and hurling matches' (*Irish Times*, September 27, 1915, 4). Commenting on a football match between Wexford and Mayo in 1916, an *Irish Times* writer observed sarcastically of the crowd:

> Were most of these youths vindicating the honour of Ireland on the icy plains of Flanders or Macedonia, or helping to fill the gaps in the ranks of their countrymen, and playing a noble game. Ireland could hold her head high. In a lull in the game one could hear the cries of the vendors of popular sheets, and see placards bearing such inscriptions as "The Volunteers and Conscription." As far as one could see, however, they had not a very large sale. The game was the thing. Wexford was hailed the winner amid a scene of enthusiasm. The crowd poured out through the gates discussing the merits of the teams. The "honour" of Mayo and Wexford was vindicated and young Ireland went home via special train to shop and farm. (*Irish Times*, December 18, 1916, 5)

Continued participation in Gaelic games, then, it was assumed, was the proclivity of the farmer's son and the shop assistant and became conflated with shirking and idling. Another *Irish Times* correspondent, reflecting on a visit to the National Library, was surprised that the reading room had been filled with 'lusty young fellows' whose general appearance 'indicated many hours on the football or hurley field' (*Irish Times*, February 24, 1916, 4). The writer went on to suggest that the National Library authorities should not issue readers' tickets to men of military age. This was carefully contrasted with the sacrifice made by rugby union. A satirical column in 1916 made reference to the GAA, hinting at its dishonourable record compared to rugby:

> The cry from the front seems to fall on deaf ears, or the joyful clamour in the Saturday and Sunday football fields is so great that it drowns the cry of the gallant lads in the trenches, who are scrummaging with the Germans and, in the intervals of the goals shouting back to Ireland that shout that gets no answer – "Come over and help us". (*Irish Times*, November 11, 1916, 8)

Moreover, with the GAA now implicated in the 1916 Easter rebellion, any existing suspicion of the organisation among unionists was heightened.

It was bad enough that the GAA should shirk the war by continuing its programme of fixtures, and, supposedly, prevent farmers' sons from enlisting but it compounded its offensiveness in several other ways. When the government introduced its Entertainment Tax in 1916, for instance, the GAA campaigned to be exempted from it and refused to cooperate with its levying. The *Irish Times* took grave offence and Rugby football, again, was favourably compared:

> Rugby football has sent far more Irishmen to the war than Gaelic football. It is played in the open air. Is a healthy sport, and has given generous help to charitable objects; but it has not sought, and – would not seek, exemption from the new tax ... The Gaelic Athletic Association need not sacrifice to the State a single halfpenny of the next big "gate" which it devotes to the Royal Dublin Fusiliers Bureau or the Red Cross funds. (*Irish Times*, April 13, 1916, 7)

A similarly angry and sarcastic letter to the same newspaper, responding to calls in parliament by nationalist MP John O'Connor for the GAA's exemption from the tax, again attempted to draw a clear distinction between rugby and GAA:

> He [O'Connor] should have demanded on behalf of the Gaelic Athletic Association in Ireland complete exemption from all taxes, both present and future. Further, the Government should provide premiums or bounties for Gaelic football, so many of its fellows having magnificently manifested their attachment to the green sod of Erin by their unwillingness to quit the same at any price. It is monstrous that a Government whose professed ambition is to prove its paternal care and love for our country, and which has already granted as a measure of ... justice total exemption from the burdens and hardships of war to our faithful and hardy tillers of the soil, should now seek to penalise their well-earned recreations by the imposition of a novel and unmerited tax ... Rugby footballers, whose mistaken ideas of patriotism led them far from their native shores, where they were worthily upholding their peculiar form of sport, to perish in unmarked and unknown hands of brutal Turks and Huns. Rather should he have "passed" and stuck to his own "corner". (*Irish Times*, April 17, 1916, 5)

The GAA's attempts to secure excursion trains for major fixtures, and their supposed attendances of up to 40,000 also gave drew a shrieking response in the *Irish Times*:

> Is there any other belligerent, Allied or enemy, against which this scandalous charge – an army corps of men watching football in wartime – could be laid? ... Today Ireland, playing her football, leaving her own soldiers to their fate ... is a disgrace to herself and her allies. (*Irish Times*, November 30, 1916, 5)

All of this occurred as the military authorities grappled with a lack of manpower as the bloodbath at the Somme took its toll on the British Army. The *Irish Times* favoured conscription and saw the apparently large reserves of manpower that had hitherto avoided their duty as a potential target. According to an editorial in late 1916:

> The views of prominent Unionists in Dublin upon this mater are quite unanimous. National service in Ireland is regarded by them as a national necessity from the Irish standpoint ... They hope that the thousands of farmers' sons and shop assistants will be made to realise their duty to the State and that instead of being provided with special trains to witness football matches they will be placed under Government control to do national work. (*Irish Times*, December 21, 1916, 5)

The political disloyalty displayed by the GAA was compounded by cultural differences. Of the GAA's staging of fixtures on Sundays, one correspondent to the *Irish Times* sarcastically implored the Catholic Truth Society to put a stop to the 'Sunday desecration' of the 'able young men off to a football, or some other, match at Jones' road [sic.]. A rougher lot I do not think you could find in the city of Dublin' (*Irish Times*, October 23, 1915, 5). The rugby authorities, by contrast, had long attempted to prevent their sport from being played in Sundays, much to the dissatisfaction of the game's followers in Limerick and Connacht.

To some degree, this was all just prejudice and hyperbole. As William Murphy has pointed out, it is likely that GAA members in not insignificant numbers volunteered for the front with Laurence Roche, a senior GAA official who served with distinction in France, providing one such example (Murphy 2009). Yet, despite targeted recruitment efforts, the enlistment of GAA members was likely to have varied depending on locality, and was possibly curtailed to some extent by both the anti-Britishness of the Association and the fact that Gaelic games was popular among the agricultural classes – the sector of society among whom enlistment numbers were least impressive (McElligott 2013). Moreover, as they served no rhetorical purpose for their favoured sporting organisation (quite the opposite, perhaps), GAA members who joined the war effort were not feted in the manner of their rugby counterparts, and their historical footprints, therefore, are obscure.

4. Irish rugby and the First World War in context

If such a notion was measured on perceived sacrifice and loyalty, Irish rugby, on the face of it, had a 'good war.' This, in turn, was even more apparent when the sport's wartime record was subject to comparison with other codes. As one writer surmised,

> everyone knew that Rugby football was preeminent among all games and sports for the manly qualities which it engendered – above all for that spirit of fair play for which our soldiers, in contrast with those of the enemy, had gained a reputation throughout the civilised world. (*Irish Times*, May 15, 1915, 7)

Yet establishing causal links between rugby playing or membership of a rugby club, and war service is difficult. The rhetorical weight afforded rugby's wartime record by elements of unionist opinion conceals a relationship between sport, Irish society, and the war that is a good deal more complex.

In the first instance, the IRFU was not representative of the entire Irish rugby community. The Union, at administrative level, was almost uniformly protestant and largely composed of men from Dublin and Belfast. Although we cannot be certain, it is safe to assume that a solid share of committee members and officers were unionists. NIFC of Belfast, when announcing its discontinuation of rugby in favour of drilling and the cause of unionism, gave some indication as to the essence of the rugby establishment: 'The

North of Ireland Football Club' is the leading Rugby football club in Ulster and shares with Dublin University the front position in Ireland, and its members are all of the public school and university class, some of the leading Belfast merchants and professional men (*Irish Times*, December 23, 1913, 4). Dublin University, in turn, was a bastion of Protestantism and unionism, 'a little piece of Britain that happened to be in Ireland' (Cronin 2011, 2756).

Something of the social and cultural profile of the Irish rugby 'establishment' can be gleaned from examining the backgrounds of contemporary elected officers. The president of the IRFU in 1909–1910, Connel Alexander, was an unrepentant unionist and war supporter. An engineering professor at University College Cork, Alexander made energetic efforts to persuade students at the college to enlist. He also threatened to fail students who openly sympathised with the 1916 rebels (O'Callaghan 2011). Alexander's successor was the Trinity educated doctor and future president of the Royal College of Physicians, Francis Purser. In 1912, Major Robert Stevenson was elected president of the IRFU. Stevenson, an Ulsterman, served in the First World War and commanded the South Tyrone Brigade of the Ulster Volunteer Force during the Home Rule crisis (*Irish Times*, August 27, 1960). The officers and committee elected at the IRFU's last general meeting before the war broke out included just two Catholics from 16 men elected to office of some description.[6] Of the Catholics, Mossie Landers was a Corkman from a fairly modest background, whereas Andrew Clinch, as a Trinity-educated medic, certainly was not out of place (O'Callaghan 2011). The point here is that the IRFU, and the unionist press by extension, only spoke for one element of the broader Irish rugby community. When exalting the heroic sacrifice of Irish rugby players, it was largely the sacrifice of protestant unionists that they spoke for. The rugby constituencies of Munster, Connacht and provincial towns did not figure in much of this commentary.

The Irish rugby war experience was not the unambiguous story of sacrifice and heroism that the rugby establishment would have had one believe. In the midst of the Entertainment Tax controversy, all of the sanctimony emanating from the *Irish* Times was too much for one correspondent to the *Limerick Leader* whose letter was summed up as follows:

> He refers to the silly protest of the *Irish Times* against the government's decision [to exempt the GAA] and dealing with the outcry raised by that journal that the rugby players have responded to the call for army recruits in larger numbers than Gaelic players, he asks, "how many Limerick Ruggerites, whom the *Irish Times* and the class for which it caters always patted on the back, have joined the colours?" (*Limerick Leader*, April 21, 1916, 5)

Indeed, there is evidence that in Limerick, rugby players satisfied their need to participate in sport by taking up hurling and Gaelic football (*Limerick Leader*, October 13, 1915). There is more evidence of stay-at-home rugby players. At a meeting of the GAA's Central Council on 1918, a discussion took place regarding letters received from individuals who had played soccer and rugby but who were now 'asking to be admitted as members [of the GAA] and promising whole-hearted support to the Association in future' (*Irish Independent*, July 22, 1918, 5). In 1917, the secretary of the Dublin County Board claimed (rather curiously) that the number of affiliated clubs would rise significantly if rugby and soccer players were allowed to join (*Irish Independent*, April 4, 1917, 2).

The rugby men who stayed at home also struggled to maintain their war enthusiasm. Within 2 months of the IRFU Volunteer Corps' foundation, concern was already expressed that the initial flurry of enthusiasm has subsided and attendance at parades had fallen. Concern was also frequently expressed at the lack of actual 'home defence' duties assigned to the corps by the War Office and by 1915, 55 (around a third) of its members had fallen behind on their subscriptions with many of these assumed to have left their membership lapse (IRFU M/065 VC minutes 18 July 1915, 21 December 1915, 5 April 1916).

Recent scholarship on Irish soldiers at the front has pointed to a myriad of potential motivations for enlistment including economic considerations, idealism, political inclination (whether of the Redmondite[7] or Unionist vintage), camaraderie, adventure and so on (Dennehy 2013; Jeffery 2002). Rugby playing or club membership could be associated with any of these factors but it is difficult to make the case that it was a key motivational factor for enlistment in and of itself.

If we look at those who did serve, the demographic characteristics of Dublin rugby players who enlisted suggest that factors beyond mere association with rugby football may have influenced recruitment. We have demographic data from three different organisations: the rugby pals regiment, Clontarf Football Club and Wanderers Football Club.[8] What we can conclude from these sources is that enlisted rugby men in Dublin were generally young, protestant and (mainly lower) middle-class. In terms of occupation, clerks and civil servants predominated. For instance, 55% of the rugby pals fitted into either of these categories. Although it should be noted that 'clerk' was a broad category that could range in status and prestige from those working in banks and insurance agencies to those standing at shop counters. Likewise, around one-third of the Clontarf men were clerks. The Wanderers sample encompassed men of a higher status with almost 40% being professionals of some description. The equivalent figures for Clontarf and the pals were 17% and 16% respectively. Though it is tempting to conclude that war service was dominated by comparative under-achievers, the occupational profile of these samples was largely a product of the average enlistment age. The approximate[9] average age of the men in the pals, Clontarf and Wanderers samples were 24, 23 and 25.5 years, respectively. In the 1911 census abstracts, few men of any religion were established as fully practising doctors, lawyers or engineers under the age of 25, although protestants did occupy a disproportionate number of these positions.

What is clear here is that older men, perhaps established in careers and married did not enlist in large numbers, whatever the inclination their experiences on the rugby field may have given them. At the outset of the IRFU recruitment efforts, Browning made it clear that service was not to 'interfere with home or business relations' (*Irish Independent*, August 11, 1914, 3). At a stroke, it seemed, moral pressure to sign up was less for men who were either married or had a good job. If the average age of the enlisted rugby player is anything to go by, these were get-out clauses availed of with some alacrity by rugby men above the age of 30 years.

It is difficult to assess the success of the IRFU's aim to run a volunteer corps 'of non-political and non-sectarian status' (IRFU M/065, VC minutes, DL McCarrison to Corps members, November 1914). Men of differing political backgrounds were clearly accommodated. In any grouping largely made up of protestants (in this case around 80%) there was likely to have been unionists. Yet there was diversity. Michael Fitzgibbon, a Catholic killed in the bayonet charge at Kireçtepe, was the son of the nationalist MP and former political prisoner John Fitzgibbon (Bligh 2013). Where these samples seem to be unrepresentative is in the religious patterns. Only one-fifth of the 'rugby pals' sample were Catholic whereas there was just one Catholic in the combined Clontarf and Wanderers samples. Though these are likely to be a slight underestimates,[10] Catholics are most likely under-represented in these samples.[11] We cannot accurately determine the precise proportional breakdown of each religious group in contemporary Dublin rugby but Catholics most certainly occupied a more prominent position than these figures suggest.

Rugby at schools level, since the 1880s, was dominated by Catholic institutions. The Leinster Schools Senior Cup (inaugurated 1887) had, by 1914, only been won four times by protestant schools. Schools, in turn, were key rugby nurseries in Dublin. There were plenty of young Catholic men playing rugby in Dublin and many of these, we can presume, joined the colours. Yet they clearly preferred other regiments besides the 'rugby pals' for reasons that can only be conjectured upon.

There is little or no evidence that a soldier's association with rugby was the essential motivational element in his joining the war effort. If this were to have been the case, one would expect to observe patterns of enlistment in certain regiments, especially a preference, perhaps, for the IRFU pals outfit. Yet the 30 Trinity rugby players of the season 1913–1914 scattered to 15 different military outfits. There were some discernible patterns. Student medics (eight) tended to join the Royal Army Medical Corps and student engineers (two) joined the Royal Engineers. Birthplace and locality may have been a factor. Norman Bor, who played for Trinity in 1913 but was born in county Galway, joined the Connaught Rangers (*University of Dublin War List*, 1922). Likewise, James Ogilvie, another to turn out for the Trinity rugby team in 1913, was born in Cork and joined the Royal Munster Fusiliers (*University of Dublin War List*, 1922). Moreover, only two of their number joined the rugby pals regiment. Of the 129 Clontarf RFC men who fought in the war only 11 (9%) joined the IRFU regiment while the equivalent figure for Wanderers FC was 14 out of 219 (6%). The 40 Clontarf men for whom biographical data was gathered ended up in 21 different regiments. The 24 Clontarf men who played for the club in 1913–1914 and subsequently enlisted were found spread across 14 different regiments. Just two joined the rugby pals. Indeed, it seems likely that a significant proportion of the rugby pals never played rugby at all. The company was, after all, open to athletes from all codes.

These low rates of enlistment in the pals company from specific clubs are suggestive. By dint of social background and ambition, some level of career- or class-based calculation must have entered the thoughts of at least some enlisting rugby men. Within one company, there were a finite number of available commissions. Something of the class-based calculation that could influence enlistment was evident in a speech made by Mr Justice Barton at a meeting of the IRFU training corps. Asserting that it was 'one of the consolations of this was that men of different ages, creeds and views were drawn together by a national danger,' he credited the rugby football corps with sending 'hundreds of men into the Army since the war began as officers, as non-commissioned officers, and – still more to their credit – as privates' (*Irish Times*, May 13, 1915, 7). Clearly, for a rugby football man, taking up the rank of private was a sacrifice in and of itself. Another officer, reflecting on the rugby pals, asserted that

> The preservation of rigid military discipline among men who were the equals of their officers in social position was not easy, but the breeding and education of the "Pals" justified the high hopes that had been formed of them when their Regiment was bitterly tested at Suvla. (Cooper 1918, 15)

5. Conclusion

Ultimately, it seems that rugby may have had exaggerated claims made on its behalf. The sport was just one component of these men's identities and just one of many agents of social interaction that formed these identities. Something of this is captured in a letter published in the *Irish Times* in 1915 written by Lt Stephen Feary, then serving in Gallipoli. Writing in his capacity as a former pupil of the Mountjoy School and a graduate of Trinity College Dublin, Feary included the following pithy description in his letter:

> A few days later … I went down to see how the football boys had fared. I found that Hugh Anderson had been wounded and sent back, that Kee, for this remarkable good work, had been

recommended for a commission from the ranks ... George Harte and RV Murphy were both very fit and had done remarkably good service all through as well as Forbes. I could not get any information about other Mountjoy [School] boys. I am afraid that, unfortunately, all the best men in Trinity have been wiped out ... The Engineering School has, I am afraid to say, had a number of casualties among its members; quite a number have been killed. (*Irish Times*, October 13, 1915)

Here we have key social configurations such as school, university and faculty being recognised as components in identity formation. More evidence of this was provided posthumously by war commemorations. In many cases, rugby clubs shared the memory of fallen members with other institutions such as schools, churches and work places. Of the many examples, two are illustrative. Poole Hickman, one of the officers in the pals company killed at Kiraçtepe, was included on the rolls of honour at Wanderers FC, The High School in Dublin, Avaron School in Bray and at the Four Courts barristers' memorial; whereas FD Downling's memory was preserved at Clontarf FC, Wesley College and Clontarf Methodist Church (www.irishwarmemorials.ie).

This is where the role of rugby must be subject to critical scrutiny. For it cannot be too wide of the mark to speculate that many of these men, by occupational and cultural predisposition, would have served in the First World War with or without the lessons learned on the football field. That the *Irish Times* should offer an unsatisfactory rendering of the wartime record of rugby and the GAA was not significant. What was important was the creation of a loyalty/disloyalty binary and the foisting of this upon activities that were ideologically malleable. In a period where King and Country needed reminding of Ireland's loyalty, rugby possessed the ideal blend of popular appeal and perceived manly virtues to show that Irishmen were steadfast in their commitment to the Empire. The sport, on the basis of assumptions about its social, cultural and political constituency, became a useful rhetorical device for the *Irish Times* and speech-makers in private schools.

Of the rugby pals who survived Suvla Bay Henry Hanna wrote, with a hint of melodrama:

> As these survivors looked back from the transport at the scene of so much unavailing bloodshed, they were only human if they hoped that there might be some little recognition or word of praise for them. But it was not to be ... (Hanna 1916, 129)

His words, written in 1916, were prophetic. David Fitzpatrick has written that in Free State Ireland, the rhetorical legacy of revolution meant that Irishmen who served in the Great War were 'damned by the flag under which they had served' (Fitzpatrick 2001, 191). The efforts of the IRFU, in this context, suffered a rather pitiable demise. If the rugby pals were on the wrong side of history, then the Rugby Football Volunteer Corps who stayed at home were on the wrong side of history in the making. On returning to Dublin from a training exercise at Ticknock on Easter week 1916, the corps came under attack from the rebels, ironically enough, in the vicinity of the Lansdowne Road football ground. Browning, who led a detachment onto Haddington Road, came under attack from rebel snipers and sustained fatal wounds (*Irish Times*, May 3, 1916). CA Owen of the Dublin Veteran Corps would later write:

> Heedless of his own danger, though under hot fire and unable to move, his concern was for the safety of others; grievously wounded and hurriedly carried by unskilled men, he bore his pain like a hero once in comparative safety, his first thought was for those near and dear to him. (IRFU M065 VC minutes, Owen to Stuart Kenny, June 23, 1916)

Another member of the Corps, a young Catholic and Belvedere College boy named Reginald Clery, was also killed in the attack. The final acts of the IRFU Volunteer Corps, before it disbanded in October 1916, was to pay for the headstones of Clery and Browning and to pass on the proceeds of a collection among the surviving 'pals' in the Balkans to Browning's widow (IRFU M065 VC minutes, October 11, 1917). The War and the new political dispensation in Ireland that followed did not signal a dramatic demise in the fortunes of the perceptibly Anglophile sport of rugby union. The game was already well-established among elements of the new social and political elite and would re-emerge strongly after the Anglo-Irish War.

Disclosure statement

No potential conflict of interest was reported by the author.

Notes

1. The Third Home Rule Bill offered Ireland a devolved parliament in Dublin. This was resisted bitterly by northern protestants who did not wish to be ruled by a Catholic-dominated parliament in Dublin and who wishes to remain within the union. This resistance was given military expression in the formation of the UVF. The subsequent founding of the Irish Volunteers was the Irish nationalist response to unionist militarism.
2. This is a subjective term that includes the IRFU's key administrators, influential clubs in Dublin and Belfast, and sympathetic elements of the sporting press, particularly the *Irish Times*.
3. For the political and cultural position of the *Irish Times*, see d'Alton (2010).
4. A small database was created recording names taken from team lists published in the *Irish Times* on the following dates and page numbers: September 29, 1913, 7; October 3, 1913, 2; October 13, 1913, 9; October 18, 1913, 4; October 30, 1913, 4; November 3, 1913, 3; November 10, 1913, 5; November 13, 1913, 4; November 17, 1913, 8; December 2, 1913, 4; December 4, 1913, 8; December 8, 1913, 8; December 19, 1913, 8; January 16, 1914, 8; January 22, 1914, 8; February 19, 1914, 5; February 23, 1914, 8; March 4, 1914, 4; March 5, 1914, 8; March 12, 1914, 5; March 18, 1914, 5; March 28, 1914, 2; April 4, 1914, 4; April 13, 1914, 2; April 14, 1914, 9. The names compiled were cross referenced with the following sources and the statistics thus derived: Clontarf Football and Cricket Club Roll of Honour, available at http://www.irishwarmemorials.ie/Place-Detail?siteId=68 (accessed 20 June 2014); Wanderers Football Club Roll of Honour. Available from http://www.irishwarmemorials.ie/Place-Detail?siteId=173; University of Dublin War List February 1922.
5. This was the majority group that favoured war enlistment when the Irish Volunteers split in 1914 on the issue.
6. Names of officers taken from *Irish Times*, November 15, 1913, cross referenced with Census returns 1911 (online). Some biographical detail already recorded in O'Callaghan (2013).
7. That section of Irish nationalism that supported the War.
8. Incomplete data in call cases? On 216 out of 297 men from the pals regiment, 41 out of 129 members of Clontarf FC and 40 out of 219 in the case of Wanderers FC. All of these data were derived from the 1911 census returns (online).
9. We cannot determine the average age of the soldiers with complete accuracy as the 1911 census (taken in April) only allows us to calculate the average age of recruits in April 1914, and not in August when the war broke out.
10. One of the pitfalls of using census data in an Irish setting, especially an urban one, is that surname replication of common Irish names will always see numbers of Catholics underestimated in samples.
11. The majority of southern Irish enlistments were drawn from the Catholic working classes.

References

Bligh, J. 2013. "Fitzgibbon, John". *Dictionary of Irish Biography*. Cambridge: Cambridge University Press.
Bowman, T. 2007. *Carson's Army: The Ulster Volunteer Force 1910–22*. Manchester: Manchester University Press.

Campbell, F. 2009. *The Irish Establishment 1879–1914*. Oxford: Oxford University Press.
Collins, T. 2002. "English Rugby Union and the First World War." *Historical Journal* 45 (4): 797–817. doi:10.1017/S0018246X02002686.
Collins, T. 2009. *A Social History of English Rugby Union*. London: Routledge.
Cooper, B. 1918. *The Tenth (Irish) Division in Gallipoli*. London: Herbert Jenkins.
Cronin, M. 2011. "Trinity Mysteries: Responding to a Chaotic Reading of Irish History." *International Journal of the History of Sport* 28 (18): 2753–2760. doi:10.1080/09523367.2011.626223.
d'Alton, I. 2010. "A Protestant Paper for a Protestant People: The *Irish Times* and the Southern Irish Minority." *Irish Communications Review* 12: 65–73.
Dennehy, J. 2013. *In a Time of War: Tipperary 1914–1918*. Dublin: Merrion.
Fanning, R. 2013. *Fatal Path: British Government and the Irish Revolution*. London: Faber.
Fitzpatrick, D. 2001. "Commemoration in the Irish Free State: A Chronicle of Embarrassment." In *History and Memory in Modern Ireland*, edited by I. McBride, 184–203. Cambridge: Cambridge University Press.
Hanna, H. 1916. *The Pals at Suvla Bay*. Dublin: Posonby.
Jeffery, K. 2002. *Ireland and the Great War*. Cambridge: Cambridge University Press.
McElligott, R. 2013. *Forging a Kingdom: The GAA in Kerry 1884–1934*. Cork: Collins Press.
Murphy, W. 2009. "The GAA during the Irish Revolution, 1913–23." In *The Gaelic Athletic Association 1884–2009*, edited by M. Cronin, W. Murphy, and P. Rouse, 61–76. Dublin: Irish Academic Press.
O'Callaghan, L. 2011. *Rugby in Munster: A Social and Cultural History*. Cork: Cork University Press.
O'Callaghan, L. 2013. "Rugby Football and Identity Politics in Free State Ireland." *Eire Ireland* 48 (1–2): 148–167. doi:10.1353/eir.2013.0009.
Seldon, A., and D. Walsh. 2013. *Public Schools and the Great War*. Barnsley: Pen and Sword Military.
War List. February 1922. *University of Dublin War List*. Dublin: Hodges and Figgis.
West, T. 2003. *150 Years of Trinity Rugby*. Dublin: Wordwell.

Hardy Fingallians, Kildare trippers and *'The Divil Ye'll Rise'* scufflers: wrestling in modern Ireland

Paul Ignatius Gunning

Sligo, Republic of Ireland

> This article advances a synoptic monograph of the principal representations that particularise Ireland's wrestling arena from modern times to the twentieth century. Providing a delineated critique of themes that include participation, patronage and promotion, particular focus is centred on providing an enhanced understanding of the predominant Irish wrestling style, namely Collar-and-Elbow, considering the *Carriaght* (Backhold) style also. Evaluating Irish wrestling's scant historiography, the codified practices and structures of Collar-and-Elbow, relevant similarities to folk wrestling styles within the Atlantic Archipelago are also catalogued. When detailing wrestling's role as public entertainment, attendant expressive episodes of social disorder are explored. Customary contentions that the principal cause for the sport's ultimate decline was British coercive legislation are challenged. The validity of recent assertions concerning the sport, to include a claim that Irish wrestling was irregularly conducted after the 1830s, are calibrated.

Origins, rules and festive sports

The history of prehistoric Gaelic sports catalogues various exhibitions of wrestling. During the ancient Festival of Tailteann's *Cuiteach Fuait* wrestlers commemorated the dead through sport (Nally 1922, 71). Though wrestling arguably was the pre-eminent unarmed hand-to-hand combat sport throughout much of modern Ireland, it has been spectacularly discountenanced from the historiography of Irish sports. Little attempt has been made to delineate Irish wrestling's respective modalities and to explore the circumstances surrounding its arc of continuance and/or subsequent demise. Recent scholastic errors include a diagnosis, that asserts wrestling effectively ended as a regular sport by the 1830s (Kelly 2014, 311), despite it being relatively vibrant in Dublin city into the 1880s, while another asserts wrestling's provincial arena, quite likely, never existed (Hunt 2007, 143).

Ireland's predominant style of wrestling, Collar-and-Elbow style, seemingly emerged during the fifteenth/sixteenth centuries (Wilson 1959, 5; Obi 2008, 82). In late Georgian Ireland two distinct 'species of [wrestling] exertions' were fleetingly detailed: *Carriaght*, quite likely a backhold throwing style, similar to the Scottish style, saw combatants engage 'the whole body' (Owenson [Lady Morgan] 1809, 178) while the second style, *Sparnaight* (O'Brien 1832, 410, 448; Macleod and Dewar 1839, 119) translates into English as a *scuffle* or *a contention* or *wrestling* (Coneys 1849, 338) and witnessed the combatants engage 'the arms only' (Owenson [Lady Morgan] 1809, 178) and may connote with *Handygrips*. Collar-and-Elbow derived its name from the contest's classical opening stance. Rivals engaged a square-hold while clasping their left hand upon their opponent's right elbow and simultaneously holding a rival's collar with their right hand. This opening hold sped up the encounter's proceedings and served to avoid dangerous rushes. Dublin city combatants, in the late Victorian era, gripped their opponent's shoulder rather than the collar and clutched their adversary's hip rather than elbow (O'Casey 1954, 94). The style's fixed-hold wrestling element compelled combatants – as in the Cumberland and Westmoreland or Scottish back-hold styles – to hold locked points both prior to and throughout the contest but when a wrestler's grip was lost new holds were permitted. Collar-and-Elbow contained composite elements of the belt-and-jacket and catch-hold wrestling styles. Similar to the Cornish and Gouren (Breton) wrestling styles, contestants wore a *surtout* jacket (known, when translated into Hiberno-English, as a 'set-to' jacket), according to 'The Gaelic American', (*Leinster Leader*, March 16, 1907) belted trousers and worsted stockings. By the late nineteenth century Dublin city's wrestlers wore a *surtout* described as 'a sleeved waistcoat of the jerkin variety' (*Irish Independent* September 15, 1936) whereas wrestlers in the Midlands wore a durable 'tight fitting frieze coat' (O'Galloglaigh 1938–1939). Pre-fight disputes could occur if a combatant attempted to engage in gamesmanship regarding their fighting apparel as in 1862 when Patrick Cullen of Rathcoole, county Dublin insisted upon sporting a full length *surtout* frock coat, whereupon the supporters of his opponent (Paddy Dunn of county Kildare) protested the coat's long skirts would prevent Dunn seeing Cullen's legs clearly, 'The Gaelic American' cited.

Traditionally, Collar-and-Elbow wrestlers contested in their stocking feet but latterly, as in the Devonshire style, footwear was permitted. Considerations regarding whether footwear was worn depended upon the era, region and/or the combatants' agreement. By 1873 boots were almost always worn during Dublin-style Collar-and-Elbow wrestling (*Freeman's Journal* [Sydney, NSW] March 29, 1873) but with certain exceptions, as when *The Coachman,* a renowned combatant, kicked with such prodigious skill he was ordered not to wear boots, *Suirman* noted in 'Memories of Dublin Bouts' (*Irish Independent*, September 15, 1936). The rules of an inaugural 1887 Irish Collar-and-Elbow championship, hosted at the Phoenix Park's Polo Grounds in Dublin, obliged protagonists to wear socks or Indian rubber shoes when wrestling. But when onlookers complained as to the absence of a toss both wrestlers were subsequently permitted to wear shoes in their fifth and conclusive bout (see *Dundalk Democrat,* September 5, 1887: October 29, 1887). It was permissible, presumably subject to private agreement, for the opposing combatants to respectively wear distinct types of footwear as when 'Rafferty of county Kildare' wore light elastic boots while the physically imposing George Hoey of Lusk, county Dublin, styled the Champion of Ireland *(Freeman's Journal,* May 16, 1900) and purportedly almost 7 feet tall, weighing 18 stone and very muscular, donned a pair of borrowed heavy shoes. After the fight, Raffery repaired to a nearby stream to wash his mutilated and blood-stained shins that looked like 'raw beefsteaks' (Sherry 1937–1938).

Irish advocates of Collar-and-Elbow judged its gladiatorial spectacle as superior to the Greco-Roman and/or Lancastrian Catch-As-Catch-Can styles. The divergence between the two aforementioned styles and Irish wrestling was comparable to the disparity between 'scientific boxing to a rough and tumble fight', 'The Gaelic American' declared. To American eyes, England's North Country wrestling appeared 'rather silly looking' whereas the American-style Collar-and-Elbow was popular as it provided a more coordinated mode of combat (Wilson 1959, 22).

Principally a standing style of combat, Irish Collar-and-Elbow wrestling was regarded as a 'pretty style of play' (*The Japan Weekly Mail,* 1891) with its techniques termed 'simplicity itself' (Chambers 1901, 752). The fighting style, was aptly termed, in an Australian journal, as a 'fist-fight with the feet' with the substantive mode of engagement accompanying the contestant's tussling being fending and foiling footwork (J.W.G., *Poverty Bay Herald*, December 21, 1907) were various leg-locks, sweeps and knocks repeatedly employed. Moves, intended to knock an opponent off balance, included the inside crook, outside slap, back-heel and side-wipes (*Dundalk Democrat*, September 24, 1887). Integral elements of this 'eminently scientific and picturesque' style according to 'The Gaelic American' included the widely recognized cross-buttock throw allied with determined foot-sparring, primarily tripping, hooking and blocking *(Leinster Leader*, March 16, 1907). A throw, or toss, was also executed when using the hip-trip, half-inside, leg-dive, toe-trip and/or a leg-lock, etc. Rapid and superior footwork was necessary to secure success in Collar-and-Elbow wrestling that was termed a 'scuffling' style (Beekman 2006, 10) in antebellum America (introduced there by Irish immigrants) and a 'heel duel' (*Irish Magazine*, February 1812) in Regency Dublin. As 'feinting and manoeuvring' *(Freeman's Journal*, November 5, 1887) were important stratagems, the concomitant relationship between dancing and wrestling was referenced in 1890 regarding the agility of the 'Kildare Trippers' (*Kildare Observer*, June 28, 1890). Strength in both hands and wrists was important to assist the contestants execute wrestling movements and throws ('The Gaelic American', *Leinster Leader*, March 16, 1907).

To gain victory a contestant generally secured two back falls out of three contests. The fall was secured after an opponent was 'thrown clean off his feet and face out' (*The GAA Rule Book*, 1887) onto the ground whereupon three points of the opponent's prostrate body (to include either two shoulders and one hip or alternatively both hips and one shoulder) were simultaneously landed or pinned. An exposition of the Kildare Collar-and-Elbow rules noted if any part of the body above the knee touched the ground this constituted a fall. To avoid gamesmanship if a knee was dropped to the ground on three consecutive occasions, either wilfully or otherwise, this action was penalized and counted as a fall ('Wrestling – Westmeath v Kildare: A Famous Contest', *Roscommon Herald*, March 16, 1907). Ground wrestling was generally not permitted. However, a somewhat discordant Irish exposition of Collar-and-Elbow's rules (which brusquely noted the latter's rubrics were analogous to Cornish methods) detailed if a man was thrown and 'any part of the body' touched the ground if the consequent effort 'was continuous' a fall could be awarded (*The GAA Rule Book*, 1887). In Dublin when an opponent's 'hand, knee, back or side' touched the ground a fall was awarded (Robinson and Gilpin 1893, xlvi) that (as the elbow was not mentioned) arguably connotes with elements of the American-style as witnessed during a world championship bout in 1884 involving James McLoughlin and Henry Dufur where the 'bridge' was utilised to avoid a fall (Journal of Manly Arts 2003).

The 'lasting greatness' of the American-styled Collar-and-Elbow wrestling was 'the changeover' from its standing style to ground wrestling without minimising on skill (Wilson 1959, 23). The emphasis of Irish Collar-and-Elbow wrestling was on skill over gratuitous brutality. A wrestler wasn't permitted to 'cross his hand on his opponent's throat' (*The GAA Rule Book*, 1887) as choking and strangleholds were strictly illegal ('The Gaelic American', *Leinster Leader*, March 16, 1907). Minor injuries were regularly sustained, for example, facial bruising during a fall or from unintended jabs received when standing or during ground skirmishing etc. Serious injuries typically were confined to shoulder dislocations and/or leg breaks. As exhibitions of shinning were permitted (similar to the Devon style), quite predictably, when footwear was worn, shins were routinely gored and/or bruised. A less than complimentary review of Collar-and-Elbow wrestling condemned it as a brutal display of 'who owns the toughest shins' particularly when blood was seen pouring over wrestler's shoes due to the punishment inflicted by an opponent's 'iron shod heel or toe' (*Dundalk Democrat*, September 24, 1887). It was claimed when sophisticated fighting science was exhibited by skilled contestants 'a square toed kick' rarely was landed upon the other's shins (J.W.G., *Poverty Bay Herald*, December 21, 1907). Kicking above the shins was illegal ('The Gaelic American', *Leinster Leader*, March 16, 1907). Alarming injuries could arise following disagreements concerning the interplay or flouting of the 'shinning' and 'kicking' rules. This included the possibility of intentional and, seemingly permissible, leg breaks, when innately dangerous leg holds were executed as demonstrated during a late Georgian championship contest between 'Big' James Dwyer of Grange, county Carlow and an unnamed county Dublin champion. When Dwyer warned his opponent *'kickin is not wrastlin'* he was informed kicking would only raise the Carlovian's 'dander' (Brophy 1888, 69). This rationale elicited the darkly ominous retort, *'id's not dandher but the divil ye'll rise in me'* whereupon Dwyer quickly completed the 'break-leg cross', deemed an 'iron grip' move, that smashed the Dubliner's leg with an accompanying 'pistol shot' crack (Brophy 1888, 69). Meanwhile at Annesley Bridge, Dublin in 1841 the *Freeman's Journal* noted that a 'brawny, strapping' county Meath wrestler, who tried a fall for a half-pint of alcohol with an inner city *'flag snob'*, upon discovering his new overcoat was stolen by the latter picaroon's accomplice, cynically inflicted unsporting injuries, having 'put the barrogue' on his opponent to 'draw him over his hip' and 'plant him fair in the gravel'. The Meath-man euphemistically noted he struck his knee in 'the right place' and confessed this manoeuvre would not be inflicted upon an 'honest boy' (*Freeman's Journal*, October 25, 1841).

Legend suggests the existence of rustic academies where only the more brilliant students were taught secret wrestling skills, such as the *'trascairt'* (meaning *overthrow*) which was a 'quick and irresistible' switch move taught in Kilmockler, north of Moondharrig, county Waterford. The victim having experienced a prolonged application of force was suddenly jerked in the opposite direction with a rapid 'steel bar' leg-lock or leg-dive applied to the knee with the option either to fall or suffer 'dislocated bones' (Dollard, *Meath Chronicle,* January 4, 1913). Quite conceivably mirroring the Cornish scheme of rule-giving (Tripp 2009, 20), Collar-and-Elbow wrestling's rules, though possibly unwritten, were customarily accepted and understood when diffused orally and inter-generationally. However even between bordering counties 'striking and extraordinary differences' in wrestling styles existed as evidenced by Meath and Louth having 'distinct modes of wrestling'(*The Portfolio of Entertaining and Instructive Varieties* 1827, 218). Legend noted the young peasantry of provincial Georgian Ireland 'greatly prized' their wrestling prowess and displayed combative gymnastic exertions with 'Spartan-like warrior energy' (Owenson [Lady Morgan] 1809, 178) during rustic festive amusements and religious feast-day celebrations such as Shrove Tuesday, May Day or 'Patterns' (equivalent to the 'Pardons' of Cornwall and Brittany).

For the participants, as Michael Huggins notes, wrestling provided prestige, rank and status (Huggins 2001, 37). The esteemed 'Kildare Trippers' were accompanied to 'an adjoining county or parish' by either sweethearts or community notables *(Kildare Observer,* June 28, 1890). Having secured an inter-county prize a successful wrestler returned home 'a demigod among the peasantry' (Brophy 1888, 70). Though competitors fought 'to the bitter end' to uphold their district's honour generally no attendant 'ill-feeling of any description' was displayed among combatants (O'Galloglaigh 1938–1939). In the 1750s 'conquerors generally received a prize' during popular Feast Day wrestling competitions (MacGeoghan 1832, 65). Vast concourses were attracted to grand matches at Patterns in the 'western and eastern provinces' during the 1820s, which 'frequently occupied a large share of public attention' (*The Portfolio of Entertaining and Instructive Varieties* 1827, 218) and during the Sabbath, feasts or fairs, engaged in 'fighting, wrestling, drinking and other evil practices' (*The Christian Observer* 1827, 632). In Dublin city a professional wrestler attended 'every fair and market town' within reasonable walking distance of the capital. Before a metropolitan Police Court in 1858 he was described as 'the hero of a thousand falls ... adept in all the tricks and dodges of his art' and was 'up to his eyes in business' so much so he was scarcely able to attend to his 'extensive practice' (*Freeman's Journal*, December 14, 1858).

The ring and pre-fight preliminaries

'Matchmakers' who knew every heavy, middle or light-weight 'worth knowing' organised contests in Victorian rural Ireland (O'Galloglaigh 1938–1939). Minimal infrastructure was required to host contests. Customarily these rudimentary rings' dimensions varied depending on either the era and/or location of a bout. In 1820s county Kildare the ring was 200 yards in diameter, formed in the centre of a field and maintained by five men on horseback ('The Gaelic American', *Leinster Leader*, March 16, 1907) whereupon, presumably, numerous contests took place simultaneously. At Bangs Meadow on Lusk Common, county Dublin, a coat when hoisted onto a riding whip signalled that non-competitors must clear the ring (Sherry 1937–1938). Crowds in 1860s county Westmeath were kept out by 'two ring masters' armed with 'stout blackthorn sticks' (O'Galloglaigh 1938–1939). During the early 1840s, in Swords, county Dublin, a robust 15-stone 'Baluister' Connor somersaulted 'seven consecutive times' to form the arena for 'ten pairs of competitors' (Kettle 1958, 2).

Ireland's wrestling headquarter was Dublin's Phoenix Park (which was opened to the public in 1745) but it had no built infrastructure to accommodate the sport. Its ring was not enclosed by stakes or ropes (without even a white line evident on the grass) but rather was formed when encircled by on-lookers (Stoker 1907, 32–33). In 1877, Bram Stoker (the author of Dracula and formerly a distinguished athlete at Trinity College, Dublin) outlined the pre-fight organisation of the capital's wrestling arena was controlled by a few 'men of authority' whose methods to create the ring though 'exceedingly violent' were 'unscrupulously fair'. One big powerful fellow armed with a drayman's heavy whip was joined by another man who took off his cap and put it before the former's face whereas a third man guided them from behind. Stoker stated that anyone who did not move had to accept the consequences of this fiercely falling whip.

When enclosed sports grounds were utilised and/or when publicans hired fields for wrestling these new arenas presented separate organisational considerations. The ambitions to designate specific locations for wrestling and/or solicit admission fees from spectators were coterminous in 1891 at Richmond Hill, Inchicore, Dublin, when the St Patrick's GAA club, having organised a sports gala, was advised to erect a 'wooden addition' to the boundary wall to prevent the 'avarious' from enjoying a free view (*Kildare Observer*, March 7, 1891).

The challenge rituals and pre-fight spectacle witnessed in 1870s Dublin involved two wrestling coats being placed at the centre of the ring whereupon one wrestler donned a coat as a challenge for another to take up the remaining *surtout* (Robinson and Gilpin 1893, xlvii). Alternately wrestlers walked the ring's circumference to invite would-be adversaries to compete. When upon the green sward at 'The Hollow' in the Phoenix Park (*Irish Independent*, November 26, 1951) a champion wrestler tucked up a trouser leg to show a 'gaudy garter' that served to unveil previously acquired martial decorations and invite suitable contestants to partake in a bout (O'Casey 1954, 94). With a referee appointed and the rules agreed upon, the wrestlers walked into the middle of the ring, shook hands and commenced their tussle ('Wrestling – Westmeath v Kildare: A Famous Contest', *Roscommon Herald*, March 16, 1907).

Boisterous games, death and prizes

Wrestling in early modern Ireland was evidently a popular form of public entertainment (Ahern 1989, 11). Successful wrestlers could derive a living from this trade as it was customary for a city to support a champion (Hyde 1905, 49). Seventeenth century fairs, in legend and literature, are recorded as providing 'rural boisterous games' for the 'less refined' (*Dublin University Magazine*, 1840, 217) while the champions did 'hug', artfully 'trip' and 'with strength...tug' (Moffet 1724, 29). The risk of sustaining serious injury was inherently associated with early modern wrestling (Hyde 1905, 49) as exhibited in the 1630s during the guileless, but powerful, belt-hold wrestling exploits of 17-year-old Thomas Costello, nicknamed *Laidir* (meaning *Strong*), from Tullaghanmore on the north Roscommon/east Mayo border (MacDermot 1996, 514). A mere wrestling novice, Costello accepted a challenge issued by a wrestling champion or 'bully' – who had previously 'killed a number of wrestlers' and was then resident in the borough of Sligo (Hyde 1905, 49). The contest held upon a town lawn attracted a vast attendance. The rivals gripped their opponent's leather girdle with both hands before wrestling in earnest, but such was Costello's strength upon the second squeeze of his rival's belt the erstwhile champion fell down dead with his spine broken (Hyde 1905, 49). Another wrestling fatality was recorded during an undated (though presumably early modern) contest at Malinbeg, south county Donegal, where one contestant fashioned a *caestus* from 'the draughts in the plough-harness' ('Kinnfaela' [T.C. McGinley] 1867, 123). Despite the vanquished acknowledging defeat and energetically begging for a release, victory could not be claimed until the opponent was thrown to the ground whereupon fatal injuries were sustained, Kinnfaela recorded. John Dunton in 1699 opined the wrestlers of Fingal (historically a Norse-Irish sub-region comprising of north county Dublin and maritime county Meath) were Ireland's elite wrestlers – though inferior to the exponents at Moorfields in London (Dunton [Ed. Andrew Carpenter] 2003, 92).

A vignette of wrestling in Georgian rural Ireland is revealed in the elucidatory footnotes of Lady Morgan's epistolary novel *The Wild Irish Girl* when referencing the '*Carriaght*' or Backhold wrestling style as exhibited during a May Day celebration (Owenson [Lady Morgan] 1809, 184). This style was described as 'almost identical' to the Scottish Western Isles method and before a bout commenced the referee shouted '*lamh an iochdair, lamh an uachdar*' meaning 'one hand down, one hand up' (Baxter 1998). The victorious wrestler was nominated the 'King of the May' and ceremonially placed his sporting crown before a local beauty (Owenson [Lady Morgan] 1809, 184). The fidelity of this account is built upon the author's attendance at a wrestling event in county Tipperary in 1802 (Owenson [Lady Morgan] 1809, 177) and, quite likely, legends associated with her grandfather, a noted wrestler in county Sligo where wrestling was performed with 'singular skill and adroitness' (Dixon 1862, 42). In 1720 county Dublin, 'jolly rusticks' in their 'best array' competed for 'caps, ribbons and beer' when displaying 'artful grappling' during a football match's wrestling where locked arms and thighs dashed a 'fierce opposer' (Carpenter 1998, 93). By the eighteenth century Irish wrestling 'shed much of its lethal roughness' and while 'a bit on the rough-and-ready side' (Wilson 1959, 5) its association with vigorous rustic gatherings (*Dublin Magazine 1840, 217*) and Dublin city's underground sport events continued.

Sabbatarianism, disorderly mobs and 'the wrestling doctor'

A 1723 history of Dublin claimed the Irish took 'pleasure in imitating' English customs that included 'manly exercises sports, recreations and vices' with back-sword, cudgels, boxing and wrestling listed ('A Citizen of London' 1732, 23). By 1818, the standard of wrestling in Dublin purportedly excelled the London arena (Warburton and Whitelaw 1818, 1174). Wrestling was held on Sunday evenings in back fields and certain squares around Dublin city with two rings, one for wrestling and the other for 'fighting', noted during a 1780s gathering (Kelly 2014, 310). Spectators – often the city's transport workers or employees drawn from breweries, distilleries, bakeries and dairies – were identified as among 'the disorderly mob' (D'Arcy 1988, 13–14). Wrestling was also actively associated with the wickedness of anti-Sabbatarian activity as in 1785 when the Sherriff of Dublin's attempt to suppress Sunday wrestling was openly defied whereupon this official summoned the infirmary guard (Kelly 2014, 310).

A county Carlow historian claimed wrestling during this era experienced a high pitch of popularity and was 'all the vogue' nationwide (Brophy 1888, 70). Large attendances in Dublin are evidenced as in 1805 when a police spy observed 1000 spectators at a wrestling contest and football match at Stoneybatter (D'Arcy 1988, 13–14). In 1824, 1200 persons assembled near Ranelagh to watch a wrestling contest (*Dublin Evening Mail*, April 21, 1824). The sporting précis of John 'Turpentine' Brenan MD, known widely as 'the Wrastling Doctor' and who dubbed himself the 'Prince of Idoagh, the King of all the Wrestlers of all Ireland' (*The Dublin Quarterly Journal of Medical Science* 1870, 254), was regarded as late Georgian Dublin city's principal wrestling promoter. The extent of metropolitan plebian participation in wrestling is demonstrated in his forceful and indiscriminate taste for contest where he had:

> blackened himself in the embraces of the athletic coal-porter, was whitened again in the arms of the flour-carrier, hugged the brawny drayman and grown greasy in the clutches of the butcher's swab. (O'Rourke 1825, 156)

An instantly identifiable figure when wearing a blue *surtout* at Dublin's Strand or the Phoenix Park, Brenan was 'that pink of gymnastic amateurs' when supervising contests whilst astride a small bay pony (O'Rourke 1825, 156). The editor of the controversial *Milesian Magazine*, Brenan was berated by a rival editor for drinking beer with 'the wrestling sailors' at Watkin's on George's-quay *(Irish Magazine*, January 1812) and termed 'a Porter House Buffoon, a Punch House Wag … Arbitrator of Bullies and a degraded kind of Prize Fighter', who spent his weekdays arranging wrestling challenges and devoted the Sabbath to deciding these contests (*Irish Magazine*, September 1811). It was asserted, this 'valiant umpire of the Broadstone Combatants', as a friend of Dublin's Town Major, Henry Sirr,[1] was a police agent, spy and denunciator (*Irish Magazine*, July 1811) who allegedly claimed rebels within secret political societies or rural syndicalists, such as the Caravats and Canal-Breakers, attended wrestling merely to spread secret political information (*Irish Magazine*, July 1812). Indeed, during late Georgian Dublin, the revolutionary United Irishmen[2] rendezvoused at wrestling matches held in Astley's Circus (Bartlett 2004, 47). Meanwhile on 12 July 1812 crowds were 'highly entertained' at *Surtout* Brenan's alleged 'spy concern' near the Broadstone, at the Grand Canal, where two 'Orange vagabonds' (presumably soldiers), having wrestled for an hour, were thrown into the waterway and prodded with their own bayonets 'something in the way a pot stick is applied in making stirabout' (*Irish Magazine*, August 1812). The zenith of wrestling's tangential confluence with subversive politics occurred in 1882 when the Lord Lieutenant and others mistakenly believed the knife-wielding assassins of the Chief Secretary, when outside the Phoenix Park's Vice-regal Lodge, were merely 'the humbler classes' involved in 'horseplay or wrestling'[3] (see, *North Wales Chronicle*, May 13, 1882; *Freeman's Journal*, May 8, 1882). Police activity at wrestling matches in late Hanoverian north Leinster was pervasive.

The *Belfast Newsletter* on June 21, 1811 reported that at New Dominick Street, Dublin a wrestling group was attacked indiscriminately by sword-wielding policemen with one man reportedly killed by pistol shot. During the mid-1820s, the magistracy of Kells, county Meath employed every 'legal and gentle means' to suppress wrestling but during a 'melancholy affair', a sergeant and a force of 14 policemen instructed to break up a well-attended wrestling contest, resulted in one man being shot along with others brought to Navan Infirmary for treatment (*Belfast Newsletter*, July 21, 1826). In 1824, Dublin's Chief Peace Officer, Horse *Patrole* and several Foot Police – upon the arrest of a wrestler near Charlemont-bridge – were stoned during 'a continued attack' by a 1000-strong crowd. The police secured reinforcements before responding with gunfire to 'intimidate' the mob to make further arrests (*Dublin Evening Mail*, April 21, 1824).

Apparently by the 1820s Dublin's ancient amusements of bull-baiting, hurling, cudgel-playing and wrestling were 'almost wholly laid aside' (McGregor 1821, 313). Dr Brenan's death in 1830 deprived Georgian Dublin of its last great wrestling promoter (Wilde 1850, 17). However, a contention that wrestling had become an 'occasional' sportive recreation (Kelly 2014, 311) requires calibration as though listed among 'the plagues of Dublin' (Herbert 1836, 90) campaigns to suppress this potentially volatile recreation garnered indeterminate successes. In the 1830s it was argued wrestling should be permitted if managed 'without riot' and 'annoyance' to the public (Herbert 1836, 90) but threats to the sport's viability included the decline of Dublin's chief May Day sports at Finglas where wrestling was previously engaged. The Government and Privy Council had received supplications to prohibit this aforesaid amusement but it was allegedly the 1833 cholera panic and a teetotalism campaign that finished off Dublin's most popular revel (Wilde 1852, 64). During the 1830s wrestling, boxing-matches, bull-baiting, dog-fighting, throwing at cocks and football were still regarded as societal ills, but wrestling alone was considered a 'manly, harmless and amusing trial of skill' (Herbert 1836, 90).

A recent extrapolation – that refers to an 1824 sub-theatrical demonstration by 'Jack' Langan of wrestling, so necessarily connected with … pugilism' – infers the former sport 'no longer functioned in Ireland as a separate sport' (Kelly 2014, 284) would appear ill-considered. Firstly, the former Mud Island sawyer-cum-sailor-cum-publican-cum-pugilist was known to execute 'the Donnybrook twist' (*New York Clipper*, July 29, 1854), which was quite likely a locally adapted cross-buttock throw, being a move still permitted in prize-fighting. Secondly, harvesting admission fees from the capital's sizeable wrestling cohort was undoubtedly a consideration as Tom Reynolds (formerly a sparring partner, promoter and good friend to the Dubliner boxer) noted of Langan 'gold was … his god' (New York Clipper, March 29, 1884). More fundamentally, when assessing Ireland's rough sport landscape, Kelly's assertion that the Irish wrestling arena did not demonstrate the parallel phenomena as experienced in England, where the wrestling styles of Devon, Cornwall or the North County respectively rivalled prizefighting as a popular recreation, (Kelly 2014, 284) is correspondingly open to challenge. Much empirical evidence cataloguing the totality of provincial Ireland's rough sports landscape points to the contrary being the case generally and more particularly when sub-regional considerations (principally in west and north Leinster) are evaluated.

Arguably, the relative paucity of contemporaneous wrestling reportage was not reflective of the sport's prevalence but rather that plebian and/or rural involvement in wrestling was largely regarded as either underground and/or unremarkable in nature. Therefore coverage largely appeared only as a consequence of outbreaks of indiscriminate violence when law-and-order concerns were voiced, as in May 1835 when a strong group of 100 men, having left a wrestling competition at the Phoenix Park, bludgeoned passersby on Parkgate Street (*Roscommon Journal*, May 9, 1835). The following month when thousands of men from counties Meath and Kildare assembled for a wrestling competition at the Phoenix Park's Seven Acre Field this event was abandoned amid a 'furious' shillelagh battle (*Dublin Penny Journal* 1835, 388). In 1843 when a policeman, sent to prevent a Phoenix Park wrestling match, sparked a riot and was in 'grave danger' when viciously stoned, a magistrate, though 'not adverse to young men enjoying themselves in a rational manner', advised attendees to 'act quietly and keep the peace' (*Freeman's Journal*, April 25, 1843). Wrestling's typical association with lawlessness was exhibited in February 1845 with a magistrate requesting the constabulary to send a reinforcement of 30 policemen to a weekly wrestling contest at Leopardstown as 'the Dublin men had come to fight the mountain men' (D'Arcy 1988, 14). Though wrestling was possibly 'another casualty of the embrace of respectability' (Kelly 2014, 310), it was tenaciously supported for decades beyond its ostensible 1830s demise due to its long-standing and robust popularity among the sportive plebian and peasantry population of county Dublin and beyond. Equally, Collar-and-Elbow was never subsumed within boxing.

Patronage and participation in provincial wrestling

Tripp's (2009, 28) commentary that various Cornish landowners viewed their patronage of plebeian sports as an old-fashioned paternalist responsibility can be applied to a select number of the Georgian and Victorian Anglo-Irish landlord milieu who arguably recognised sport's worth when fostering psychic social capital among their tenantry. Equally, a powerful (possibly dissident political) display of wrestling's popularity, prestige and pageantry was exhibited in 1826 when an estimated 20–30,000 spectators attended an inter-county match at Loughinure, Clane, county Kildare, to witness county Westmeath's champion Richard Carey of Mullingar contest with James Larkin of Clane ('The Gaelic American', *Leinster Leader*, March 16, 1907). The ceremony and hospitality associated with wrestling was demonstrated when Carey (already accompanied by 50 supporters on horseback) rendezvoused with a further 200 mounted horsemen at Kinnegad, county Westmeath before being escorted to the venue. This event alone confutes the unaccountably negligible historiography of Westmeath's wrestling arena (Hunt 2007, 143).

A notable example of pre-Famine landlord patronage of wrestling was exhibited at the second Earl of Howth's birthday, hosted at his north Dublin castle grounds, where crowds enjoyed racing, wrestling and other amusements (Binns 1837, 18). This noble's large open-carriage, illustrated with panels of 'all manly sports, boxing, hunting, wrestling, racing', created a 'spirit-stirring sight' (*The New Sporting Magazine*, May 1833, 177). Inter-county wrestling matches were organised by an unspecified 'Lord Howth' for wrestlers from Lusk, county Dublin and county Kildare (Sherry 1937–1938). Conversely, in April 1845 the Terry Alts, a secret agrarian society, in Roscrea, county Tipperary, asserted their opposition to the conacre land system of short-term holdings and uncertain tenure, when utilising wrestling to transmit social and political disaffection. Having occupied lands, they threatened farm staff with pistols, before engaging in wrestling and leaping (*Nenagh Guardian*, April 23, 1845).

In advance of the harrowing calamity of the 1840s Great Famine many Irish sports had already declined but by the 1850s sport re-emerged fitfully. Certain sportive Anglo-Irish landlords encouraged wrestling with a vigour beyond mere tacit acquiescence. On Lord Bellew's estate at Barmeath, county Louth, in May 1850, wrestling was promoted as 'an innocent and healthy amusement' by the territorial magnate's *heir presumptive*, Edward Bellew with foot-racing, donkey-racing and wrestling enjoyed by a large gathering from

Dunleer (*Dundalk Democrat*, May 25, 1850). In March 1861 a sports day inaugurated by Lord Lansdowne's agents on his estate in Kenmare, county Kerry, witnessed tremendous public excitement during a wrestling final between Townsend Trench, a land agent and a tenant, Humphry Murphy, with vigour, ability and an 'admirable display of sinew' demonstrated (*New York Clipper*, March 30, 1861).

Wrestling was demonstrated at festive estate celebrations and within programmes designated to provide structured agricultural instruction that strengthened social bonds between the landed classes and the tenant masses. In March 1861 during the New Ross Union Farming Society's entertainments on Mr BWK Whitney's grounds at Old Ross, county Wexford wrestling figured prominently (*Irish Times*, March 2, 1861). In February 1862 at the Westmeath Farming Society's annual gathering on Henry Parnell's Anneville estate, outside Mullingar, large multitudes amused themselves with foot races and wrestling matches where the 'utmost good feeling' was displayed (*Irish Times*, February 14, 1862). On C.W. O'Hara's Annaghmore estate in county Sligo, during an annual fete in May 1868, collective delight was expressed that wrestling, throwing the sledge and other sports 'so eagerly enjoyed a century ago' were 'reinstated' under the landlord's patronage (*Sligo Chronicle*, May 23, 1868). At the Rockingham estate in Boyle, north county Roscommon, with entertainment and sports organised for harvesting labourers in August 1882, Col. King-Harman presented prizes to the best runners and wrestlers (*Roscommon Herald*, August 12, 1882). However during the Land War campaigns and amid Home Rule demands, such sportive Anglo-Irish patrons apparently shied away from these aforementioned estate sponsored sporting events, focussing patronage instead on sports such as horse-racing.

Rational recreations versus turbulent sports

From an apparent late Georgian peak of interest (Brophy 1888, 69) wrestling declined from the 1830s, particularly outside of Leinster. In 1830s Ulster the 'Irish accomplishments' of 'wrestling, ball-playing, and cock-fighting' had waned (*Cavan Weekly News*, December 27, 1878). *Viator* from Blarney, county Cork, in 1844, urged land magnates and agricultural societies to encourage 'running, hurling, wrestling and other exercises' as such 'fine old customs' were 'almost entirely banished' (*Cork Examiner*, July 17, 1844). Expressing typical concerns regarding sporting violations of the Sabbath, as prescribed under statute 7th Wm. IV c.17., in 1839 Dublin's Lord Mayor ordered that no public pastime, to include wrestling, was permitted during the annual Donnybrook Fair (*Belfast Newsletter*, August 23, 1839) and by 1855 this event, once regarded as Dublin's principal public entertainment, was abolished. An increased focus on the provision of rational Sunday recreation in 1860s Dublin included wider access being provided for the masses to the Zoological Gardens and Botanical Gardens. By 1858 rational amusements had assisted in halting the incidents of 'fighting and wrestling previously so prevalent' around the Phoenix Park (*The Reasoner* 1858, 251). Sunday sports enjoyed at the Phoenix Park included leaping, throwing-a-weight, football and hurling, the high level of car-driving was termed 'perfectly surprising' while nearby stallholders sold fruit, cake and ginger beer (see, 'A Sabbath in Dublin', *The Christian Treasury* ... 1849, 77; O'Rourke. 'A Sunday Stroll: The Hermit In Ireland, Vol. IV.', *The Dublin and London Magazine* 1825, 154). But rational amusements had not extinguished the disorderly mob's sporting proclivities. A Dublin police memorandum of 1857 catalogued 'disgraceful' scenes and anti-Sabbatarian activities with open-air wrestling, dog fighting, cockfighting, boxing, gambling and drinking at public houses in Ringsend, Irishtown, Harold's Cross, Phibsboro, Dolphin's Barn and the Phoenix Park (D'Arcy 1988, 13–14).

Ireland's wrestling arena, similar to that in the North Country (Tripp 2009, 101) and Cornwall, experienced Victorian era vicissitudes and participatory flux (Huggins 2001, 38). Either side of the Great Famine relatively prominent wrestling events were hosted in metropolitan Dublin. In June 1837, a 'great wrestling match' was organised at the city's Royal Coburg Gardens with a silver cup and minor prizes supplied (*Freeman's Journal*, June 22, 1837). During the 1840s–1860s certain Dublin theatres and music halls showcased Irish wrestling (*Freeman's Journal*, March 7, 1855; *Freeman's Journal*, March 30, 1865; *Bell's Life in London and Sporting Chronicle*, October 8, 1843). In 1864 the city's Royal Recreation Grounds on Upper Wellington Street hosted the 'Great All-Ireland Wrestling match' with a 'splendid champion gold and silver belt' on offer (*Freeman's Journal,* September 19, 1864). Though the Donnybrook Fair's demise was 'a service to civilisation' (Elrington Ball 1903, 57) its spirit flickered on St Patrick's Day 1865 at *Floraville*, Donnybrook with a pony steeplechase, foot-racing, weight throwing and wrestling on offer. Wrestling was apparently the chief physical sport for county Kildare's men during the 1850s–1870s with an estimated 10,000 attending a tournament near Timahoe in 1865. ('The Gaelic American', *Leinster Leader*, March 16, 1907) In late 1870s Dublin city wrestling was 'very popular' among the 'labouring classes' whereupon 'each Sunday some young man who won victory in Navan, or Cork, or Galway or wherever exceptional excellence was manifested' travelled to 'the Phaynix' to try conclusions (Stoker 1907, 32). For an impecunious provincial wrestler the biggest obstacle to compete there was the 'prohibitively high' transport costs, which were often defrayed by subscriptions raised among his associates (Stoker 1907, 33). During this era, GAA stalwart Dan Fraher recalled various inter-county wrestling matches involving counties Waterford, Cork, Wexford and Tipperary while contests involving south Kildare versus Queens (Laois) generating great excitement (see, *The Western People*, January 7, 1933; *Kildare Observer*, June 28, 1890).

Wrestling may have become increasingly unpopular among the skilled working classes desirous of securing increased respectability (D'Arcy 1988, 13–18) due to its episodically rowdy association with the city's life. In 1874, wrestling (with spontaneous ease) even intruded upon the city's high status annual regatta with crowds reportedly surging around the combatants and drinking stands imperilled (*The Irish Times*, July 7, 1874). In 1876–1877, Dublin's Metropolitan Police chief John Mallon ordered plain clothes detectives to gather information to quash wrestling at the Phoenix Park (D'Arcy 1988, 13, 20) but illustrative of wrestling's continued popularity was a contest there in 1876 with an estimated 7–8000 in attendance (Robinson and Gilpin 1893, xlvi). While newspaper reports and police memorandum recurrently detailed wrestling's association with lawlessness, nevertheless the sport in north Leinster displayed particular resilience and relatively high levels of participation into the 1880s.

Wrestling at 'The Phaynix' – 'Sport, Pure and Simple'?

During the Hanoverian era certain speculative Anglo-Irish landlords who promoted their own wrestling champion arguably hoped to bask in a reflected sportive glory and secure gambling winnings. At 'the championship of Ireland' organised by an unnamed Dublin Marquis in the Phoenix Park, a Carlow landlord when on horseback amid a large crowd entered 'his man' against the Marquis' champion, before entrusting the large stake to an illusively entitled 'Captain W__' (Brophy 1888, 70–71).

Tripp (2009, 174) outlines the emergence of money prizes in nineteenth century Cornwall fashioned a greater incentive to swindle while 'sham-fights' were a problem addressed by the North Country's governing body (Huggins 2001, 37). Prizes in late Victorian county Dublin's Collar-and-Elbow wrestling arena, while symbolically important, were of meagre financial worth with belts and/or ladies elastic garters commonly presented (Sherry 1937–1938). Bram Stoker claimed prizes were not offered nor was betting conducted in Dublin city as wrestling was undertaken as 'sport, pure and simple' (Stoker 1907, 32–33). However private side wagers, most likely, did occur. In Victorian rural Ireland with 'no prizes for the winners ... heavy wagering' took place among the large attendances (O'Galloglaigh 1938–1939). County Kildare's Mike Kelly, regarded as Ireland's 'best wrestler' during the 1800s, 'could be backed ... for £500 against any man in the world' (*Bell's Life in London and Sporting Chronicle*, May 5, 1850) and with money to be made it is worth speculating certain organisers at the very least facilitated bookmakers. By the 1880s wrestlers placed newspaper advertisements when offering money stakes to induce named wrestlers to a challenge, however a 'scarcity of competitors' could result in disappointed crowds (see, *Freeman's Journal*, February 12, 1891; *Sport*, November 18, 1882).

Stoker was astonished by the Phoenix Park crowd's extraordinary fairness as onlookers were not permitted to speak out regarding defence or attack. The rationale behind this honour-code was while local supporters might cheer their man 'to the echo' the stranger was at a disadvantage (Stoker 1907, 33). However, during a rural north Dublin contest, in stark contrast to this aforesaid alleged impartiality, the herculean George Hoey was roared on by followers that included a large contingent of city jarveys who previously had lost 'a packet of money' to Hoey's opponent – the latter having previously vanquished one of the jarveys' Phoenix Park 'fancies' (Sherry 1937–1938). Confirmation of wrestling's betting and cash prize culture (even within the aegis of the avowedly amateur GAA) was witnessed in 1908 at The Thatch in Drumcondra, Dublin, when side bets were not permitted as the winner would receive two-thirds of the gate-money and the loser to receive the remainder (*Freeman's Journal*, June 16, 1908).

Presentational changes attempted

While the establishment of a rule-making body is declarative of a transition from an informal pastime to the status of an institutionalised sport (Huggins 2001, 41), an independent and/or centralised national association to govern wrestling was arguably never developed in Ireland. Irish wrestling's long-standing robust communal rituals, bolstered by regular meetings, sustained the sport. However in December 1876 a new highpoint of organisational ambition was demonstrated when influential wrestlers advertised an enclosed meeting (organised in conjunction with the Irish Champion Athletic Club) at Lansdowne Road, Dublin, to put 'the now almost national pastime of wrestling' on a 'satisfactory basis' (*The Irish Times*, December 26, 1876). Events were scheduled for St Patrick's Day 1877, with a county Dublin championship on Easter Monday and the Championship of Ireland arranged for Whit Monday.[186] Hopes that Cornish, Devonshire and Cumberland athletes, and 'perhaps some Frenchmen', would compete with Irish champions conveyed the organisers' intention to create new or renewed interest in the sport and/or provide future international competition upon a sophisticated stage (*The Irish Times*, December 26, 1876). The March 1877 event was 'interesting' and 'tolerably well' carried out (*The Irish Times*, April 3, 1876) with a partially covered grandstand reserved by the police for 'tradesmen's wives and daughters' on Whit Monday (*Freeman's Journal*, May 16, 1877). But the latter contest witnessed a resurrection of the 'Donnybrook spirit' when disorderly 'roughs' (who entered without paying) wreaked havoc, raided drink stands and assaulted attendants (*Irish Times*, May 22, 1877). Though the event was a financial success, this was poor compensation for the destruction to property and the damage wrought upon wrestling's reputation. Remarkably the organisers staged another tournament in August 1877 with wrestlers from counties Dublin, Meath, Kildare and Wicklow invited to compete for silver medals (*Freeman's Journal*, August 15, 1877). However, the Whit Monday outrages, quite likely, cast a long shadow over this event's prospects as this format was apparently discontinued at the genteel surrounds of Lansdowne Road.

Public houses, factions fights and wrestling suppressed

During the 1870s the sporting culture displayed at the Phoenix Park, now widely recognised as Ireland's premier wrestling arena, was generally a complimentary mix of good-humoured order that melded a sophisticated fight mentality with fair play. But outside such long-standing non-partisan demotic sporting confines, and/or arising from the failure or unwillingness to facilitate wrestling at Ireland's elite athletic grounds, this partial vacuum was filled by enterprising patrons who hosted wrestling events at south county Dublin public houses. However arising from a 'fearful faction fight' in May 1880 at Killiney, county Dublin, described as 'playfully murderous' as the battles between the Shanavests and Caravats, the magistrates of Tallaght Petty Sessions ordered a stop to the 'legitimate amusements' of wrestling (*Irish Times*, May 27, 1880). After hundreds from Terenure and county Dublin's mountain villages clashed, the police threatened to close all local public houses unless wrestling was discontinued (*Irish Times*, May 27, 1880). To avoid police detection in August 1880, the public house wrestling arena moved from Firhouse to Redcow in county Dublin. Further trouble erupted when 100 men from the Crumlin and Dolphin's Barn areas assaulted stragglers (*Irish Times*, August 19, 1880) while 'a band of thirsty wrestlers' from the city's Coombe and Smithfield districts were cautioned by the police (*Weekly Irish Times*, September 4, 1880). Another significant clash occurred in September 1880 at Clondalkin among combatants from counties Dublin, Wicklow, Meath and Kildare. With an estimated 10,000 men prepared to undertake a mass faction fight, members of the Roman Catholic clergy called upon a prominent wrestler, Patrick Cullen of Rathcoole, to dissuade the would-be-combatants from clashing. With 100 summonses issued (but not served), the charges against 12 defendants (described as agricultural labourers or farmers, aged between 18 and 40 years and 'fine, strapping fellows') were dismissed with the Bench's Chairman (somewhat expediently) noting the relevant legislation, Wm III, chap 17, sec 3, was antiquated (*Weekly Irish Times*, September 4, 1880). The combined forces of clerical intervention, a pragmatic magistracy (who ordered the suppression of wrestling but did not issue punitive fines and/or jail terms) allied with a vigilant constabulary had broken the turbulent nexus between public house organised wrestling and faction fighting.

By April 1884 wrestling's more typical peaceable character was displayed at the Phoenix Park (*Freeman's Journal*, April 9, 1884) and again 2 months later when wrestlers from the city, Rathcoole, Newcastle, Saggart, Clondalkin and Balbriggan challenged those from Wicklow and Kildare as while an estimated 3000 people were in attendance no disorder was reported (*Weekly Irish Times*, June 7, 1884). Organised events continued throughout rural county Dublin on Balrothery Green, the Commons of Lusk, (see Sherry 1937–1938; Mag Fhionnbhairr 1937–1938) at Balbriggan Strand, (*Freeman's Journal*, April 18, 1889) Saggart, 'The Boot' at Ballymun and at the Spring Gardens, home of the 'Ballybough Bridge Brigade' (*Irish Independent*, November 26, 1951). While late

Georgian Ireland's canal network facilitated wrestling in Dublin, a rare example of rail travel promoting a 'great wrestling match' at the Curragh noted the venue was one mile from Kildare's train station (*Freeman's Journal*, March 9, 1882). In 1891 a GAA-promoted wrestling championship at Inchicore, Dublin drew significantly larger crowds than a nearby boxing event and provided the city's labourers and mechanics with 'wholesome' pastimes (*Kildare Observer*, March 7, 1891).

Wrestling, other sports and the GAA

The longstanding bifurcation within wrestling was referenced by Archbishop T.W. Croke who in 1884 lamented 'the lost arts of wrestling and handygrips' (Birley 1993, 281–282). Historically combat sports were integrated within folk hurling and football. In north Connacht, wrestling was an intrinsic part of 'hurling' with competitors drawn from 'the gentry, farmers and squirearchy' (Dixon 1862, 42). The wrestling and tripping techniques displayed during a 1720 county Dublin football match included a 'dextrous crook' that grounded a 'grovelling champion' (Carpenter 1998, 93). Football and wrestling contests were also hosted successively. In Killucan, county Westmeath, 100-a-side teams terminated their match with wrestling (Hunt 2007) with attendance figures suggestively high as in 1801 when 50 men were arrested during a similar event in Rathmines, Dublin (D'Arcy 1988, 144).

Collar-and-Elbow wrestling was permitted during 21-aside football in Dublin city, Padraig Pirseal wrote (*Irish Independent*, December 11, 1964). In county Tipperary when two players collided one fall was allowed however the referee intervened when the interlocked players attempted a second fall (King 2005, 31). An 1870s hurling match outside Cork city between Aglish and St Finbarr was stalled, from the outset, with every player wrestling (O'Dubagan, *Meath Chronicle*, August 1, 1914). The GAA purged handygrips – a grappling form of hand-to-hand combat (Drake 1755, 188) – from its football and hurling codes in 1886. During the GAA's early years wrestling was a scheduled curtain-raiser for hurling matches in counties Leitrim, Roscommon, Longford and Sligo, while the attendees enjoyed a 'regular feast' of wrestling afterwards (*Roscommon Herald*, May 31, 1919). In 1885 during an inaugural county Louth GAA athletics event wrestling generated the greatest levels of public enthusiasm (Coyle 2003, 23) and was widely undertaken at various county Dublin GAA events (see, *Freeman's Journal*, August 16, 1886: *Freeman's Journal*, March 7, 1891). However, a revival was required as the wrestling arena, even in once vibrant provincial strongholds, by 1885 had 'almost completely vanished' (*Roscommon Herald*, February 14, 1885). Though Collar-and-Elbow wrestling was listed in the GAA's first constitution and rulebook, and was sanctioned at the January 1888 Thurles convention, the organisation's promotion of wrestling was 'partial and halting' (Devlin 1908, 27). Indeed, the GAA's second edition rulebook indifferently noted Ireland's Collar-and-Elbow wrestling rules equated to Cornwall's and were provided not as the GAA's rules 'but only as an outline for those who may wish to encourage wrestling' (*GAA Rulebook* 1887, 20).

Wrestling's decline – disorganised or discountenanced?

In 1887 a new promoter stepped into the organisational void when a Dublin championship was promoted by the *Athletic and Cycling News* (*Dundalk Democrat*, October 29, 1887), which was the official organ of the Irish Amateur Athletic Association, an organization regarded as aggressive to the GAA's programme. While in 1890 *Sport* facilitated a new grand wrestling tournament in the capital (*Freeman's Journal,* December 30, 1890). However without an independent governing authority, Collar-and-Elbow wrestling exhibited its typically fluid structure when relying upon key wrestling individuals and stalwart communities to sustain the sport. In 1907, the celebrated Irish pedestrian athlete, John Ennis, argued it was the 'duty' of the GAA and Irishmen 'to resuscitate and cultivate' wrestling clubs and with competent instructors appointed, he claimed, wrestlers equal the champions once the 'pride of Kildare and Westmeath' could again be produced ('The Gaelic American', *Leinster Leader,* March 16, 1907). Indeed, despite operating under 'every vicissitude and disability' keen interest in wrestling was still manifest in districts bordering Dublin (Devlin 1908, 27). However, while the 'rank and file' (see, *The Western People,* January 7, 1933: Devlin, *The Irish Year Book 1908,* 27. An Caman, 'Irish Wrestling and Wrestlers: *A Neglected Native Pastime*', 1932, 13) were interested in wrestling the GAA's governing bodies took no steps to 'preserve or encourage' the pastime ('Wrestling – Westmeath v Kildare: A Famous Contest', *Roscommon Herald,* March 16, 1907).

When evaluating the decline of Collar-and-Elbow wrestling, two leading Irish sportsmen, based in America, provided convergent assessments that principally blamed the British government. Ennis condemned the rigorous application of coercive laws during the 1860s Fenian scare and 'the troublous days of Land League agitation' where large secular gatherings were 'strictly prohibited' ('Wrestling – Westmeath v Kildare: A Famous Contest', *Roscommon Herald,* March 16, 1907). A leading Boston-based Fenian, O'Reilly argued wrestling was 'frozen out by the landlord government' (O'Reilly 1888, 42). The 'English rulers' had 'discountenanced' Irish sports to 'unman and degrade Irishmen' until ignorant of conflict 'even in sport' and 'robbed them of self-confidence' to place them in 'hopeless subjection' (O'Reilly 1888, 42). However, throughout the Atlantic Archipelago, wrestling's viability was increasingly challenged by the damaging effects of emigration that Ennis accepted was a secondary cause of wrestling's decline in Ireland. The draw of counter-attractions, as in Cornwall, (Tripp 2009, 144) in particular a robust mass support for football codes and hurling games during the 1880s significantly undermined wrestling's popularity. Equally, in 1904 a sportive cultural malaise was reported as the football matches, religious festivals and wrestling competitions that once kept up 'the country's vitality' were practically non-existent (*Dundalk Democrat,* March 26, 1904).

Wrestling's international dimension was demonstrated during the 1890 Belfast Highland Games with the eye-catching title of the 'all-round wrestling' world champion and Scottish-style wrestling on offer (*Belfast Newsletter,* August 11, 1890). Commercial theatrical wrestling was increasingly popular in Dublin with the Rotunda's Round Room hosting grotesque vaudeville demonstrations where even collar-and-elbow wrestlers 'guzzled' opponents by the throat (*Weekly Irish Times,* April 26, 1884). Catch wrestling competition was available exclusively for Dublin's garrisoned British soldiers at the city's Empire Theatre (*Freeman's Journal,* February 13, 1884). Circuses offered battles with putative world champions where local competitors could demand 'Fingallian style' (described as 'a combination of Cornish and Catch-as-catch-can' wrestling) as they did not tolerate 'furrin rastlin'' (Archer 1906, 61, 67). In April 1892 an 'enormous salary' secured for 'positively six nights only ... the great Irish-American' Collar-and-Elbow World Champion, John McMahon and England's Catch champion Tom Connors (also an Irish wrestling exponent) at Belfast's Alhambra Theatre (*Belfast News-Letter,* April 15, 1892). In Munster, a catch-hold wrestling stronghold, (An Caman 1932, 13) regional Catch-as-Catch-Can championship titles were contested for in Cork and Limerick. In 1900, 'bumper audiences' witnessed Cornish-American legend, Jack Carkeek defeat Cork Catch-hold wrestlers, including Jack Horgan in the Graeco-Roman fashion, (*Skibbereen Eagle*, November 10, 1900) while at Dublin's Lyric Theatre, Carkeek simultaneously fought O'Connor and Nolan for £10 (*Freeman's Journal*, June 2, 1900).

Gallant but belated revival efforts

However, Dublin's Collar-and-Elbow enthusiasts did not accept Irish folk wrestling's demise with fatalistic resignation. Commercial entertainment avenues were explored during a 'gallant' revival effort, with the promotional efforts of GAA and wrestling champion Dick Curtis and publican Mr P Nolan of 'The Thatch' in Drumcondra, Dublin, particularly conspicuous. In October 1906, Collar-and-Elbow wrestling re-emerged under the GAA's auspices when the County Dublin Wrestling Committee was organised (*Freeman's Journal*, October 16, 1906). Traditional wrestlers appeared at the Empire Theatre, Dublin and renewed interest was evident when English wrestler George Dinnie challenged George Hoey, Edward O'Connor of Balcunnin or Dick Curtis to fight for any sum up to £50 (*Freeman's Journal*, October 16, 1906). Hoey offered to wrestle the Irish Catch-as-Catch-Can champion, Patrick Connolly, for the national title 'in an open field, Irish style' (*Nenagh Guardian*, August 22, 1906) and though 'past his prime' Hoey valiantly wrestled against 'the Russian Lion' George Hackenschmidt, then the world champion in Dublin's Theatre Royal (Sherry 1937–1938). Further resuscitative action saw more than 100 Collar-and-Elbow matches organised at 'The Thatch' in August 1907, with prize money and medals available (*Freeman's Journal*, August 27, 1907) but these revival efforts were marred by crowd disorder (see, *Irish Independent*, September 23, 1907; *Freeman's Journal,* October 18, 1907). Though a wrestling championship was advertised for St Patrick's Day in 1908 (*Freeman's Journal*, March 7, 1908) such events were 'spontaneous and isolated' (Devlin 1908, 27). The crossover experiment degraded into participation in all-in 'body wrestling' with Dublin's wrestlers competing against rivals in the Cumberland or Devon styles at the Rotunda Theatre (*Freeman's Journal*, June 16, 1908). By 1910 Ireland's theatrical hippodrome wrestling allegedly was no more (*Irish Press*, November 11, 1932).

Traditional backhold wrestling lingered in rural West of Ireland amongst schoolboys who engaged in '*Barrog*' (*Irish Independent*, December 1, 1951) meaning 'a tight-grip', and also among 'Tattie Hoakers' who were seasonal Irish migrant labourers based in Scotland (Baxter 2014). In the Irish enclave of Warwick, Queensland, Australia during celebrations to honour St Patrick in 1892, the Collar-and-Elbow and Irish Body-hold styles were hosted simultaneously (*Warwick Argus*, March 19, 1892). In Dublin, Collar-and-Elbow's future viability flickered with a club operating at Henrietta Street (*Irish Independent*, January 30, 1957) however by the outbreak of World War I wrestling in Britain 'passed into oblivion' (Oakley 1971, 26) while in Ireland the War of Independence (1919–1921) and the Civil War (1922–23) 'played havoc' with 'manly outdoor sport' and efforts to locate Dublin's wrestling county championship were 'to no avail' (*Sunday Independent*, June 11, 1922). Though wrestling exhibitions were given at the Irish Free State's Portobello Army Barracks, Dublin, with plans to subsume the All-Ireland Army Athletic Association into the GAA (*Fermanagh Herald*, June 10, 1922), the prospects for a new wrestling agency were arguably uncertain. Indeed, by April 1922 the GAA was ready to omit handball, wrestling and tug-o-war from its rulebook (*Irish Independent*, April 18, 1922). Wrestling, according to 'Vigilant' was 'a lost art' (*Nenagh Guardian,* April 29, 1922) and did not warrant inclusion in the proposed revivalist *Aonach Tailteann* games

(*Sunday Independent*, June 11, 1922). Belatedly, wrestling was listed for inclusion (though seemingly not under Collar-and-Elbow rules) alongside gymnastics, literature and motor car racing (*Irish Independent*, April 19, 1923).

By the 1930s Collar-and-Elbow wrestling was 'almost, if not altogether, forgotten' (O'Galloglaigh 1938–1939) as in Lusk, north county Dublin (possibly the last significant wrestling stronghold) the sport was recently 'abandoned for hurling' (Sherry 1937–1938). *An Irishman's Diary* in 1949 confirmed the Collar-and-Elbow style up to 'a few years ago' remained a popular pastime in Fingal (*Irish Times*, October 26, 1949) however boxing, once considered 'too gross and vulgar for the direct descendants of Irish princes' (Barrington 1832, 254) is now Ireland's pre-eminent rough sport.

Conclusion

The Collar-and-Elbow and *Carriaght* styles were once significant confrères within the Atlantic Archipelago's stable of folk combat sports. Widely demonstrated during the festive sporting occasions of ancient Hibernia to late Hanoverian Ireland, though the sport experienced vagaries it remained relatively resilient (particularly in north Leinster) into the mid-late Victorian era. With *Carriaght* an increasingly peripheral sport, the causes for the late Victorian decline of Collar-and-Elbow wrestling included: emigration; counter-attractions; the lack of an independent centralised sporting organisation; a public sportive malaise; the marginally negative potential of fight-fixing, politically motivated police surveillance, a sense the sport was outmoded and/or unrespectable with acts of lawlessness occurring at organised events.

Wrestling's belaboured efforts to adapt and survive were inadequate. The GAA's support for this 'popular and meritorious' (Devlin 1908, 27) sport was deemed inexpert. Expectations that Elbow-and-Collar's belated and short-lived twentieth century quasi-autonomous, self-regulated and subregional controlling body could reverse the protracted demise of this ancient rough sport, though well-intentioned, ultimately, proved inadequate. Correspondingly, Irish wrestling, despite its prominent sporting lineage, stretching back to the *Fair of Tailte,* suffered its final fall.

Disclosure statement

No potential conflict of interest was reported by the author.

Notes

1. *Irish Magazine*, July 1811, 301. Major Henry Charles Sirr in 1796 was appointed Dublin's Town Major which was effectively the Police Commissioner. He was one of Dublin Castle's leading agents in the campaign against the United Irishmen. He apprehended Lord Edward Fitzgerald and Robert Emmet. When the post disappeared in 1808, he was permitted to keep the title and remained in office as an assistant magistrate until he retired in 1826. See Madden, *The United Irishmen, Their Lives and Times* (1857, 394–395) regarding 'Secret Service' moneys, were it is noted there was 'little doubt' that the 'well-known Wrestling Doctor, of the *Milesian Magazine*, was pensioned for lampooning the Catholic leaders from 1816 to 1825 and received a pension of £200; page 369 detailing a payment in March 1798 of £22 15 shillings; page 370 regarding a payment in May 1798 of £11 – with both payments from Major Sirr.
2. (See Bartlett, R*evolutionary Dublin: The Letters of Francis Higgins to Dublin Castle, 1795–1801,* 2004, 47) regarding the Society of United Irishmen that was established in Belfast and Dublin in 1791 – with the later grouping comprising of Dublin's middle class society and divided between Protestant and Catholic. The society's ideology combined the new radicalism

inspired by the American and French Revolutions along with older British traditions regarding Commonwealth doctrines, and Irish patriotism. Its main aims were parliamentary reform and the removal of English control from Irish affairs. In 1798, Lord Edward Fitzgerald and others advocated immediate insurrection, but were opposed by moderators such as Robert Emmet who later engaged in insurrection 1803.
3. The assassination of the newly appointed Irish Chief Secretary, Lord Frederick Cavendish and the Under-secretary, TH Burke, was carried out by the Invincibles. These murders forced the British Prime Minister Gladstone to maintain coercion in Ireland.

Archival references

Mag Fhionnbhairr, S. 1937–1938. "Wrestling." Balrothery NS, 38: Irish Folklore Commission. http://www.ucd.ie/irishfolklore/en/ and http://www.duchas.ie/en/cbes/4498253/4383749/4506973

O'Galloglaigh, C. March 1938–January 1939. [Untitled]. Irish Folklore Commission. Rathwire NS, Killucan, County Westmeath. 340–342. Microfiche. http://www.ucd.ie/irishfolklore/en/

Sherry, E. 1937–1938. "Wrestling: Collar-and-Elbow." Milverton NS, Irish Folklore Commission, 142–145. http://www.ucd.ie/irishfolklore/en/ and http://www.duchas.ie/en/cbes/4498263/4383622

References

Ahern, Richard. 1989. *'Limerick in 1689': The Old Limerick Journal*. Limerick: Winter Edition.
Archer, Patrick. 1906. *The Humours of Shanwalla*. Dublin: M.H. Gill & Son.
Barrington, Jonah. 1832. *Personal Sketches of His Own Times*. Vol. III. London: Colburn and Bentley.
Bartlett, Thomas. 2004. *Revolutionary Dublin, 1795–1801: The Letters of Francis Higgins to Dublin Castle*. Dublin: Four Courts.
Baxter, William. 1998. "Wrestling, 'Wrestling, The Ancient Modern Sport'." In *Popular Games: Eclipse and Revival. From Traditions to the Regions of the Europe of Tomorrow*. Jugaje Info No. 27. Paper presented at European Traditional Sports and Games Association (ETSGA), Carhaix, France.
Baxter, William. (Private Correspondence with Author) 2014.
Beekman, Scott. 2006. *Ringside a History of Professional Wrestling in America*. Westport: Praeger.
Bell's Life in London and Sporting Chronicle. 1850, May 5.
Binns, Jonathon. 1837. *The Miseries and Beauties of Ireland*. Vol. 1. London: Orme and Browne.
Birley, Derek. 1993. *Sport and the Making of Britain*. New York: Manchester University Press.
Brophy, Michael. 1888. *Carlow Past and Present: A Brochure Containing Short Historical Notes and Miscellaneous Gleanings of the Town and County of Carlow*. Carlow: The Nationalist and Leinster Times Office.
Carpenter, Andrew, ed. 1998. *Verse in English from Eighteenth-century Ireland*. Cork: Cork University Press.
Chambers, WR. 1901. *Encyclopaedia*. Vol. X. Philadelphia: J.B. Lippincott Company.
The Christian Observer. 1827. Vol. 26. London: Hatchard & Son.
Coneys, Thomas De Vere. 1849. *Focloir Gaoidhilge-sacs-Bearla, or, An Irish-English dictionary*. Dublin: Hodges and Smith.
Coyle, Joe. 2003. *Athletics in Drogheda 1861–2001*. Victoria: Trafford.
D'Arcy, Fergus A. 1988. "The Decline and Fall of Donnybrook Fair: Moral Reform and Social Control in C19th Dublin." In *Saothar 13*. Dublin: Journal of Irish Labour History Society.
Devlin, PJ. 1908. "Irish Athletics From the National Standpoint." In *The Irish Year Book*. The National Council. Dublin: James Duffy; MH Gill; Sealy, Bryers and Walker.
Dixon, William Hepworth. 1862. *Lady Morgan's Memoirs Autobiography, Diaries and Correspondence*. London: W.H. Allen.
Dollard, James. January 4, 1913. "The Gaels of Moondharraig or The Modern Fianna." *Meath Chronicle*.
Drake, Peter. 1755. *The Memoirs of Capt. Peter Drake*. Dublin: S. Powell.
The Dublin Quarterly Journal of Medical Science. 1870. Vol. XLIX, February–May, 1870. Dublin.

The Dublin University Magazine: A Literary and Political Journal, July–December, 1840. Vol. XVI. Dublin. 1840.

Dunton, John, and Andrew Carpenter. 2003. *Teague Land, Or, A Merry Ramble to the Wild Irish (1698)*. Dublin: Four Courts Press.

Elrington Ball, Francis. 1903. *History of Dublin*. Vol. II. Dublin: Alex., Thom.

The GAA Rule Book 1887, 2nd ed. Dublin: A & E Cahill.

Hardy, P. D., ed. 1835. *Dublin Penny Journal, 1833–34*. Dublin: J.S. Folds.

Herbert, J. D. 1836. *Irish Varieties, for the Last Fifty Years: Written from Recollections*. London: W. Joy.

Huggins, Michael. 2001. "The Regular Re-Invention of Sporting Tradition and Identity: Cumberland and Westmorland Wrestling c. 1800–2000." *The Sports Historian* 21: 35–55.

Hunt, Tom. 2007. *Sport and Society in Victorian Ireland: The Case of Westmeath*. Cork: Cork University Press.

Hyde, Douglas. 1905. *Love Songs of Connacht, Being the Fourth Chapter of the Songs of Connacht*. Dublin: Gill & Son.

The Irish Fancy. 1827. *The Portfolio of Entertaining and Instructive Varities in History*. Vol. IV. London: J. Duncombe.

The Japan Weekly Mail. 1891. "Blackwell, AH [Ed]." Vol. 15, pp. 543. http://books.google.ie/books?id=r0oxAQAAMAAJ&q=The+Japan+Weekly+Mail+Collar+and+Elbow+1891&dq=The+Japan+Weekly+Mail+Collar+and+Elbow+1891.

Journal of Manly Arts, March 2003. http://ejmas.com/jmanly/articles/2003/jmanlyart_duformclaughlin_0303.htm

Kelly, James. 2014. *Sport in Ireland 1600–1840*. Dublin: Four Courts Press.

Kettle, L. J., ed. 1958. *The Material for Victory: Being the Memoirs of Andrew J Kettle*. Dublin: CJ Fallon Ltd.

King, Se. 2005. *A History of Hurling*. Dublin: Gill & Macmillan.

Kinnfaela (T.C. McGinley). 1867. *The Cliff Scenery of South-Western Donegal*. Londonderry: Journal Office.

MacDermot, Dermot. 1996. *MacDermot of Moylurg: The Story of a Connacht Family*. Manorhamilton: Drumlin Publications.

MacGeoghan, James (Ed – P O'Kelly). 1832. *History of Ireland: Ancient and Modern, taken from the most Authentic Records*. Vol. III. Dublin: T. O'Flanagan.

MacLeod & Dewar. 1839. *A Dictionary of the Gaelic Language*. Glasgow: W.R. McPhun.

Madden, Richard R. 1857. *The United Irishmen, Their Lives and Times: With Additional Authentic Documents and Numerous Original Portraits. The Whole Matter Newly Arranged and Revised*. Dublin: James Duffy.

McGregor, J. 1821. *New picture of Dublin: Comprehending a History of the City*. Dublin: CP Archer.

Moffet, William (really Walter Jones). 1724. *Hesperi-neso-graphia: or, A description of the Western Isle [viz. Ireland] in Eight Cantos*. Dublin: Carson and Smith.

Nally, TH. 1922. *The Aonac Tailteann and the Tailteann Games: Their Origin, History and Ancient Associations*. Dublin: Talbot Press. 71.

Oakley, Atholl. 1971. *Blue Blood on the Mat: The All-In Wrestling Story*. London: Stanley Paul.

Obi, M. Thomas J. Desch. 2008. *Fighting for Honor: The History of African Martial Art Traditions in the Atlantic World*. Columbia: University of South Carolina Press.

O'Brien, J. 1832. *An Irish-English Dictionary*. 2nd ed. Dublin: Hodges & Co.

O'Casey, Sean. 1954. *Sunset and Evening Star*. London: MacMillian.

O'Reilly, John Boyle. 1888. *Ethics of Boxing and Manly Sport*. Boston: Ticknor and Company.

O'Rourke, Rory, ed. 1825. "'A Sunday Stroll – The Hermit In Ireland, No., I.V." *The Dublin and London Magazine*. London: James Robins & Co.

Owenson, Sydney (Lady Morgan). 1809. *The Wild Irish Girl: A National Tale*. Baltimore: Geo. Dobbin & Murphy.

Poverty Bay Herald, Vol. XXXIV, Issue 11157, December 21 1907, . . . J.W.G., in Argonaut. http://paperspast.natlib.govt.nz/cgi-bin/paperspast?a=d&d=PBH19071221

The Reasoner. 1858. "Volumes 23–24. George Jacob Holyoake." http://books.google.ie/books?id=Jel6AQAAMAAJ&q=The+Reasoner,+1858,+251.+Phoenix+Park

Robinson, J, and Sidney Gilpin. 1893. *North County Sports and Pastimes*. London: Bemrose & Sons.

A Sabbath in Dublin. 1849. *The Christian Treasury*. Vol. 4. Edinburgh, London, Glasgow, Belfast: Johnstone and Hunter. http://books.google.ie/books?id=GDcUAAAAYAAJ&pg=PA77&dq=The+Christian+Treasury+Phoenix+Park+Sabbath

Seamus. 1932. "Irish Wrestling and Wrestlers: A Neglected Native Pastime." *An Caman* 1 (28): 13. Baile Atha Cliath: Comh Coiste na gCumann nGaedhealach.

Stoker, Bram. 1907. *Personal Reminiscences of Henry Irving*. London: Heineman.

Tripp, Michael. 2009. "Persistence of Difference: A History of Cornish Wrestling." Vol. 1. PhD diss., University of Exeter.

Warburton, J., and James Whitelaw. 1818. *History of City of Dublin*. London: Cadell and Davies.

Wilde, William Robert Wills. 1850. *The Beauties of the Boyne and Its Tributary the Blackwater, by William R. Wilde*. Dublin: J. Mc Glashan.

Wilde, Robert W. 1852. *Ireland: Her Wit, Peculiarities, and Popular Superstitions with Anecdotes, Legendary and Characteristic*. Dublin: McGlashan & Gill.

Wilson, Charles Morrow. 1959. *The Magnificent Scufflers: Revealing the Great Days When America Wrestled the World*. Brattleboro: Stephen Greene Press.

The National Athletic Association of Ireland and Irish Athletics, 1922–1937: steps on the road to athletic isolation

Tom Hunt

Social and Sports Historian, Ireland

> The interplay between politics and Irish sport is seldom far from the surface and has often been detrimental to its development. Athletics exhibit this characteristic more than any other sport. A unity of sorts was achieved in 1924 with the final metamorphosis of the National Athletic and Cycling Association of Ireland (NACAI). This unity was not to survive as a range of political interests produced a tripartite institutional split by 1938 that inflicted near terminal damage on the sport and established a type of athletic apartheid as the practitioners of the sport in rural Ireland were deprived of international competition due to their membership of the unrecognized NACAI.

Introduction

The decade of revolution that began in Ireland in 1912 ended with the establishment of the Irish Free State in 1922. The calamitous 11-month Civil War that followed concluded on 24 May 1923 (Hopkinson 2004, 34). The establishment of the Irish Free State effectively completed the partition of Ireland as the Government of Ireland Act (1920) had already established the Northern Ireland state. Ireland was now divided into two political units: the 26-county Irish Free State, a self-governing dominion of the British Empire with the same constitutional status as Canada, and the 6-county semi-autonomous Northern Ireland, which remained within the UK (Buckland 1981, 20 and 21; Fanning 2013, 1–3).

The new political landscape had implications for the federations responsible for the management of Irish sport that was organized on an all-island basis prior to 1922. Their responsibilities now covered two political jurisdictions and they had to deal with two separate government authorities and cope with the difficulties associated with combining unionists and nationalists in the same body. Unity was maintained in some federations only by considerable compromise as issues of political symbolism were tailored to accommodate diverse political and cultural backgrounds. Rugby football was a game that attracted a broad cultural constituency in Ireland (O'Callaghan 2011, 29–64). This placed the Irish Rugby Football Union (IRFU) in an invidious position regarding the use of national symbols and ceremony, as a significant section of the country's rugby membership was drawn from Northern Ireland's Protestant and unionist community. The bar on Sunday rugby was continued and the playing of international matches was alternated between Belfast and Dublin. In 1925, the IRFU adopted a neutral flag carrying the emblems of the four provinces to be flown at all international matches played in Ireland. This decision was made to avoid potential controversy caused by the flying of the Union Jack at matches in Belfast and the tricolour in Dublin. This policy continued until 1932 when the IRFU was challenged by Paddy McGilligan, the Minister for External Affairs, at a time when Munster and Connacht clubs expressed disquiet at the flag policy and the *Irish Press* newspaper gave extensive coverage to the issue (Morris, 2005, 190, 193). The Golfing Union of Ireland also adopted the flag of the four provinces as did the Irish Hockey Union (*Irish Times*, September 20, 1928, June 22, 1929). The latter body used the *Londonderry Air* as its anthem and the men's branch of the IHU refrained from entering the Olympic Games qualifying competition until the Barcelona quadrennial to avoid division.

Irish partition also had implications for the international federations who dealt with the new political reality. Their decisions in turn had sometimes a dramatic impact on the national federations. There was no consistency in how international federations managed the change. The most diligent was the *Fédération Internationale de Football Association* (FIFA). The Irish Football Association, established in 1880, split prior to partition as a result of long-standing political, organizational, and cultural differences between the Belfast and Dublin strongholds of the game. The breakaway Football Association of Ireland (FAI) was established on 2 September 1921. This was planned as an all-Ireland body and its affiliates included the Falls League in Belfast. Recognition of the new association by FIFA came 2 years after its foundation and was only possible because of partition. At FIFA's first postwar congress, held in Geneva in May 1923, its Emergency Committee was delegated to ascertain whether the Irish Free State possessed the political status claimed and to determine whether the FAI 'conformed to the principles laid down for national associations'. The association was admitted to membership on 1 September following FIFA consultation with the British Foreign Office on the constitutional status of the Irish state. The newly designated Football Association of the Irish Free State (FAIFS) was now free to take its place on the international stage (*Irish Times*, May 26, 1923, Lanfanchi et al. 2004, 64–68; Garnham 2004, 181).

The International Olympic Committee (IOC) admitted J. J. Keane as the member in Ireland in June 1922 without defining the unit he represented. An attempt by Colonel Reginald Kentish to debate the issue was prevented as it introduced politics to the discussion (McCarthy 2010, 305–315). The implications of this decision only emerged in 1934 when the IOC attempted to limit Irish Olympic selections to the territory of the Irish Free State. This was fiercely resisted by the Irish Olympic Council from 1935 to 1956 and inspired the decision not to compete at the Berlin Games in 1936. Irish Olympic officials eventually secured the right to select Irish nationals, regardless of their place of residence, as well as the right to be recognized as Ireland for Olympic competition.[1] The International Amateur Athletic Federation (IAAF) and the *Union Cycliste Internationale* (UCI) initially recognized the National Athletic and Cycling Association of Ireland (NACAI) as the governing body for their sports in Ireland without exercising any FIFA-type diligence.

This article examines how athletics adjusted to the new political order and explores how a single controlling body, the NACAI, split into three separate institutions over a 15-year period between 1922 and 1937. Historical analysis of this development has been mainly from the Irish perspective; this article takes a broader focus with the international dimension explored and the positions and involvement of Northern Ireland and British officials and politicians considered.

J. J. Keane engineers a fragile unity

J. J. Keane was the architect of the fragile unity achieved by the establishment of the NACAI as the single controlling body for athletics and cycling on the island in 1922. The Gaelic Athletic Association (GAA) and the Irish Amateur Athletic Association (IAAA) controlled Irish athletics between 1884 and 1922. The nationalist GAA embraced rural and urban Ireland, promoted Sunday sport and placed special emphasis on weight throwing and jumping. The politically more inclusive IAAA had its power-base in Dublin and a less significance presence in Belfast and Cork. Sunday track and field meets were rigorously proscribed by the IAAA, a constraint that inevitably limited its influence in rural Ireland and its class appeal. Cooperation between the two bodies effectively ended in 1906 (O'Donoghue, n.d., 6). Neither the GAA nor the IAAA were recognized by the IAAF. The United Kingdom of Great Britain and Ireland was admitted to membership of the IAAF at its inaugural meeting held in Berlin in August 1913 with the Amateur Athletic Association (AAA) the recognized authority (*Spalding's Athletic Library* 1914, 23, 26). The IAAA was essentially a subcommittee of the AAA, responsible for managing athletics on the island of Ireland. In the early months of 1922, Keane persuaded the GAA to abandon its nominal interest in athletics; he also worked closely with Dr Robert Rowlette (President of the IAAA, 1908–1920) who played the lead-role in encouraging the IAAA to also disband. However institutional unity was not immediate. British soldiers, navy-men or police on active service in Ireland were initially ineligible for membership of the NACAI (Mandle 1987, 205). As a result, a number of mainly Belfast-based clubs formed the Amateur Athletic Association of Ireland to cater for those who refused to join the NACAI (*Irish Times*, August 5, 1922). In May 1923, at the general meeting of the central executive council of the NACAI, Keane successfully proposed the removal of the exclusion rule and in doing so exhibited a pragmatism seldom recognized by historians (*Irish Times*, May 11, 1923). Intense negotiations between the interested parties in Northern Ireland and the NACAI concluded with a conference held on 2 February 1924 when it was unanimously agreed that the various Northern Ireland bodies would recommend that their clubs joined the NACAI (Griffin 1990, 68–72). The agreements were ratified at the first congress of the NACAI. All amateur athletes resident in Ireland, irrespective of creed, class or occupation, were now eligible for membership of the NACAI; it was also agreed to stage the national championships in alternative years on Saturdays and Sundays as far as possible (*Irish Times*, May 12, 1924). For the first time since 1885, the control of athletics and cycling in Ireland was vested in a single body. International recognition was approved by the council of the IAAF in January 1924 and confirmed at its Congress in Paris on 4 July 1924 (IAAF (International Amateur Athletic Federation) 1926, 28). The AAA apparently had no difficulty with this development and no objection was made to the decision.

Ireland played an active role in the IAAF after membership was granted. NACAI delegates attended the federation's annual congresses, contributed to debates and were appointed to sub-committees. For instance, J. J. Keane and Dr Rowlette contributed to the debate at which it was decided to remove the 10,000-m walk, the 5000-m cross country race, the 3000-m team race and the pentathlon from the Olympic programme (IAAF (International Amateur Athletic Federation) 1926, 42 and 43). Keane also argued that the Irish version of handball should be placed under the jurisdiction of the IAAF and Sean O'Hanlon was nominated as a member of the subcommittee formed to examine the issue (IAAF (International Amateur Athletic Federation) 1926, 84 and 85, 95). In 1924, the NACAI organized the Ireland team that competed in the triangular series with England and Scotland for the first time. The series continued without interruption until 12 July 1930 when the last event was held at Crewe (Murphy and Murphy, 2013, 98–150). NACAI athletes were also included on the Ireland team that competed in the 1924, 1928 and 1932 Olympic Games. It is clear from this abbreviated summary that Ireland as a 32 county entity was a fully integrated member of the international athletics community, and for most of the 1920s, the AAA had no difficulty with this position.

Membership of the IAAF brought with it certain responsibilities and when the executive of the NACAI implemented IAAF regulations, it initiated a series of events that ended with the suspension of the association. The crisis was precipitated by an event organized by Belfast Celtic Football Club, the great sports' institution of nationalist west-Belfast. The new northern state was born in violence and in the early 1920s Belfast was immersed in a sectarian conflict that was bloody and vicious. The numbers killed in Belfast alone from 1920 to 1922 reached nearly 500 with over 2500 injured. The victims were mostly civilians, innocent and vulnerable targets on both sides of the sectarian divide, although Catholics suffered disproportionately. IRA actions, loyalist violence, and violence by state forces all played their part (English 2007, 314 and 315). The annual carnival promoted by Belfast Celtic with its combination of whippet racing, pony trotting, boxing, cycling and athletics provided an oasis of normality in the strife-torn city. These carnivals flourished during the early 1920s (Coyle 1999, 41–46; Flynn 2009, 90–103).

On Easter Monday 1925, Belfast Celtic, a limited company with a policy of promoting cycling and athletics enshrined in its Articles of Association, organized its annual athletic sports with a whippet handicap and an open trotting handicap as part of the programme (Coyle, 51). The Ulster Council of the NACAI, but not the associations Central Council, granted Belfast Celtic the necessary permit to hold the meeting. NACAI officials were now obliged to enforce international regulations and ensure the amateur purity of all licenced sports meetings. Clubs were informed that the rules forbidding betting at athletics meetings were to be rigidly enforced. Dog and pony races were not permitted and members of professional clubs were ineligible for membership of the NACAI.[2] J. J. Keane informed 'the members of the Committee and everyone connected with the affair' of their automatic suspension through an interview in the *Belfast Telegraph*. Another period of intense negotiations concluded with the lifting of suspensions on condition that no permits were issued by anybody in Ulster and that those issued be withdrawn (Griffin 1990, 76 and 77).

'All the elements of a first class split are in place (*Irish Times*, May 23, 1925)'

The fault lines for the future institutional development of Irish athletics were established at the NACAI congress held in Jury's Hotel on 17 May 1925. Only the six northern delegates, all from the Antrim-Down region, supported a motion seeking to abolish the rule prohibiting betting and gambling at sports meetings. This was a problem not of J. J. Keane's making and neither Keane nor his fellow officers were in any position to compromise on this issue. They were now responsible for the implementation of the IAAF's regulations. Keane informed the delegates that the 'rule regarding amateurism must be kept'; Dr Rowlette made it cleat that they 'were up against hard and fast IAAF rules'. After losing the vote, the Ulster delegates withdrew from the meeting (*Irish Times*, May 18, 1925). Events now moved quickly along a path to separation. In July 1925, the Northern Ireland Amateur Athletics, Cycling and Cross-Country Association (NIAACCA) was founded under the presidency of Thomas Moles MP, at a meeting held in the Belfast Celtic headquarters in Celtic Park. In September, the split was solidified when the Belfast county board of the NACAI disbanded and transferred its assets to the new northern association (*Irish Times*, 11, 25 July, September 17, 1924; Coyle, 51). The split was essentially on non-sectarian lines with clubs such as Queens' University, Willowfield, North Belfast Harriers and the RUC (Belfast) opting to remain within the NACAI fold.[3]

However, what was to this point a domestic dispute soon took on an international dimension and became politicized. Unionist-minded administrators and Northern Ireland politicians used the opportunity to pursue their agenda of separate recognition for Northern Ireland in sport. It soon became clear that when J. J. Keane attempted to establish a unifying body for Irish athletics he was attempting the impossible. As Richard English has pointed out (317) the Irish Revolution, apart from being a struggle between Ireland and Britain, was also a struggle between the Irish people themselves. Keane's attempt to achieve a grand coalition of disparate groups in the interest of Irish athletics was doomed to failure. An umbrella group capable of coalescing nationalist and unionist, republican and Home Ruler, pro-Treaty and anti-Treaty men, IRA and RUC as well as those engaged in the promotion of amateur and professional sport had yet to be designed. Fracturing was the inevitable result when issues of principle emerged. The NACAI's standing as a newly founded organization added to its vulnerability. Officials from disparate political backgrounds had no experience of working together in the common cause of athletic promotion, there was no tradition of tolerance or compromise established between those of opposite ideological perspectives and the mission to promote athletics was replaced by a battle for the control of the sport. National federations with a long-term history (with the notable exception of football) continued to manage their sports on an all-island basis in post-partition Ireland.

The NIAACCA failed to gain recognition from the AAA but that body did suggest a meeting between itself, the NACAI and the new northern association. This suggestion was rejected at the NACAI congress of 1926 (*Irish Times*, May 24, 1926). In October 1929, a request made to the Scottish AAA by the northern association for recognition was discussed at a meeting of the representatives of the home nations held at Crewe. A resolution was adopted inviting both Irish associations 'to meet to consider the formation of a new association to govern athletics in the six northern counties, with a joint council, composed of the National Athletic and Cycling Association and the new Northern body to promote All-Ireland championships, select All-Ireland teams, and control all matters of a national character (*Irish Times*, October 7, 1929; Reynolds 2008, 26–28). This chaotic meeting, which solidified divisions and enhanced mutual suspicions, was held in Dundalk on 14 December 1929 under the chairmanship of George Hume, secretary of the Scottish AAA (*Irish Times*, December 16, 1929). Eoin O'Duffy, later explained that 'the NACA could not forego its authority and the rules already gave such a wide measure of autonomy to the Ulster Council that no practical suggestions could be made for improving them in this respect'.[4] It was eventually decided that the Ulster Council of the NACAI and the northern association would jointly call a meeting of all northern athletic clubs to explore the formation of the new association as suggested at Crewe. The meeting took place on 30 December 1929 with Queen's University the only NACAI club represented and the outcome was not what was initially intended. A new approach was adopted to the quest for international recognition. It was unanimously decided to form a northern branch of the AAA (NIAAA). Walter Marrs explained the rationale for such an intervention.

> We will have the fullest international recognition that any country can possess. We will be surrounded and supported by the full authority, prestige and powerful influence of the AAA and the NCU, and we shall be masters of our own household, having our own autonomy.

This was approved by the general committee of the AAA on 15 February 1930 (subject to the approval of the AAA general meeting scheduled for April). At this stage, the UCI had decided that Northern Ireland was within the jurisdiction of the British National Cyclists' Union. The affiliation of Great Britain to the IAAF was now defined to mean the affiliation of the United Kingdom of Great Britain and Northern Ireland and the jurisdiction of the AAA was extended to the counties that formed the Northern Ireland state. The jurisdiction of the NACAI, as far as the AAA was concerned, was limited to the 'area known as the Irish Free State' and it delegated to the new northern body 'full powers to control amateur athletics in the area known as Northern Ireland'. The AAA officers were still anxious to see both bodies united for international purposes and 'recommended that a joint body of representatives from both associations' be formed to explore that possibility. It was also agreed that if both associations in the future expressed a unified wish to 'participate in all international competitions as a unified geographic whole, the AAA will use every endeavour to secure that the International Olympic Committee should recognize such a unity for the purpose of international competitions'. The resolutions were passed by a large majority at the annual meeting of the AAA held on 5 April 1930. A few days later the NIAAA were informed of their status as the sole governing body for athletics and cycling in Northern Ireland (Reynolds 2008, 28–30; *Irish Times*, February 17, 1930; Griffin 1990, 90, 100 and 101).

Recent research by Dónal McAnallen has revealed that these decisions were made after considerable lobbying by Northern Ireland political figures, some of which had taken place prior to the meeting at Crewe. The lobbyist-in-chief was Sir Richard Dawson Bates 'a man who knew the mind of Ulster better than almost anyone else' according to Sir James Craig. As Minister for Home Affairs, Bates was one of the leading architects of the Northern Ireland state but one with a deep distrust of the nationalist community. His responsibilities included electoral affairs, local government and law and order. In the words of Patrick Buckland (1981, 23–33), he was 'a small man physically and intellectually, [he] was unable to give such questions the careful and sympathetic handling they so urgently required, particularly since he looked upon all Catholics as nationalists and all nationalists not just as political enemies but as traitors'. In Donal McAnallen's opinion (2010, 169) 'the Northern Ireland cabinet played 'a crucial and quite covert role in enforcing the partition of Irish athletics'. Implementing might also be an appropriate term as athletics was effectively partitioned at this time; all that was needed to validate the reality was the creation of an institutional framework to cater for the respective positions. On 16 May 1929, Bates, following an approach by officials of the NIAAA, contacted Harry Barclay, secretary of the AAA, to elicit support for the 'very considerable justification' of the claim made for independent recognition and for its desire 'to work under the auspices of the British association'. Bates explained that 'under present political conditions' there were 'two associations of comparatively equivalent standards, one in Northern Ireland and the other in the Irish Free State'; 'Northern Ireland politically, socially and economically is more closely allied to Great Britain than to the Irish Free State'. He claimed that it was in the interest of sport as a whole that clubs were allowed to hold events under Northern Ireland auspices 'closely related to, allied to or affiliated with the British parent organisation'. Bates found it particularly frustrating that RUC and Army athletes could not compete in Northern Ireland without the risk of incurring suspension as he had 'by every means possible been endeavouring to encourage athletics and athletic events among the members of the RUC'.[5]

In February 1930, Hugh Pollock, the acting Prime Minister of Northern Ireland, prompted by Thomas Moles MP, also contacted Barclay and gave his full support to the application. Pollock requested that the AAA 'accede to their request as soon as may be convenient' in the 'best interests of sport'. He also offered to make representations to the IAAF if it was thought 'advisable' as similar representations had been successfully made to the UCI, 'at the instance of the [British] National Cyclists' Union' prior to the Zurich conference which recognized the Northern Ireland federation as a branch of the British cycling body.[6] Barclay's response was non-committal; the matter would be discussed by the association's general committee; the AAA was 'most anxious for a settlement of this question one way or the other'.[7] Prior to the AAA meeting, Lord Craigavon (Sir James Craig) returned from New Zealand and resumed his duties as Prime Minister of Northern Ireland. He contacted Lord Desborough to thank him for 'promising to do what you can' to support the efforts to affiliate to the English AAA 'which will be a great boon to us here'. He emphasized the 'anxiety of the Ulster people to be treated on exactly the same lines as the rest of the United Kingdom of which we are so proud to be a part'. Couched in these terms, Desborough could hardly ignore a request from someone of Lord Craigavon's standing within the UK and in his response promised to do his best to keep the AAA 'up to the mark'. He then made immediate contact with Barclay.[8]

Lord Desborough was the incoming president of the AAA and a powerful recruit to the Northern Ireland cause. William Grenfell, born in 1855 and educated at Harrow and Oxford, was an exceptional all-round sportsman as a young man and, like many of his class, an intrepid adventurer. His record as a sports' administrator and politician was equally comprehensive. He was first elected to the House of Commons as a Gladstonian Liberal but resigned in 1893 rather than support Gladstone's home rule policy but was returned to parliament in 1900 as a Conservative Party member. He was raised to the peerage in 1905. He was a founding member and first president of the British Olympic Association (BOA), a member of the IOC (1906–1913) and the inspiration behind the staging of the 1908 Olympic Games in London. He was also president of the Amateur Fencing Association, the MCC, the National Amateur Wrestling Association and the Lawn Tennis Association at different stages of an extraordinary career in sport (Lovesey 1979, 91). Although 74 when he became president of the AAA, he played an active part in the affairs of the organization.

'Police are not children'

The association of the RUC club with the NACAI was totally unacceptable to Richard Bates who was directly responsible for policing in Northern Ireland. He now intervened and pressurized the RUC to discontinue this relationship. On 2 July 1929, Bates contacted the Inspector General of the RUC, Sir Charles Wickham, after the Governor-General of the Irish Free State, James McNeill, declined to attend the annual Trinity College sports in protest against the traditional playing of *God save the king* at the conclusion of the event. McNeill was not the only one missing during Trinity Week. A number of teams withdrew from subsequent events possibly because their clubs included soldiers or Gardai who could not participate while the anthem dispute remained unresolved. Ten of the 13 crews entered for the Trinity Regatta withdrew and only two clubs competed in the Trinity Swimming Gala (Morris 2005, 80; West 1991, 68; *Irish Independent*, June 12, 1929; *Cork Examiner*, June 15, 1929). The incident generated considerable newspaper debate with unionist comment being particularly vitriolic (Morris, 83–89). The episode Bates argued 'brought matters to a head in regard to the position of the Northern Ireland Amateur Athletic Association'. Because of the 'new circumstances and spirit that have arisen' Bates requested that 'pending the recognition of the Ulster Association' no further events would be organized under Dublin control. Wickham was also requested to ensure that where events were already organized under the auspices of the Dublin association 'that the Union Jack is the dominant flag flown, and that the British National Anthem only is to be played'. Wickham was ordered

> to prohibit any members of the Force from taking part, even in their individual capacity, in events under circumstances which might place them in position of being mistaken for representatives of the Irish Free State, or where the Free State flag is flown or the "Soldier's Song" sung.[9]

Wickham was not convinced. The Yorkshire-born police officer, who served in the Boer War, First World War and with the British military mission against the Bolsheviks in Siberia, brought the perspective of an outsider to the issue. He was appointed the divisional commander of the RIC in Ulster in 1920 and in June 1922 became the inspector general of the RUC (Long 2009a, 921 and 922). Wickham resented 'the wholly unjustifiable and uncalled for reflection' by Bates and in his response exposed the inconsistencies and class bias inherent in the proposal. The notion that the RUC should not take part in any meetings at which the tricolour was displayed or the Irish national anthem played was challenged. Nobody had seriously suggested that northern owners should cease to race their horses at the Curragh or compete in the RDS in show jumping or that rugby footballers should cease to play in Dublin because the Free State anthem or emblem were evident. Neither was it suggested that northern race meetings should no longer be held under Turf Club or Irish National Hunt Steeplechase Committee rules (these were the bodies that controlled Irish racing on an all-island basis). If the RUC club disaffiliated from the NACAI members of the force would be ineligible to participate in any sports meeting of any importance in Great Britain or Ireland. Other clubs and individuals would also be debarred from competing against the RUC club, its members or in its annual sports. Wickham firmly rejected the suggestion by Bates that he should issue orders prohibiting members of the force from competing in any meeting where the tricolour was flown or the 'Soldiers' Song' played. 'Orders', Wickham stressed,

> mean that failure to comply involves a disciplinary offence. I could be no party to any such order. It would be an unwarranted interference with the liberties of the men ... I can imagine no sane man preferring a discipline charge against a member of the R.U.C. for taking part in a Championship meeting in Dublin ... where he took first prize defeating representatives of H.M. Army.[10]

Wickham also contacted C. H. Blackmore, the secretary of the Northern Ireland cabinet, and pointed out that the only grounds on which an objection could be made to the existing system was on the principle that the Irish Free State was now a separate Dominion and it 'was illogical and perhaps unconstitutional that the control of athletics in that Dominion should extend into an area which is no part of it'. However this argument could not be confined to any one sport without 'admitting that you are taking sides in a quarrel largely personal' and 'without laying yourself open to the accusation that your action is at the behest of the [Belfast] *Evening Telegraph*'. A principled challenge extended to all sports would run the risk of Northern Ireland 'becoming only a third class power in the field of sport'.[11] Despite the warnings, the basic position of the Northern Ireland ministers remained unaltered. While Pollock was not in favour of the prohibition of RUC officers participating in the various talks taking place, he considered it 'desirable for the RUC to remain outside the present discussions'.[12] As a result, Bates once again instructed Wickham that 'under no circumstances' was the RUC to continue to engage in the discussions.[13]

'We must live up to modern time'

It was now the turn of the NACAI officers to move their case to the international stage. They appealed to the IAAF for protection from what was interpreted as AAA interference. The IAAF's regulations required that affiliated federations 'shall acknowledge each other as the only legislative authorities for athletes in their respective countries and the only organization authorized to regulate international agreements in athletics' (IAAF (International Amateur Athletic Federation) 1926, 24). J. J. Keane personally contacted the IAAF president, Siegfried Edström, arguably the most powerful administrator in world sport, and explained the position in great detail. Edström was the founding father of the IAAF in 1912 and its only president until he resigned in 1946 to become the president of the IOC. His response should have alerted NACAI officials to the futility of pursuing their principled championing of a 32 county body to control athletics in Ireland. 'I cannot agree with you', Edström informed Keane,

> your association governs the Irish part of Ireland. The inhabitants of Ulster (sic) belong to the English nation therefore the English governing body will take charge there. Formerly your association governed all Ireland, but since the formation of the Irish Free State things have been different and we must live up to modern time.

The belief that athletic boundaries and political boundaries should coincide became one of Edström's cherished principles. Tom Ferguson, secretary of the NACAI's Ulster Council, was also informed by Edström that 'it is quite clear to my mind that the NACAI can only govern athletics within the Free State'.[14]

On 15 December 1930, the NACAI lodged an official protest with the IAAF against the interference by the AAA with its jurisdiction in Northern Ireland and a special council meeting of the IAAF was held in London on 26 and 27 May 1931 to consider the matter. Edström chaired the meeting that was also attended by IAAF secretary Bo Ekelund as well as the Hungarian, French and UK (Harry J Barclay) members. Edström made it clear that it was planned to finally decide the issue at the meeting. This must have terrified the members of the Irish delegation for a settlement on Edström's political boundary line was totally unacceptable and would have threatened the NACAI's future participation in international competition.

Prior to the London meeting, Lord Desborough called to the Home Office on 15 May 1931 with a copy of the statement prepared by Harold Abrahams for 'official confirmation' of the case Abrahams planned to present. Desborough explained that it 'was really a matter for settlement by agreement between the athletic associations concerned' and understood that the officials could not act in a judicial capacity in settling the matter. In a later correspondence (19 May) with the officials, Desborough pointed out that the IAAF council members would have to be 'instructed as to the legal rights and wrongs as long as north and south will not join together of their own free will'. Desborough also organized a meeting between Abrahams and the Home Office officials. Abrahams called to the offices on 20 May and 'after a most interesting discussion' ambiguities in the use of the word Ireland arising from its meanings in the geographical and the political context were clarified after Home Office officials consulted with officers in the Dominions Office. The task proved to be complicated and required more alternations 'than appeared necessary at the first sight' but their combined efforts produced 'a statement of the facts which cannot be questioned'. Part of Abrahams' rephrased statement now read: 'As a single political unit there is no such country today as Ireland, and in claiming to control Ireland the NACAI did not call the attention of the IAAF to the fact that the unit they claimed to represent had since 1922 been divided into the Irish Free State and Northern Ireland'. The officials also produced a more exact explanation of the Anglo-Irish Treaty of 1921 in its use of the word Ireland and replaced 'country' with 'unit' in the three paragraphs that were altered.[15]

O'Duffy and Harold Abrahams presented the case on behalf of their respective federations (Lovesey 1979, 175–177).[16] Abrahams provided a detailed analysis of the legislation that established the Irish Free State as a 'co-equal member of the Community of Nations forming the British Commonwealth of Nations' and explained that Northern

Ireland was an integral part of the UK. Ireland as a political and constitutional entity did not exist. The affiliation of the NACAI to the IAAF was also outlined by Abrahams. This was made at a time when the AAA was affiliated to the IAAF as the body responsible for the government of athletics in the United Kingdom of Great Britain and Ireland; 'for the purpose of internal management only' the Scottish and the Irish Amateur Athletic Associations were responsible for athletics in Scotland and Ireland. Abrahams argued that the crucial issue at stake for the IAAF was to determine 'what territory was taken out of the jurisdiction of the Amateur Athletic Association by the affiliation of the NACAI'. The only point at issue was to what extent the jurisdiction of the AAA over Ireland had been modified.

O'Duffy presented a comprehensive statement of the NACAI case that ranged through the Government of Ireland Act of 1920, the concept of dominion status, the organization of Irish sport and the constitution of the IAAF which guaranteed 'that no one member can limit the jurisdiction of any other member'. O'Duffy achieved an important victory when he succeeded in persuading the council members that only an IAAF congress could decide on an alteration of the jurisdiction of the NACAI and the council members, in a private session, decided to refer the protest to the congress scheduled for Los Angeles in 1932. The NACAI and the AAA were requested to establish a joint commission under a neutral chairman to decide on all pending questions relating to disqualifications, suspensions and Olympic Games entry (*Irish Independent*, May 30, 1931; *Irish Times*, May 31, 1931).

The NACAI accepted this decision on the basis that participation would not in interfere with its national status and O'Duffy and Rowlette represented the NACAI when the commission met in London on 24 November 1931.[17] It was agreed that both associations would carry on without prejudice to the claims of either party during the period before the next congress. Athletes could not change their affiliation during this period and the fixtures of the rival bodies would receive sanction from each other; suspended athletes had their suspensions rescinded and athletes could legally take part in the meets of either association. The AAA agreed not to raise any objections to Ireland competing as a geographic unit in the Los Angeles Olympic Games. Most importantly, a council was to be established consisting of representatives of both organizations to seek a permanent settlement (*Irish Times*, November 28, 1931).[18]

Eoin O'Duffy now accepted that an IAAF solution would most likely confine the NACAI's jurisdiction to the territory of the Irish Free State and the necessity for a negotiated settlement with the northern association became a priority. According to his own account, O'Duffy and Douglas Lowe (newly elected secretary of the AAA) 'were in constant communication and always in the friendliest way'. O'Duffy used Lowe's influence to organize the northern body to attend a conference to explore the possibility of a permanent settlement.[19] O'Duffy came prepared to compromise when delegates from both associations engaged in conclave in Belfast on 6 January and 22 January with O'Duffy and Thomas Moles leading the respective delegations.

O' Duffy was the chief sports' evangelist of the Irish revolutionary generation. Outside of his work, as Commissioner of *An Garda Síochána* most of his time was devoted to the promotion of sport. He was elected president of the NACAI on 19 January 1931 and then president of the Irish Olympic Council on 10 October; without his influence and energy it is possible that Ireland would not have been represented at Los Angeles. O'Duffy immersed himself in his new positions with missionary zeal as he preached his 'gospel of national virility' the length and breadth of the country (Long 2009a, 432–434; McGarry 2007, 141–169). O'Duffy, the pragmatic nationalist and Moles, the dogmatic unionist, shared several characteristics with the latter in many ways the Northern Ireland equivalent of Eoin O'Duffy. Politically active and committed to the unionist cause, a sports fanatic, a superb propagandist and the chief advocate of separate federations to manage sport in Northern Ireland, he was a member of Edward Carson's 'inner cabinet' in the anti-home rule campaign and was the leading propagandist of the unionist cause as a columnist, letter writer and pamphleteer. He was elected to the Westminster parliament in 1918 and he remained an MP until 1929. Apart from athletics his sporting interest embraced cycling, football, boxing and shooting and he held positions on the governing bodies of five different sports. He also had a long association with the Masonic order, was prominently identified with the Orange Order and was a member of the Walker Club apprentice boys of Derry (Bryson 2009, 546 and 547).

Remarkably it was agreed to recommend the establishment of autonomous bodies in the Irish Free State and Northern Ireland that would unite to form a single 12-member authority, the Irish Amateur Athletic Union (IAAU) to manage national and international events. At a third conference held in the Grand Central Hotel in Belfast on 28 February 1932, it was unanimously agreed that a flag depicting the arms of the four provinces on a field of 'St Patrick's blue' with a central crest bearing the letters IAAU, would be flown at international events. The tricolour would be flown at events held in the Irish Free State with the flag flown at Northern Ireland events to be the choice of the northern federation. The question of the flag used in the Olympic Games was a matter for the members of the Irish Olympic Council (*Irish Times*, February 29, 1929). O'Duffy outmanoeuvred Moles on this issue as the tricolour was the chosen Olympic flag and this was a non-negotiable issue. The proposals were discussed at a special congress of the NACAI held at the Dolphin Hotel in Dublin on 3 April 1932. O'Duffy (at this stage in a state of temporary resignation as president of the NACAI) in a letter to the delegates urged that the matter be approached in 'a calm, impersonal and dispassionate manner'. He warned that if the NACAI was deprived of international recognition, its athletes and cyclists would be condemned to athletic isolation.

> There will be in the Six-County area a branch of the English Association whose members will have international privileges, and at whose sports meeting athletes from abroad may compete. I believe the NACA would not long survive under such circumstances. If the NACA and its supporters all over Ireland desire to be cut-off from the rest of the athletic world, then we need not trouble further about flags, boundaries or anything else. The Irish Free State as such will have international recognition without question, but the NACA will not be allowed to draw on a single athlete outside the territory ... You are either for isolation or you are not. No amount of bluff or empty platitudes can evade this issue. (*Irish Times*, April 4, 1932)

The delegates with a few notable exceptions ignored O'Duffy's appalling athletic-vista. Peter O'Connor, the Olympic triple jump champion of 1906, urged the delegates to make concessions 'to prevent disunion that would set Irish athletics back into the wilderness for another twenty years'. They were 'up against a stone wall': 'In the North they loved their Union Jack and in the South they hated it'.[20] Mr Briggs, a delegate from County Down also pointed out the obvious: 'The tricolour was obnoxious to some persons in the north and from experience he knew that the Union Jack was equally obnoxious to others' and: 'for a satisfactory settlement, the Union Jack and the Tricolour would have to go and they would have to have a flag that would satisfy all factions'. Dr Eamonn O'Sullivan was the chief spokesman for the uncompromising majority; 'It was their duty as a national body to recognise the national flag and a compromise flag was only worthy of an organisation that was prepared to compromise itself'. The proposed settlement 'would irrevocably split the association and it would renew divisions in existence before 1922 ... No matter what they might lose internationally regarding this northern crux, their first duty was to the nation'. Dr Sean Lavan, who represented Ireland in the 1924 and 1928 Olympic Games, was absolute in his rejection of the proposed settlement. He would 'rather have the twenty-six counties cut-off in loyalty to a thing that the majority of the people were loyal to than go selling a thing that was hard won' (*Irish Press*, April 4, 1932).

This congress was arguably the most important in the association's history. O'Duffy's flexibility and pragmatic anti-partitionism was thwarted by those who valued sovereignty (McGarry 2007, 153). The delegates approved by a margin of 41-6 of the agreement 'as set out in the proposals agreed by the Belfast Conferences, *with the proviso that the flag to be used for all international purposes to be the Tricolour* [author's italics] '. Unfortunately this was not the agreement negotiated in Belfast. No vote was taken on the flag issue as it was clear that the proposal would be beaten by a large majority. Athletic division and ultimately international isolation was the inevitable result of this decision. O'Duffy's post-Congress ambivalence destroyed any possibility of reopening talks with the NIAAA. He claimed that it was not possible to draw a distinction between Olympic and other international contests and therefore if the tricolour was used for the Olympic Games, its use was also essential for all international contests. The central council of the NACAI decided in June that no useful purpose would be served by convening another congress to discuss the flag issue. The dispute was now headed for the IAAF congress scheduled for Los Angeles in August (Reynolds 2008, 35–39; *Irish Press*, May 3, 1932; *Irish Times*, June 6, 1932). Several Belfast clubs severed their connection with the Ulster Council of the NACAI after the Dublin decision to reject the flag compromise (Griffin 1990, 117).[21]

The 'protest from the NACAI against the AAA of Great Britain concerning questions in Northern Ireland' formed Section 20 of the agenda at the IAAF Congress held on 8 August in Los Angeles. Sigfrid Edström explained that due to the complicated nature of the issues both associations had been invited to make written statements of their views, which were then circulated to all members of the IAAF. He was satisfied that all those present had studied the documents carefully. After enjoying a feast of athletics at the Olympic Games, the delegates decided that this was not an issue that captured their interests. Captain Baran (Poland) proposed that this issue was 'merely a political affair' and should not be discussed. This was immediately challenged by O'Duffy who now recognized the essential weakness of the NACAI's position. He clutched at his final straw but Edström rejected his claim that decisions of congresses were not subject to review unless circumstances had changed since the original decision was taken. The president rightly ruled that each congress was individually supreme. Captain Baran's proposal was carried by 12 votes to 6; Finland, France, Haiti, Mexico and Switzerland supported Ireland (or in some instances voted against the IAAF) when the vote was taken (IAAF 1934, 46–48).

Two months later, on 29 October 1932, events moved towards their inevitable conclusion when representatives of the AAA, the Scottish AAA and the Northern Ireland AAA approved an agreement drafted by Harold Abrahams and Douglas Lowe that established a single International Board to represent the three separate associations of the UK. Apart from dealing with the Northern Ireland difficulty, this agreement also provided a solution to what had become the Scottish problem for the AAA. After 1930, England withdrew from the triangular international series and Scotland applied to the IAAF for separate recognition. This new departure satisfied Scottish requirements and their application to the IAAF was withdrawn (Lovesey 1979, 67). In early 1933, the IAAF's council accepted this body as a replacement for the AAA. Subject to the approval of the IAAF congress this board was now the sole authority over athletics in Great Britain and Northern Ireland.

The decisions that ratified the new arrangement were made at the twelfth congress of the IAAF held in Stockholm on the 28 and 29 August 1934. The president of the IAAF, Sigfrid Edström arrived at the congress with the solution to the Irish problem. An attempt by NACAI officials to secure government support prior to the event was met with a lukewarm response. On 16 July 1934, the Irish ambassador at Washington was requested 'to do what he could on behalf of the NACA' in connection with the dispute. The president of the Executive Council of the Irish Free State and minister for external affairs, Eamon de Valera instructed that any action taken was to be 'purely unofficial'; the 'Minister Plenipotentiary' was not to appear to express the views of the government as to the position of Northern Ireland; 'he [the Minister] has promised his support to the Committee (NACAI) with a certain reluctance as he thinks that any intervention of the Government would probably be a hindrance rather than a help'.[22] Edström's plan was devised by the members of the IAAF council and simply required the approval of the delegates for the council's interpretation of Rule 1 of the IAAF's by-laws. Under the existing by-law, membership of the IAAF was confined to the athletic governing body of each country 'accepting the rules and regulations of the IAAF'; in addition, only a single association was entitled to represent a nation. The council members proposed an interpretation of this by-law based on a dictionary definition a country as 'a land under a particular sovereignty or government'. The corollary therefore was that *the jurisdiction of members of the IAAF is limited by the political boundaries of the country or nation they represent* (IAAF 1934, 78 and 79, Griffin 1990, 116–124). These words were then added to the IAAF's Rule 1. The NACAI President P. C. Moore argued once again to have a decision postponed until the next IAAF congress because of the seriousness of the change. No attempt was made to challenge the dictionary definition of a country offered or to explore the idea that the people who formed the Irish nation resided in both jurisdictions on the island. Moore's suggestion went unsupported. Delegates voted by 12-0 in support of the council's proposition which later received a certain amount of retrospective approval from *An Taoiseach*, Eamon de Valera in 1939 when he informed an NACAI delegation that he could not see how the international federation could be induced to change a rule 'which experience and expediency had taught them to be the only practicable rule'.[23] The boundary definition was debated in conjunction with the discussion on whether to admit the International Board to membership of the IAAF. Harold Abrahams presented the British point of view and P. C. Moore and E. C. Fleming, the NACAI perspective. Both sides justified their claim for athletic jurisdiction of Northern Ireland with customary legal and constitutional argument. Only the Italian delegate, Dr Nai was sufficiently engaged to respond and he enquired about the possibility of an amicable solution. Edström explained that 'this question was of many years old and much time and effort had been spent in the endeavour to reach a mutual understanding without any result whatsoever'. Delegates believed that the question was a politically inspired one and had little or no interest in exploring its nuances, a point made by the delegate from Switzerland when he explained his reason for abstention. The International Board, as the body responsible for managing athletics in Great Britain and Northern Ireland, was approved for membership of the IAAF by 9 votes to 1 with 10 abstentions (Reynolds 2012, 33; Griffin 1990, 134; *Irish Times*, April 2, 1935).

'The unity of sport in Ireland at the moment is gone (Griffin 1990, 130)'

The jurisdiction of the NACAI was now limited to the territory of the Irish Free State. If it was to remain within the international athletic community it now had no option but to accept the constitutional change. Officials of the NACAI now found themselves in a position analogous to that of the Sinn Féin Party prior to the Anglo-Irish Treaty debates that began in December 1921. Like its political counterpart, the grand coalition of athletic nationalists was unable to reach a consensus. The idea that the Irish formed a single nation was a central tenet of Irish nationalism (Bowman 1982, 300 and 301). Unfortunately, for the future of Irish athletics, a majority of those responsible for the promotion of the sport in Ireland chose to vote in accordance with their political consciences and voted (31 votes to 23) not to accept the new IAAF by-law at a special NACAI congress. This decision was later endorsed at the annual congress held on 3 February 1935 when delegates voted by 27 votes to 24 to again reject the new IAAF regulation (Griffin 1990, 124).

Those in favour of abiding by the constitutional change argued on the importance of the promotion of athletics and the centrality of international competition to this. Prior to the second congress, J. J. Keane entered the debate and made one of his last public contributions to Irish athletics when he appealed through the medium of the *Irish Independent* to the congress delegates to reverse their earlier decision (*Irish Independent*, February 2, 1935). In a powerful analysis of the certain fallout from a rejection, Keane again revealed his pragmatism. He explained that during his career he 'did everything humanly possible to work in harmony with those in the North'. The members of the clubs in Northern Ireland were always anxious to retain a connection with the rest of Ireland but 'unfortunately four or five officials, who were more extreme in both their political and religious views, were able to exercise a controlling influence over the others'. Therefore, Keane argued it 'was in the best interests of the rest of the country to devote all our attention to the welfare of athletics within the political boundaries'. He always found Edström 'an exceptionally capable President'; 'for the past three or four years he has postponed bringing the Irish question to a head in the hopes that an amicable settlement could be arrived at domestically'. If the Dublin amendment was rejected 'the North will carry on with a free hand, the British Association will continue to recognise them' and the IAAF 'will not suffer in any way through the absence of an Irish delegation'. The Tailteann Games would be ended 'for no athletes can come here from any other country, when we are suspended, and the whole object of the Tailteann Games-a reunion for Irishmen all over the world will be gone'. Rejection would mean the isolation of Ireland, 'cut off from intercourse with any other country' and athletes such as the 1932 Olympic champions, Dr Pat O'Callaghan and Bob Tisdall, 'will no longer be able to make the name of Ireland ring in the ears of the world'. For hundreds of young Irish boys 'the incentive to emulate these heroes will be gone, and with it the future of athletics in this country'. Keane appealed to the delegates not to let 'political considerations' interfere in the matter for 'it is not a question of politics, it is a question of the future of Irish athletics (*Irish Independent*, February 2, 1935)'. Unfortunately, in the context of the time, for many the political dimension was paramount and to accept the IAAF rule was also a vote for partition. Dr Eamonn O'Sullivan argued that the loss of international competition was a small price to pay for unity; it was important to only a small fraction of the association's membership. Dr Pat O'Callaghan proposed that a decision on the matter be postponed. The support of the Munster delegates and the Army and Garda representatives was crucial on this occasion. Seven of the votes cast to reject the motion were those of policemen or soldiers (Griffin 1990, 126–131).

It is difficult to think of a more damaging decision made by an Irish sporting federation. Vincent Comerford (2003, 233) has correctly observed that 'Irish athletics in the mid-1930s provides a notable instance of an inflexible nationalism thwarting the interests of nationality. Though not uncommon, this is rarely so visible'. In 1937, clubs began to resign from the NACAI and formed the Amateur Athletic Union of Eire (AAUE) that was affiliated to the IAAF in 1938; prior to this the NACAI was suspended 'forever' from the IAAF (Griffin 1990, 139–148). Athletics on the island was now mismanaged by three controlling bodies that broadly reflected the political divisions of the island: the advanced nationalist NACAI, the unionist NIAAA and the more moderate and pragmatic nationalists who controlled the AAUE and worked within the constitutional requirements of the IAAF. The AAUE attracted little popular support; its influence was mainly concentrated in the Dublin region and catered for less than 20% of those involved in athletics in Ireland. Athletes who remained loyal to the NACAI were excluded from all international competition. Irish Olympic Council meetings in the late 1940s and early 1950s provided a forum for both athletic associations to articulate their animosities with the result that both were excluded from membership in 1952. The division also prevented successive Republic of Ireland governments from investing in sport and it was only after the athletic division was 'settled' in 1967 that serious consideration was given to government investment in Irish sport.

Acknowledgements

This essay was based on material mined in writing the official history of the Olympic Council of Ireland. In research for this project, Dr Dónal McAnallen and Pearse Reynolds made their respective theses available to this author. Their academic generosity is greatly appreciated. Thanks also to Pierce O'Callaghan who supplied a set of IAAF Handbooks.

Disclosure statement

No potential conflict of interest was reported by the author.

Notes

1. For a detailed examination of this issue see Hunt 2015.
2. National Library of Ireland (NLI), O'Duffy unsorted papers, Accession 5694, Box 3, File 29, The struggle for Irish athletic unity, 4.
3. NLI, O'Duffy unsorted papers, The struggle for Irish athletic unity, 5.
4. NLI, O'Duffy unsorted papers, The struggle for Irish Athletic unity, 7.
5. Public Records Office of Northern Ireland (PRONI), Cab. 9/b/160/1, RD Bates to Harry J Barclay, May 16, 1929. I am indebted to Dónal McAnallen for alerting me to the presence of this wonderful archive. At this stage, the northern body had yet to achieve any type of recognition so if policemen or army athletes competed under its auspices they risked suspension for competing in unsanctioned competition.
6. PRONI, Cab. 9/b/160/1, Note from WJ Trueman, Ministry for Finance to CR Blackmore, secretary of NI Cabinet; H Pollock to Barclay, February 5, 1930.
7. PRONI, Cab. 9/b/160/1, Barclay to Pollock, February 12, 1930.
8. PRONI, Cab. 9/b/160/1, Lord Craigavon to Lord Desborough, March 19, 1930; Desborough to Craigavon, March 22, 1930.
9. PRONI, Cab/9/b/160/1, Bates to Charles Wickham, July 2, 1929.
10. PRONI, Cab. 9/b/160/1, Wickham to Pollock, July 8, 1929.
11. PRONI, Cab. 9/b/160/1, Wickham to Blackmore, July 9, 1929.
12. PRONI, Cab. 9/b/160/1, Minute of discussion between Pollock and Wickham, January 13, 1930.
13. PRONI, Cab. 9/b/160/1, Correspondence from Bates to Wickham, January 11, 1930.
14. NLI, O'Duffy unsorted papers, The struggle for Irish athletic unity, 8 and 9.
15. National Archives (UK), HO 45, 15758; C462369. Minutes of meetings with Lord Desborough and Harold Abrahams concerning the relationship of the IAAF to athletics in the Irish Free State and Northern Ireland and related correspondence.

16. Abrahams at this stage was a member of the General Committee of the AAA and one of the most influential figures in the sport. The Olympic 100 m champion of 1924 combined his professional career as a barrister with an incredible devotion to athletics. He was the voice of British athletics as a result of his broadcasting career with the BBC, his journalism with the *Sunday Times* and his authorship of several athletics books. He has been described as the architect of the modern laws of athletics (Lovesey, AAA, 175–177).
17. NLI, O'Duffy unsorted papers, The struggle for Irish athletics unity, 16.
18. NLI, O'Duffy unsorted papers, The struggle for Irish athletic unity, 17. Olympic champion, Dr Pat O'Callaghan had his suspension lifted as a result.
19. NLI, O'Duffy unsorted papers, The struggle for athletic unity, 18–20.
20. There is some irony attached to Peter O'Connor's position as he has earned a certain amount of infamy in Olympic history. At the Intercalated Games of 1906, O'Connor climbed a flag pole at the victory ceremony for the long jump competition and waved the tricolour in protest against the use of the Union Jack to mark his runner-up position.
21. The Ulsterville, North Belfast, Duncairn Nomads, Albertville, 9th Old Boys and Queens' University clubs disaffiliated.
22. National Archives (Ireland), DFA/6/415/32, Memo to Secretary Department of External Affairs, January 6, 1948.
23. National Archives (Ireland), TSCH/3/S11053A Memorandum of meeting between NACAI and *An Taoiseach* and Minister for External Affairs, Eamon de Valera, January 23, 1939.

References

Bowman, John. 1982. *de Valera and the Ulster Question, 1917–1973*. Oxford: Clarendon Press.
Bryson, Anna. 2009. "Moles, Thomas." In *Dictionary of Irish Biography*, edited by James Maguire and Patrick Quinn. Vol. 6, 546–547. Cambridge: Cambridge University Press and Royal Irish Academy.
Buckland, Patrick. 1981. *A History of Northern Ireland*. Dublin: Gill and Macmillan.
Comerford, R. V. 2003. *Inventing the Nation: Ireland*. London: Hodder Arnold.
Coyle, Padraig. 1999. *Paradise Lost and Found: The Story of Belfast Celtic*. Edinburgh: Mainstream Publishing.
English, Richard. 2007. *Irish Freedom: The History of Nationalism in Ireland*. London: Pan Books.
Fanning, Ronan. 2013. *Fatal Path, British Government and Irish Revolution 1910–1922*. London: Faber and Faber.
Flynn, Barry. 2009. *Political Football: The Life and Death of Belfast Celtic*. Dublin: Nonsuch Ireland.
Garnham, Neal. 2004. *Association Football and Society in Pre-Partition Ireland*. Belfast: Ulster Historical Foundation.
Griffin, Padraig. 1990. *The Politics of Irish Athletics, 1850–1990*. Ballinamore: Marathon Publications.
Hopkinson, Michael. 2004. *Green Against Green, The Irish Civil War*. Dublin: Gill and Macmillan.
Hunt, Tom. 2015. "'In Our Case It Seems Obvious the British Organising Committee Piped the Tune': The Campaign for the Recognition of 'Ireland' in the Olympic Movement, 1935–1956." *Sport in Society*. doi:10.1080/17430437.2014.990689.
IAAF (International Amateur Athletic Federation). 1926. *Handbook of the International Amateur Athletic Federation, 1924–26*. Västerås: IAAF.
IAAF (International Amateur Athletic Federation). 1934. *Handbook of the International Amateur Athletic Federation, 1932–1934*. Västerås: IAAF.
Lanfanchi, Pierre, Christiane Eisenberg, Tony Mason, and Alfred Wahl. 2004. *100 Years of Football: The FIFA Centennial Book*. London: Weidenfeld and Nicolson.
Long, Patrick. 2009a. "O'Duffy, Eoin." In *Dictionary of Irish Biography*, edited by James Maguire and Patrick Quinn. Vol. 7, 432–434. Cambridge: Cambridge University Press and Royal Irish Academy.
Long, Patrick. 2009b. "Wickham, Sir Charles George." In *Dictionary of Irish Biography*, edited by James Maguire and Patrick Quinn. 9, 921–922. Cambridge: Cambridge University Press and Royal Irish Academy.
Lovesey, Peter. 1979. *The Official Centenary History of the AAA*. Enfield: Guinness Superlatives.
Mandle, W. F. 1987. *The Gaelic Athletic Association and Irish Nationalist Politics, 1884–1924*. Dublin: Gill and Macmillan.

McAnallen, Dónal. 2010. "Playing on the Fourth Green Field: The Gaelic Athletic Association and the Northern Ireland State, 1921–1968." PhD diss., National University of Ireland, Galway.

McCarthy, Kevin. 2010. *Gold, Silver and Green: The Irish Olympic Journey. 1896–1924*. Cork: Cork University Press.

McGarry, Fearghal. 2007. *Eoin O'Duffy: A Self-Made Hero*. Oxford: Oxford University Press.

Morris, Ewan. 2005. *Our Own Devices: National Symbols and Political Conflict in Twentieth-Century Ireland*. Dublin: Irish Academic Press.

Murphy, Catherine, and Colm Murphy. 2013. *Wearing the Shamrock: Ireland Internationals, 1876–1939*. Rochester: Self-published.

O'Callaghan, Liam. 2011. *Rugby in Munster: A Social and Cultural History*. Cork: Cork University Press.

O'Donoghue, Tony. n.d. *Irish Championship Athletics, 1873–1914*. Dublin: Self-Published.

Reynolds, Pearse. 2008. "The 'Split': Divisions in Irish Athletics (1920–1940)." . MA diss., De Montfort University, Leicester.

Reynolds, Pearse. 2012. "'A First-Class Split': Political Conflict in Irish Athletics. 1924–1940." *History Ireland* 20 (4): 30–33.

Spalding's Athletic Library - Official Minutes and Rules Promulgated by the Second Congress of the International Amateur Athletic Federation held at Lyons, France, June 10–12. 1914. New York: American Sports Publishing Company.

West, Trevor. 1991. *The Bold Collegians: The Development of Sport in Trinity College, Dublin*. Dublin: The Lilliput Press.

Index

Note: **Boldface** page numbers refer to figures and tables, page numbers followed by "n" denote notes.

All-Ireland Army Athletic Association 125
Allen, J.A. 39
Amateur Athletic Association (AAA) 132
Amateur Athletic Union of Eire (AAUE) 144
American football 24
American-styled Collar-and-Elbow wrestling 112
Ancient Order of Hibernians (AOH) 9, 19n45; Fermanagh Division of 14–15
Anglo-Celt 5
Anglo-Irish patrons 119
Anglo-Irish Treaty 143
anti-Sabbatarian activity 116
AOH *see* Ancient Order of Hibernians
Aonach Tailteann 30, 36n4
Association football 28; Gaelic Athletic Association *vs.* 14–16
Australia, emergence of hurling in: codification and Michael Cusack 64–7; Gaelic Athletic Association (GAA) code of 1884 62; Irish communities 62; ongoing problems in 67–8; Rose, A. J. 63; Western Australia 68–71
Australian hurling code 65

Bale, John 75, 76, 91
Bates, Richard Dawson 135, 136
Battalion of the Royal Dublin Fusiliers (RDF) 98
Belfast Celtic Football Club 133
Belfast Defence Corps 99
Belfast Newsletter 40, 41
Belgian tour 1910 29–34, 36
Belew, Edward 118
Birrell, Augustine 53, 55
Blake, Richard 9
Boyle, Peadar 59
Bracken, J.K. 51
Brennan, John 'Turpentine' 116
Brett, Jasper 100
Brian Boru team 71
'British garrison' 12

British Home Championship 1914 38, 41, **41**, 42, 44–9, **47**, **48**
British National Cyclists' Union 134
Burke, Frank 59

Caledonians football club 39
Carson, Edward 98
Catholic Truth Society 103
Chamberlain, Neville 55
Clontarf Football Club 105
Collar-and-Elbow style wrestling 110–11, 125–6; decline of 124; in Dublin city 123; rules of 113
Collingwood Hurling Club 65–6
Collins, Michael 56–7, 60
Collins, Tony 95
commercial theatrical wrestling 124
Cork Sportsman: GAA's Belgian tour 1910 and 29–34; relationship between sport and press 24
Cornish and Gouren (Breton) wrestling styles 111
Cornish scheme of rule-giving 113
Corry, Eoghan 11
County Dublin Wrestling Committee 125
cricket: campaigns against 11–14; revival 7–8
Croke, T.W. 51, 123
Cuiteach Fuait wrestlers 110
cultural nationalism 30; emergence of 9
Cusack, Michael 51, 53, 64, 72; codification and 64–7

Davitt, Michael 51
de Búrca, Marcus 52
de Valera, Eamon 142
Delaney, Enda 74
Desborough, Lord 136, 138
Devonshire style wrestling 111
'disorderly mobs' 115–18
'Donnybrook twist, the' 117
Doone, Allen 71
Dublin Association Football Club 41
Dublin rugby, ammunition for 101
Duffy, John 82

147

INDEX

Easter 1916 59–60
Easter Rising 1916 96
economic depression 4
Edström, Siegfrid 138, 141
Edwards, Ruth Dudley 75
emigration 4
employment industry 4
England's Football Leagues, Irish-born players in: Bale, John 75; birthplaces of Irish Football migrants 75–8; initial recruiting clubs 88–90; McGovern, Patrick 74; Northern Ireland-born footballing migrants 81–3; recent growth of scouting networks and regional structures for Football 86–8; Republic of Ireland-born football migrants, birthplaces of 78; Republic of Ireland Source Clubs 78–80; schoolboy leagues in Provincial Ireland 84–6; slow development of schools' soccer 84–6; sports and lack of schools' football, competition with 83–4
'Erin-go-Bragh' 71

FA *see* Football Association
FAI *see* Football Association of Ireland
FAIFS *see* Football Association of the Irish Free State
Feast Day wrestling competitions 113
Fédération Internationale de Football Association (FIFA) 131
Fermanagh County Board 15
Festival of Tailteann 110
'Fingallian style' wrestling 124
First World War, Irish rugby and *see* Irish rugby and First World War
Fitzgerald, Dick 58–9
Fitzgerald, Fenian P.N. 51
Fitzpatrick, David 52, 107
fixed-hold wrestling 111
Fontenoy 32
Football Association (FA) 39
Football Association of Ireland (FAI) 131
Football Association of the Irish Free State (FAIFS) 131
Football Sports Weekly 27
Foyle Cup 85
Free State Ireland 107
Freemans Journal 46

GAA *see* Gaelic Athletic Association
'Gaelic American, The' 111, 112
Gaelic Athlete 27, 54
Gaelic Athletic Association (GAA) 1, 25, 38, 67, 96, 131; *vs.* Association football 14–16; Belgian tour 1910 and *Cork Sportsman* 29–34; code of 1884 62; Collins, Michael 56–7; critiques of 101; Croke, Thomas 51; Cusack, Michael 51; Easter 1916 59–60; establishment of 3; Fitzgerald, Dick 58–9; Fitzpatrick, David 52; Maguire, Sam 57; Murphy, William 51; national decline of 4–6; political disloyalty displayed by 103; revival and reorganization of (1898–1905) 9–11; role for 53–5; Walsh, J.J. 57–8; and war 100–3
Gaelic games 4, 5, 7, 9; determined continuation of 101; participation in 102; pre-eminence of 11
Gaelic League 9, 19n43, 31
'Gaelic Revival' 19n42
Gaelic revival movement 67
'Geography of Revolution in Ireland, The' (Hart) 60
Golfing Union of Ireland 131
Government of Ireland Act (1920) 130, 139
'Great All-Ireland Wrestling match' 120
Great Southern Railway 30
Greco-Roman style wrestling 111
Grenfell, William 136

Hackett, Thomas Kirkwood 42
Hanna, Henry 107
Hannan, Paddy 68
Hannigan, Dave 86
Hart, Peter 60
Hatte, C. G. 68–9
Home Rule 38–9; crisis 104
Home Rule Bill 96
Howard, John W. 64
Huggins, Michael 113
hurling clubs in Australia 63, **63**
Hyde, Douglas 19n43, 30

IAAA *see* Irish Amateur Athletic Association
IAAF *see* International Amateur Athletic Federation
IAAU *see* Irish Amateur Athletic Union
IFA *see* Irish Football Association
IFAB *see* International Football Association Board
initial recruiting clubs 88–90
International Amateur Athletic Federation (IAAF) 131, 132; Rule 1 142
International Football Association Board (IFAB), formation of 41
International Olympic Committee (IOC) 131, 135
IRB *see* Irish Republican Brotherhood
IRFU *see* Irish Rugby Football Union
IRFU Volunteer Corps' foundation 104–5
Irish Amateur Athletic Association (IAAA) 131, 132
Irish Amateur Athletic Union (IAAU) 140
Irish Association of Volunteer Corps 99
Irish athletics, institutional development of 133–6

INDEX

Irish-born players in England's Football Leagues *see* England's Football Leagues, Irish-born players in
Irish Catch-as-Catch-Can champion 125
Irish Collar-and-Elbow championship 111
Irish Collar-and-Elbow wrestling, emphasis of 112
Irish communities 62
Irish Football Association (IFA) 17n5, 39, 40, 44, 131
Irish Football League 44
Irish football migrants 74; in English Premier and Football Leagues, birthplaces of 75–8
Irish Free State 135, 137; establishment of 130
Irish Home Rule movement 4
Irish Independent 26, 30, 46
Irish migration to non-European countries 74
Irish nationalism 56
Irish nationalist movement 52
Irish Olympic Council 131, 140
Irish Parliamentary Party 101
Irish Republican Brotherhood (IRB) 4, 29, 36n3, 51
Irish Revolution 134
Irish rugby and First World War 95–6, 103–8; Belfast Defence Corps 99; Brett, Jasper 100; Carson, Edward 98; Collins, Tony 95; cultural conflict 100–3; Easter Rising 1916 96; Irish Association of Volunteer Corps 99; Irish Rugby Football Union (IRFU) 96, 97; Mahon, Bryan 97–8; Rugby Union Volunteers 98; social and cultural profile of 104
Irish Rugby Football Union (IRFU) 7, 46, 96, 97, 103, 130
Irish society, peaceful penetration of 56
Irish sports history 1–2
Irish Volunteer Aid Association 54
Irish Volunteers 55; formation of 54; support for 54
Irvine, Willie 83
Ives, Henry 65

Keane, J. J. 131–3, 137–8, 143
Kelly, Seamus 88
Kerrigan, Colm 38
Kerry Sentinel 5, 20n50
'Kildare Trippers' 112, 113
Killorglin Laune Rangers club 6
Knalea 29, 32–4

La Gazzetta dello Sport 24
Lancastrian Catch-As-Catch-Can style wrestling 111
Lavan, Sean 141
Legg, Marie-Louise 25
Leinster Football Association, establishment of 42

Leinster Schools Senior Cup 106
Limerick County Board 6, 12
Limerick Leader 12
Long, Patrick 66

Maguire, Sam 57
Mahon, Bryan 97–8
Malone, Tom 67
McAlery, John McCredy 39, 40
McGilligan, Paddy 130
McGovern, Patrick 74
McParland, Peter 83
Milk Cup 85
Moles, Thomas 133
Moore, Frederick 99
Munster Football Association 26, 42
Murphy, William 51, 103

NACAI *see* National Athletic and Cycling Association of Ireland
Nathan, Matthew 55
National Athletic and Cycling Association of Ireland (NACAI) 130, 131; affiliation of 139; institutional development of Irish athletics 133–6; Keane, J. J. 131–3; 'police are not children' 136–7; Ulster Council of 133; unity of sport 142–4
National Library 102
Neill, Terry 83
NIAACCA *see* Northern Ireland Amateur Athletics, Cycling and Cross-Country Association
NIFC *see* North of Ireland Football Club
Nolan, W. E. 68
Nolan, William 60
non-European countries, Irish migration to 74
North of Ireland Football Club (NIFC) 103–4
Northern Ireland Amateur Athletics, Cycling and Cross-Country Association (NIAACCA) 133, 134
Northern Ireland-born footballing migrants 81–3
Northern Ireland Schools Football Association 85
Northwest Ireland, soccer growth in 8–9

O'Beirne Ranelagh, John 53
O'Brien, William 36n1
O'Connor, John 102
O'Connor, Peter 140
O'Donnell, John 53
O'Duffy, Eoin 139–41
O'Farrell, Patrick 73
O'Leary, John 51
O'Sullivan, Thomas F. 9–10

Pan-Celtic Congress 29–31, 33
Pan-Celticism 31
Parnell, Charles Stewart 4–6, 51

INDEX

Peake, Robin 74
'Phaynix, the,' wrestling at 120–1
Phoenix Park 114, 116; sporting culture 122
'physical force movement' in Ireland 53
'political clause' 53
Pollock, Hugh 135
Power, John Wyse 51
pre-Famine landlord patronage of wrestling 118
prehistoric Gaelic sports, history of 110
Price, Ivan 55
professionalism 42, 43
Provincial Ireland, schoolboy leagues in 84–6
provincial wrestling, patronage and participation in 118–19

Quain, John 69

rational recreations *vs.* turbulent sports 119–20
Recollections of a Rebel 57
regional structures for Football 86–8
Republic of Ireland-born football migrants, birthplaces of 78
Republic of Ireland Source Clubs 78–80
Robert Emmet Club 67
Roche, Laurence 103
Rose, A. J. 63
Rowan, Paul 80
Royal Irish Constabulary (RIC) 52, 55
RUC club, association of 136
rugby 102; campaigns against 11–14; at schools level 106
Rugby Football Volunteer Corps 107
Rugby Union, expansion of 6–7
Rugby Union Volunteers 98
rural boisterous games 115
Ruxton, Cecil 99
Ryan, Eugene 70

Sabbatarianism 115–18
Scanlan 51–2
schoolboy leagues in Provincial Ireland 84–6
Schoolboys Football Association of Ireland 85
schools' soccer: competition with sports and lack of 83–4; slow development of 84–6
Scottish Football Association 39
scouting networks, recent growth of 86–8
Seven Acre Field event 118
Sheridan, Cillian 87

Siochfradha, Pádraig Ó 59
soccer: British Home Championship 1914 44–9, **47, 48**; growth in 8–9; international beginnings 39–44
'Spartan-like warrior energy' 113
Sport History Ireland 2
Stevenson, Robert 104
Stoker, Bram 114, 121

Third Home Rule Bill 108n1
Toley, A. 56
traditional backhold wrestling 125
Tralee RFC 6, 12
Trumper, Victor 70
turbulent sports *vs.* rational recreations 119–20

Ulster GAA Convention 14
Ulster GAA Council 14
Union Cycliste Internationale (UCI) 131

Victorian Hurling Club Association 62, 64, 71
Victorian Sports Revolution 1, 4
Volunteer Military Medical Corps 54
"Volunteer movement" 54

Walsh, J.J. 29–31, 34, 57–8
Wanderers Football Club 105
Wars of Austrian Succession 32
Western Australia, hurling in 68–71
Wickham, Charles 136, 137
Wilkin, Albert 98
wrestling doctor 115–18
wrestling competition 124
wrestling, in modern Ireland: boisterous games, death and prizes 115; decline of 123–5; disorderly mobs 115–18; gallant revival effort 125–6; law-and-order concerns 117–18; origins, rules and festive sports 110–14; other sports and GAA 123; at 'Phaynix, the' 120–1; pre-Famine landlord patronage of 118; predominant style of 110; presentational changes attempted 121–2; public houses, factions fights and wrestling suppressed 122–3; rational recreations *vs.* turbulent sports 119–20; ring and pre-fight preliminaries 114; Sabbatarianism 115–18; stop to 'legitimate amusements' of 122; wrestling doctor 115–18